MORE PRAISE FOR

THE INDOMITABLE FLORENCE FINCH

"A wonderfully graphic and moving account of the selfless and courageous role played during the Japanese occupation of the Philippines by Florence Finch, one of the great unrecognized heroines of World War Two."

—Saul David, author of *Crucible of Hell* and *The Force*

"Thanks to Robert Mrazek's rich and fast-paced narrative, we can add Florence Finch's name to the honor roll of World War II heroes such as Raoul Wallenberg and Oskar Schindler who risked their lives to save others from certain death. Her thrilling story, expertly told by Mrazek, proves that there are still stories of Second World War heroism that remain untold."

—Thurston Clarke, author of *Pearl Harbor Ghosts*
and the *New York Times* bestselling *The Last Campaign*

"The richly detailed account of a courageous woman's life."

—*Kirkus Reviews*

"A crisp chronicle. . . . WWII buffs will relish this inside look at life under Japanese occupation."

—*Publishers Weekly*

"Acclaimed novelist and historian Mrazek has crafted a compelling narrative, which also provides rich coverage of the overall war in the Philippines. A perfect match of author and subject."

—*Booklist*

THE INDOMITABLE
FLORENCE FINCH

THE **INDOMITABLE FLORENCE FINCH**

THE UNTOLD STORY OF A WAR WIDOW TURNED RESISTANCE FIGHTER AND SAVIOR OF AMERICAN POWs

ROBERT J. MRAZEK

hachette BOOKS

NEW YORK

Copyright © 2020 by Robert J. Mrazek
Maps copyright © 2016, 2020 by Jeffrey L. Ward
Jacket design by Amanda Kain
Jacket photographs: (top left) Photo courtesy of the U.S. Coast Guard; (top right) © Bettmann/Getty Images; (bottom) © Time Life Pictures/Getty Images; Textures: MM_photos/Shutterstock; javarman/Shutterstock
Jacket copyright © 2020 by Hachette Book Group, Inc.

Hachette Books
Hachette Book Group
1290 Avenue of the Americas
New York, NY 10104
HachetteBooks.com
Twitter.com/HachetteBooks
Instagram.com/HachetteBooks

First Edition: July 2020

Hachette Books is a division of Hachette Book Group, Inc.

The Hachette Books name and logo are trademarks of Hachette Book Group, Inc.

The publisher is not responsible for websites (or their content) that are not owned by the publisher.

The Hachette Speakers Bureau provides a wide range of authors for speaking events. To find out more, go to www.hachettespeakersbureau.com or call (866) 376-6591.

Library of Congress Cataloging-in-Publication Data has been applied for.

ISBNs: 978-0-316-42227-7 (hardcover), 978-0-316-42224-6 (ebook)

Printed in the United States of America

LSC-C

10 9 8 7 6 5 4 3 2 1

To Florence.
With unbounded admiration for this extraordinary
woman and all the unsung heroines whose stories have
yet to be told.

CONTENTS

Contents

Contents

Contents

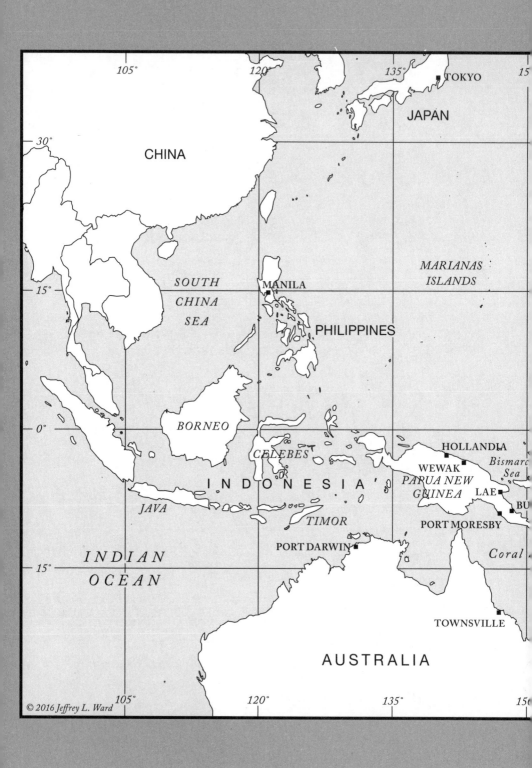

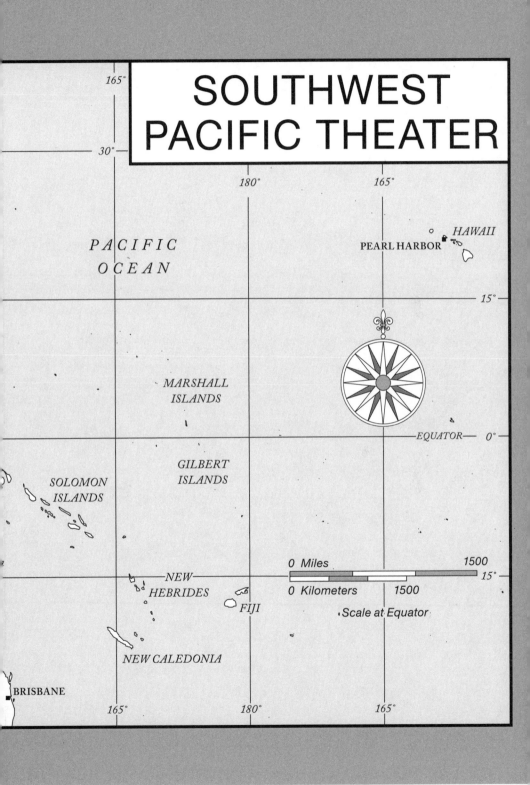

SOUTHWEST PACIFIC THEATER

165°

30°

180°   165°

○ ▪ *HAWAII*

PEARL HARBOR ▪

PACIFIC
OCEAN

15°

MARSHALL
ISLANDS

EQUATOR — 0°

GILBERT
ISLANDS

SOLOMON
ISLANDS

0 Miles   1500

NEW   15°
HEBRIDES   *FIJI*   0 Kilometers   1500

Scale at Equator

NEW CALEDONIA

BRISBANE

165°   180°   165°

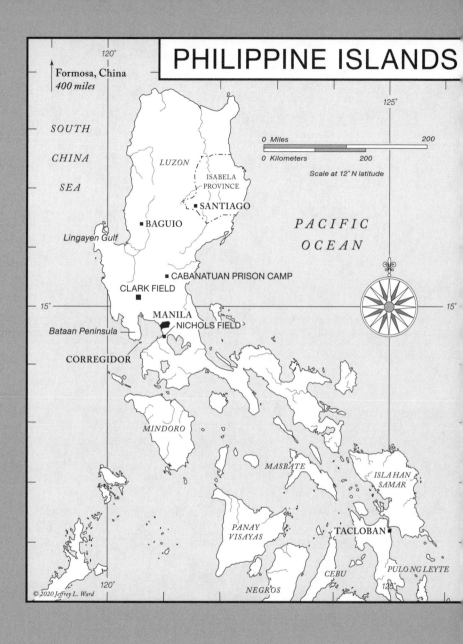

PHILIPPINE ISLANDS

Formosa, China
400 miles

SOUTH

CHINA

SEA

LUZON

ISABELA
PROVINCE

■ SANTIAGO

■ BAGUIO

Lingayen Gulf

PACIFIC

OCEAN

0 Miles   200
0 Kilometers   200
Scale at 12° N latitude

■ CABANATUAN PRISON CAMP

CLARK FIELD ■

MANILA
NICHOLS FIELD

Bataan Peninsula

CORREGIDOR

MINDORO

MASBATE

ISLA HAN
SAMAR

PANAY
VISAYAS

TACLOBAN ■

CEBU

PULO NG LEYTE

NEGROS

© 2020 Jeffrey L. Ward

THE INDOMITABLE FLORENCE FINCH

PROLOGUE

At twenty-nine, Florence Ebersole Smith knew the depths of terror as well as she knew her own family—at least those who were still alive. She had lived with fear every day for more than three years.

Two of her closest contacts in the Philippine underground had recently disappeared. She could only assume they had been taken by the Kempeitai and were being tortured to find out who had stolen the Japanese army's stocks of gasoline and diesel fuel and diverted them to the Philippine resistance. A Kempeitai officer had the unlimited power to arrest, torture, condemn without trial, or execute anyone in the Philippines. Florence hoped her friends hadn't revealed her role in the diversions.

A month earlier, the Kempeitai sent two officers to question Florence and her coworkers at the Philippine Liquid Fuel Distribution Union. Afterward, the Japanese director of the company, Kiyoshi Osawa, brought the staff together to say the Kempeitai was sure that people in the company were guilty of sabotage and stealing massive quantities of liquid fuel. The punishment for the criminals would be death.

"Steer clear of trouble," Osawa warned them. "The time will come when you will be glad you followed my advice."

Florence hadn't followed his advice. They came for her shortly after dawn.

ONE

She was born Loring May Ebersole. The name Florence came after the cataclysm.

Her earliest memories were stained with melancholy, loss, and pain. The roots of the tragedy were sown more than twenty years earlier, in 1899, when Charlie Ebersole arrived in the Philippines aboard the hospital ship USS *Missouri*. A young American medic, Charlie volunteered at seventeen in a spirit of high adventure, after reading the thrilling newspaper accounts of Teddy Roosevelt leading his Rough Riders to glory on their charge up San Juan Hill in the first year of the Spanish-American War. With his sensitive blue eyes, gentle smile, and blond hair, Charlie looked more virginal choir boy than Rough Rider.

The war began in Cuba in 1898, when its people revolted against their Spanish rulers with the United States backing them. The fighting then spread to the Philippines, a colony Spain had ruled for nearly four hundred years.

When Charlie's hospital ship arrived in Manila Bay a year later, it sailed past the wrecked warships of the Spanish fleet, which had been destroyed in the naval battle that finally ended Spanish control of the Philippines.

Emilio Aguinaldo, the Filipino leading the insurrection against the Spanish, initially welcomed the Americans as liberators. But when the United

1

States decided to make the Philippines its own possession, Aguinaldo named himself president of the First Philippine Republic and declared war once again.

In the beginning, his ragtag soldiers suffered terrible losses in traditional battles against the US Army. Aguinaldo changed to guerrilla tactics, avoiding direct conflict and making night raids and ambushes on American outposts. The idea was not to defeat the Americans but to inflict constant losses that would make them quit.

General Elwell Otis, commander of the American troops, issued secret orders to execute all enemy soldiers captured in the fighting. Publicly, he claimed that the Filipino insurgents were guilty of atrocities and that captured Americans were being buried up to their necks in ant hills.

Aguinaldo asked the International Red Cross to determine the truth. Over General Otis's objections, their representatives reported seeing burned-out villages and "horribly mutilated Filipino bodies, with stomachs slit open and men decapitated."

Charlie's ship reached Manila just as the war reached the height of its savagery in November 1899. Before he was assigned to a hospital, he was given two days' leave to visit the city and its famous walled compound, called the Intramuros. Built by the Spanish in 1571, its Romanesque churches and narrow, cobbled streets were surrounded by twenty-five-foot-high stone walls. The natives of the city did not seem dangerous to him, nor did they appear to fear his presence. He also couldn't help but notice the beauty of some of the young Filipina women.

He could only wonder where the war was. Four days later, he found out.

The army hospital he was assigned to was overflowing with wounded American soldiers and many more were battling typhoid, dysentery, and malaria. Men were dying every day, sometimes a hundred or more each week. He quickly lost his boyhood illusions of glory and high adventure, and his noble goal of saving lives was put to a stern test.

The Philippine insurrection came to an end in 1902, after Aguinaldo was captured during an attack on his headquarters north of Manila. He reluctantly signed an oath of allegiance to the United States, and President Theodore Roosevelt declared the war over.

Charlie Ebersole's three-year enlistment ended a month later. By then, he had seen the brutality of the savage conflict firsthand. It was no newspaper article; no dime novel.

At twenty-one, he knew two things with certainty: he wasn't going to stay in the army, and he wasn't going back to the Buffalo, New York, winters. Despite the inhumanity he had witnessed, Charlie came to love the Philippines for its loveliness, the warmth and hospitality of its people, and the unhurried atmosphere that allowed a man to enjoy life's pleasures.

The US Congress authorized funds for the building of modern roads, schools, and hospitals in its new possession to improve the Filipinos' quality of life. Although Charlie had no contracting experience, his service record included commendations for competence, resourcefulness, and "very good character."

Hired by one of the contractors, he soon was supervising Filipino work crews as they hacked through jungles and across rivers to connect remote cities and towns. He was earning more money than he ever had in his life and was banking most of it.

In the spectacularly beautiful northern provinces, he came upon plantations growing tobacco, rice, pineapples, and other crops. He had never farmed, but the plantations offered a pastoral lifestyle he found attractive. He began looking for one that he could afford to buy.

At the same time, another muse began whispering in his ear. Her birth name was Maria Hermoso, and Charlie met her in 1907 while overseeing a road-building project. Although he had gone out with many young Filipina women, the twenty-four-year-old Maria caught and held his attention. She was illiterate in English, but high-spirited and beautiful, and she could make him laugh. Over the years, Charlie had learned enough of the indigenous Tagalog language for the two of them to communicate.

There was only one complication: Maria was already married to a former Spanish soldier named Marcel Arzi, and together they already had a young daughter, Flaviana. The "very good character" citation recorded in Charlie's military service record didn't cover a situation like this, and the years of war and rough living had coarsened him.

With an almost reptilian cold-bloodedness, Charlie asked Maria to leave her husband and live with him as his common-law wife, assuring her they would raise Flaviana together. Swept off her feet by the handsome and successful young American, Maria agreed. Life was good for a young American with full pockets in the Philippines, who could live without fear of retribution from a cuckolded husband who fought on the losing side of the Spanish-American War.

With the money he saved, Charlie bought a plantation along the Calao River in Isabela Province, near the city of Santiago. Known as Pueblo de Carig in the Spanish days, Santiago was a gateway to the fertile plains of the Cagayan Valley.

There was a small house on the property and the plantation's acreage included fields, pastures, and pine forest running for almost half a mile along the river. To the kid from Buffalo, the groves of bananas, coconuts, grapefruit, lemons, limes, pineapples, and oranges were exotic and intoxicating, endowing the plantation with an almost Eden-like bounty—his own "Treasure Island," a favorite book from childhood.

Charlie was sure the soil would be perfect for cultivating tobacco as well. Instead of growing the harsh and bitter native blends, he ordered mild Virginia and burley seeds from suppliers in the United States, along with long-leaf plants of different blends to produce high-quality, hand-rolled cigars. In a few years he was exporting to the United States.

As the plantation prospered, he built a substantial house at the edge of the river. It followed a traditional American floor plan, with family living quarters on the first level and bedrooms on the second and third. His design included oversized screened windows in every room to allow constant airflow during the hot season. Wood stoves provided heat in the rainy and cool ones.

Charlie fell in love with the land, planting an expansive garden that included acacia trees, gardenias, white roses, golden shower trees, lei flowers, night-blooming jasmine, and mango trees. Through the open windows, the aromatic plantings filled the house with the fragrance of flowers and music of songbirds attracted by the garden.

His favorite room was the pine-paneled library, the shelves of which were soon filled with his growing collection of books. The library included favorite novels from his boyhood and contemporary works by Theodore Roosevelt and Arthur Conan Doyle. Reading became his preferred form of relaxation.

As his wealth grew, so did the four children he had with Maria, including Processo, born in 1908, followed by Edward in 1911, Norma in 1913, and Loring in 1915. The family gathered for prayers at six each evening, after which they ate together in the formal dining room.

Before bedtime, Processo and Edward spent at least an hour reading in the library with Flaviana, Maria's daughter from her first marriage. Charlie would read children's books aloud to Norma and Loring, stories that took Loring far away in her young imagination. But the good times were not to last.

Flaviana was a stunningly beautiful young woman. At age seventeen, she was a younger version of her mother, and far more sophisticated with her ability to read and write in English. She was impossible to ignore.

That year, a young man named Antonio Vasquez met Flaviana while she was visiting friends in Santiago. He asked if he could see her again and she agreed. During his chaperoned visits to the plantation, it was clear that Flaviana was taken with the handsome young man, and Maria strongly urged her to accept Antonio's marriage proposal.

Flush with success, Charlie wasn't used to having things *taken* from him—especially someone as enchanting as his Flaviana. After she and Antonio married and moved away, he began to harbor a smoldering anger that only grew with the passing days.

Two months after Flaviana's marriage, Charlie went to the village where they lived. Taking Flaviana aside, he boldly declared his love and asked her to return with him to live together as man and wife.

Perhaps Flaviana was in love with him all along. Maybe it was because she was so young and he was so powerful. Whatever her motivations, she agreed to go with him. Like Maria's husband Marcel Arzi, the young Antonio Vasquez felt powerless to challenge him.

When they arrived back at the plantation, Maria flew into a rage, accusing her daughter of seducing her husband. With the same cold-blooded attitude that had empowered him to steal Maria from her husband, Charlie gave her an ultimatum: accept his decision and stay with their children in the small house where they had first lived after he bought the plantation, or be cast out.

With no place else to go, Maria agreed.

TWO

After Flaviana assumed the role of Charlie's common-law wife, it seemed as though Maria would acquiesce to her sudden change in status. For the next two years, she didn't give up hope that Charlie would leave Flaviana and reconcile with her. She didn't blame Charlie; he was only a man. She never forgave her daughter.

Charlie was now one of the most influential men in the province, and from their small cottage, Maria and the children could often hear the sounds of music and laughter as Charlie and Flaviana entertained their many important guests in the plantation house.

Charlie remained active in the raising of his and Maria's children. A good education was his mantra, particularly for the girls, and he built a one-room schoolhouse to advance their learning. Local children in Santiago were invited to attend, and were taught in their native Tagalog. Although Charlie's children were fluent in Tagalog, they learned their lessons in English from a teacher recruited in Manila.

In 1917, Flaviana gave birth to their first child, a daughter they named Perrine, followed by Diana, born fourteen months later. Their first son together, Charles Jr., arrived in 1921.

The uneasy truce with Maria came to a sudden end when Charlie agreed to marry Flaviana at the small chapel on the plantation. Although Flaviana had never divorced Antonio Vasquez, she wanted the validation of a marriage regardless of its legality under Philippine law.

For Maria, this was the final indignity. It was clear that Charlie would never take her back. By marrying Flaviana, he was saying to all their friends that Maria was a worthless whore whose four children were illegitimate. She became increasingly despondent. During the day, she sat silently brooding, alone in her misery. Often, she wept through the night. As the weeks passed, her grief turned into sullen rage.

She erupted into angry verbal tirades toward her children. Soon, she was physically punishing them for imaginary transgressions, and seeming to take pleasure in it, as if she were punishing Flaviana for stealing Charlie away from her.

Maria would make them kneel in the beds of coarse salt used to husk rice and demand that they hold their arms straight out. When they eventually dropped them in exhaustion, she would strike each child with a long bamboo pole. The boys took the brunt of the physical beatings, but Norma and Loring received their share too.

They never knew what might set her off or when another outburst might be unleashed for failing to do a chore or simply for being there. It was hard for the children not to feel they were viewed as somehow responsible for the situation between their parents. Loring shut down emotionally and stopped speaking. She found refuge from the emotional carnage in Charlie's library, where she was able to escape into stories like *Sleeping Beauty*.

Deliverance for the children arrived when Maria met a man in Santiago named Procopio Balagot. She was still lovely, and he was very taken with her. Knowing she had never been divorced from Flaviana's father, he proposed a tribal marriage. The ceremony had no legal authority, but in a Catholic country that did not recognize divorce, it was a commonly employed ritual.

After the wedding, Maria moved with Procopio to Solano, Nueva Vizcaya, at the other end of the Cagayan Valley. Charlie decreed that the children remain behind.

One morning, Charlie brought Norma and Loring to the house and told them they would soon be leaving the plantation. He was sending them to the newly created Union Church Hall school in Manila to continue their formal education. It was a boarding school for mestizas, female children of American and Filipino heritage, and he was a friend of the school superintendent, Harvey Bordner.

Charlie told them that since they already knew basic English, they would be well prepared to attend the school, where only English was spoken. Union Church Hall had adopted the American system of a general education and most of its teachers were Americans.

With a good education, they could succeed in whatever path they chose to follow in life. Processo and Edward would remain on the plantation and learn to manage its operations while attending the local school.

The last thing he told the sisters was that he planned to legally acknowledge them as his natural children and they would receive American citizenship. Loring had no idea what this meant, nor the impact it would have on her future.

The sisters left the plantation in a horse-drawn carriage for the two-day journey to Manila. Spare clothing and a few personal possessions were packed in two suitcases. It was their first time away from home.

Seven-year-old Loring would never return.

THREE

1923
UNION CHURCH HALL
MANILA, PHILIPPINES

To Loring, her first entry into the city of Manila proved to be strange, intimidating, and exciting. As their carriage carried them through the outskirts into the heart of downtown, she was overwhelmed by the sight of huge buildings standing side by side along the broad streets. Noisy crowds of people of every skin color surged along the cement sidewalks. From open-air markets and stalls, the smell of fried meat and other foods scented the air.

The carriage deposited them at the Emerson Chapel on Padre Faura Street. The massive stone building dwarfed its smaller neighbors and looked more like a fortress than a religious sanctuary.

The chapel anchored the complex of buildings that made up Union Church Hall. The boarding school's founding charter embraced the Protestant ethic of faith and hard work along with duty and responsibility.

A school matron met Norma and Loring's carriage and walked them to one of the dormitory buildings. There, they were each assigned a cot and told they would share the room with ten other girls.

The matron said that their first responsibility was to learn the rules that governed the lives of the students. A printed schedule dictated the specific times for meals, classes, physical activity, church attendance, study hours, personal hygiene, and chores. The girls rose each morning at six and retired at eight in the evening.

Every student was assigned a job ranging from working in the kitchen and serving the other students' meals, to cleaning the dormitories, bathrooms, and classrooms. The school set aside an hour before bedtime for personal activities such as reading or family correspondence.

When the matron asked the girls to briefly tell her about their life in Isabela Province, Loring refused to speak. After learning from Norma that Loring was only seven, the matron said she would need to meet Mr. Bordner before she could be officially admitted as a boarding student.

Harvey Bordner was the superintendent of schools in Manila. Then in his mid-forties, he arrived in the Philippines with his wife Maude in 1902 after being recruited in the United States to help create an education system using English as the single medium of instruction. Together, he and Maude spent twenty years pursuing this goal in every part of the country. In Isabela Province, he met and became friends with Charlie Ebersole.

After the Spanish-American War, Bordner was deeply sensitized to the plight of children of mixed race. Many were fathered by American servicemen and treated as outcasts. Some were abandoned by their mothers and became wards of the government.

When he met Loring in his office for the first time, Bordner told her that he knew her father and was aware of the family situation. He asked if she felt comfortable leaving her parents at seven to begin a new life at their school. Loring remained silent.

Over the years, Bordner had learned how to put most children at ease, but Loring seemed almost fearful. He also discovered she seemed to flinch each time he used her name. He ended the meeting by saying he wanted to meet her again before deciding if she would be a good fit for the school.

Bordner concluded that Loring's name might be a painful reminder of the distress at home. Since she was beginning a new chapter in her life, he decided to try the idea of informally suggesting a change. During their second meeting, he told her that Florence was a beautiful name. In Spanish, *Florencia* meant blooming flower, as he hoped she would be.

Loring finally spoke and said she liked the name. From that day forward, she became Florence Ebersole. The name on her birth certificate would become a distant memory, emblematic of a childhood she desperately wanted to forget.

For the next ten years, Florence lived and worked at Union Church Hall under the guidance of the Bordners and the other American teachers and educators. It was a life without parental love and support, but one that molded her into a self-reliant and accomplished young woman.

She settled easily into the rhythms and routines of the school. It was a Spartan existence. When she outgrew the clothes brought from the plantation, they were replaced with hand-me-downs from the older students or clothing solicited in donations from the Union churchgoers.

Although Norma was two years older, the sisters took the same entrance tests and were placed in the same class. From the start, Florence mastered each subject with enthusiasm and hard effort, earning perfect grades every term.

The Union Church Hall school ended its classes after the fifth grade. At the end of the term, the fifth-graders took a general examination to determine their class placement at the Manila Central School, which was largely made up of American children.

Based on her scores, Florence skipped two grades and began in eighth. Norma was told she would have to start in the sixth grade. She took it hard, feeling angry and humiliated. Although it wasn't Florence's fault, it caused a temporary breach between the sisters and Norma received permission from Charlie to attend the less academically rigorous Ellinwood Presbyterian Bible School.

As Florence flourished, Charlie faced an ever-worsening business crisis. From 1909 until 1919, the plantation prospered with his successful tobacco export business. It was his one cash crop, and its superb quality financed the plantation's expansion and made him wealthy.

Following World War I, a glut of tobacco worldwide caused a collapse in prices. Charlie's export business slowly began to dry up. The plantation's profit margins narrowed and he started absorbing annual losses in 1924.

That same year, he was badly injured in a riding accident in which his legs were pinned under his falling horse. His health began a downward spiral and pessimism began creeping into his regular letters home to his younger sister, Mabelle, in Buffalo.

November 12, 1926. Hello Kid: I owe you an apology for not writing sooner. Here it is just one darn thing after another with the worst yet to come... I never was one to worry about the final liquidation but after limping around on crutches for two seemingly endless years, I sometimes rather wish for an end to it all.

In 1927 Charlie was forced to shutter the tobacco farm. There was no money to hire skilled help or maintain the houses and farm buildings. Charlie rented his tillable land out to tenant farmers.

By then, he and Flaviana had six children. He was also supporting Processo and Edward, and sending tuition money for Norma and Loring.

Twenty-five years of smoking had taken its toll on his lungs and he began to suffer respiratory problems followed by a diagnosis of tuberculosis. In 1928, he left the plantation and was admitted to the pulmonary tuberculosis ward at St. Luke's Hospital in Manila.

Man is weak and susceptible, he wrote Mabelle on March 28, 1928, *and has been since Adam's time.... Increase in weight is slow, a pound or two per month, yet like all optimistic fools I live and hope. Last May I did not much give a darn which way the cat jumped. Thinking of the kids is the only thing that has made me struggle to continue living.*

Charlie died at St. Luke's on August 6, 1928, at the age of forty-nine. His body was returned to Santiago in Isabela Province and Flaviana held a memorial service for him at the plantation chapel. For his contributions to the economic growth of the region, the city elders of Santiago renamed one of its prominent avenues Ebersole Street.

Charlie didn't leave a last will and testament, and a legal battle soon ensued. Maria and Processo hired a lawyer to sue Flaviana over who was the legitimate heir to the substantial estate.

Florence was deeply saddened when she received word of her father's death. Although she had never returned to the plantation, Charlie corresponded with her over the years. In his letters he praised her for her academic accomplishments and wrote that he was proud of her.

Not long after he died, Florence received a letter from Charlie's sister, her aunt Mabelle in Buffalo, New York. Mabelle wrote that she hoped to have a closer relationship with Florence and the other children even though they were separated by thousands of miles. The two began a regular correspondence in which they shared the goings-on in their respective lives. It gave Florence a window into American life and a way to feel truly connected to her father's family.

Now an honor student at the Manila Central School, Florence continued to live in the dormitory at Union Church Hall, finding a part-time job that paid for her meals, clothing, and personal needs. From the age of twelve, she was financially independent.

She continued to excel in every subject, including English, history, algebra, Spanish, and geometry, as well as three years of Latin, which was considered the most difficult academic discipline.

Florence found her greatest satisfaction in being a mentor to the young mestizas who were just starting at Union Church Hall. As much as she had personally thrived there, there was an ugly secret she had discovered about some of the white members of the congregation who supported the school.

In many encounters over the years, she was treated with the pity owed someone who was racially soiled and told how grateful she should be that the church saw as its Christian duty the need to help girls like her. Others were even more obvious in their choice of words. One parishioner referred to the girls as tar babies.

These encounters only toughened her. By being a source of strength to the younger mestizas when they confronted bigotry, she was able to prepare them for the reality of their situation as they grew older. It gave her a sense of purpose and a feeling she had helped their lives in a small way.

Her social life centered on school and church activities. A member of the choir, she sang at regular services at Emerson Chapel, as well as to patients at the Sternberg Army Hospital and to sailors aboard the American naval vessels in Manila Bay. Although she had male friends, she didn't date anyone in high school. Some of her friends called her a Goody Two-shoes.

After graduating with honors from Manila Central High School in 1934, the nineteen-year-old Florence enrolled for a year in the Insular Business College in Manila. She learned typing, shorthand, accounting principles, and other business disciplines to prepare her for a secretarial career.

Norma had followed a different career path after attending the Ellinwood Presbyterian Bible School, going on to take teacher training courses. After graduation, she was hired as a kindergarten teacher at the school established to educate children of the executives of the Peter Paul candy company, the makers of Mounds and Almond Joy, which was located fifty miles south of Manila in the town of Candelaria.

Norma and Florence reconciled a few years after their paths diverged at Union Church Hall. Norma rarely traveled to Manila but she kept in touch with letters, writing at one point that she was now in a serious romantic relationship.

In 1935, Harvey Bordner, who had remained a mentor to Florence and also served on the board of the Army-Navy YMCA, alerted her to an open position available as executive assistant to the business manager, Fred Comings.

Housed in a four-story building that spanned two city blocks, the Army-Navy YMCA was an important site for social events within the American community. The hotel had more than one hundred rooms and provided visiting accommodations for American sailors, marines, and soldiers deployed across the Pacific. The YMCA had an open patio bar, club rooms, a gymnasium, bowling alley, swimming pool, barber shop, banking office, and dining rooms.

Florence interviewed for the job with Comings and was hired as his secretary. Working at an important American-run facility was a prestigious job for a mestiza to have and she was thrilled to begin her professional career at the age of twenty.

Two years later she was promoted to executive assistant to the YMCA's general manager, H. J. Scofield. Through the next two years, Scofield assigned her a growing set of responsibilities. Whatever assignment he gave her, she performed well. Hours didn't matter. Eventually, she became a de facto assistant manager of the club, overseeing some of the daily operations of the front office, including the planning of special events, ceremonial galas, and athletic competitions. Although her salary remained that of a well-paid secretary, she took pride in her growing responsibilities.

Entering her twenties, Florence matured into a lovely young woman with delicate Eurasian features and a slender figure. Scofield became more personally attentive, and Florence sensed he was falling in love with her. A thirty-three-year-old bachelor, Scofield lived with his mother and had an earnest sincerity that Florence found endearing. Although she was not attracted to him, she didn't want to hurt his feelings.

After Scofield returned from a business trip to China, he presented her with a pair of green silk pajamas embossed with yellow threaded dragons. He introduced her to his mother, who apparently approved of Florence, because he then invited her to join him on a business trip to Baguio, the mountain resort in northern Luzon. Florence said she would accept the invitation if she could bring a girlfriend, and he agreed.

Florence handled the awkward situation with openness and honesty, always keeping things on a pleasant basis, but promising nothing further. Scofield eventually realized that his romantic feelings were not reciprocated. They remained good friends.

When the Imperial Japanese Army invaded China in 1937, the repercussions were immediate for the YMCA and its staff. Ships carrying Chinese refugees began arriving every day at the Manila docks. Many Chinese with American connections were temporarily housed at the YMCA, and Florence began to hear firsthand reports of Japanese atrocities against civilians.

In September 1939, the German army invaded Poland and war with England and France broke out after Germany refused to withdraw its troops. In Manila, Filipino political leaders began to express fears that a world war could spread across the Pacific. Florence and her friends had many discussions about how the Japanese invasion of China might affect the Philippines, which was only a few hundred miles south of the Chinese island of Formosa.

In the spring of 1940, Florence wrote to Mabelle to express her personal feelings on who was responsible for fomenting the crisis.

The military now rules Japan and has brought about the Sino-Japanese undeclared war. Chiang Kai Shek, because of his fear that his own opponents in China will overthrow him, will not use his great army to drive Japan and her menacing forces out of the country. Why the world's greatest nations do not confer with one another to prevent Japan from taking her terrible toll of bloodshed is a mystery. But "truth is stranger than fiction" so we have to just wait for what's going to happen.

A few months later, Florence received a letter from Norma in Candelaria in which she confided she was pregnant. The baby was due in September and the father was a young man named Manuel Castro. She hoped he would soon ask her to marry him.

FOUR

Charles E. Smith earned a lot of nicknames by the time he was thirty-five years old. In high school back in Cedar Rapids, Iowa, he was called Chuck. In the navy, some of his fellow sailors called him Smitty. After he became a star player of the Pacific All-Fleet baseball team, his nickname became Clutch.

Mostly, they called him Bing for the simple reason that he bore more than a passing resemblance to the legendary crooner, Bing Crosby. He liked that one most of all, although unlike the diminutive singer, he was a strapping six feet tall with an athlete's body, blue eyes, and a ruddy complexion.

Born on July 11, 1906, in Cedar Rapids, Bing's father was a lineman for the Iowa Power and Light Company, his mother a homemaker. In high school, he was an indifferent student but a phenomenal ball player. A natural leader, he was popular with his classmates and went steady with a fellow student named Alice Belle Emmons.

A restless adventure-seeker, Bing lied about his age and enlisted in the navy at seventeen. After he left, Alice discovered she was pregnant with his child, but chose not to confide the news to him. Their daughter Arlene was born in 1924 while he was attending a naval training course in Virginia. The baby was quietly adopted by Alice's married sister and raised as her child. Bing never knew.

Working his way up the ranks, Bing traveled the world aboard a slew of US Navy warships, including the *Nevada, Memphis, Whitney, Tracy, Sirius, Melville, Noa, Decatur, Zane,* and *Tatnuck.*

When his father died after a fall from the top of a telephone pole while working to restore power during an Iowa blizzard, Bing was at sea in the Pacific and unable to travel home for the funeral. Back in port, he expressed his deep regret in a letter to his mother.

He possessed a bit of a wild streak and it sometimes got him into trouble. While assigned to the light cruiser USS *Memphis* in 1925, he was declared a deserter when the ship sailed for Europe without him aboard. It hadn't been intentional; just one drink too many. He surrendered to authorities and served a month-long sentence in the prison stockade.

Later that year, his enlistment expired and he was honorably discharged. In his last fitness report, his superior officer cited his natural leadership ability and potential to be a good petty officer. Bing promptly reenlisted for another three years.

As he matured, the tempestuous side of his personality began to smooth out and in 1931 he was officially commended by his commanding officer for graduating first in class at the Destroyer Battle Force Fire Control School.

From 1932 to 1939, he received a succession of commendations and promotions until earning his permanent appointment as Chief Electrician's Mate, the highest enlisted rank in the navy within his field.

The navy saw even greater leadership potential in Bing and in 1940 he was transferred to the shore patrol headquarters in Manila, where he ran the night detail for the hundred-man force providing security for military installations and helping to keep order within the city. Although untrained in law enforcement, he became a self-taught and skilled criminal investigator, resolving many open cases involving robbery, smuggling, and even murder.

Bing enjoyed the work enough to begin studying law. Soon he was officially representing navy enlisted men charged with crimes in the Philippine civil courts. His performance was exceptional enough to earn a commendation from his superior officer, Lieutenant Philip Price.

When Lieutenant Price's tour of duty ended in 1940, he recommended Bing for a job with the Office of Naval Intelligence (ONI), where his investigation in illegal and subversive activities in Manila would be a great asset.

Transferred to the ONI at Fort Santiago later in 1940, Bing was assigned to monitor Japanese espionage activities and to conduct surveillance on Japanese civilians who emigrated from Japan over the previous decades, and who might be spies or potential saboteurs if a war did ever come.

Bing spent much of his time with ONI liaising with his old unit of the shore patrol, which was responsible for maintaining order in the capital and was now headquartered in the Army-Navy YMCA building.

One morning, Florence was overseeing activities at the front desk when she looked up to see a tall chief petty officer coming across the lobby. He was deeply tanned in dramatic contrast to his dapper white uniform. When he arrived at the desk, he asked a staff member about an upcoming event at the club. At one point he glanced in Florence's direction and his eyes lingered. Later that day he showed up at her office and asked if he could have a minute of her time. Out in the corridor, he introduced himself and invited her to lunch.

Florence saw he was a lot older than she was, but he had an air of confidence and strength, and she was intrigued enough to say yes.

FIVE

Major Edward Carl Engelhart, the deputy head of US Army Intelligence for the Philippines, struck some of his fellow officers in Manila as almost too good to be true, and it was no exaggeration. When he graduated from the US Military Academy in 1920, the editors of *The Howitzer*, the West Point yearbook, summed up his personality in three words: *Veteran Boy Scout.*

He preferred being called Carl. After twenty years in the army, Engelhart was still trustworthy, loyal, courteous, and brave, but even if he lived the Boy Scout oath, he was no one's fool. At forty, he still retained the slender athlete's body that made him a West Point fencing standout as well as an expert marksman. Of medium height with brown eyes, his only concession to age was the nearsightedness that required him to wear wire-rimmed glasses. A gifted student of human nature, he had become a brilliant intelligence officer with particular insight into Japanese military intentions.

In 1937, the Japanese demonstrated their thirst for conquest by invading China. The United States demanded their withdrawal, but Japan refused. In 1941, the Japanese sent troops into French-held Indochina, which also threatened British-held Malaya.

President Roosevelt now demanded that the Japanese forces withdraw from both China and Indochina, but the Japanese government ignored

21

him. In response, Roosevelt stopped shipments of scrap iron to Japan and closed the Panama Canal to its ships. Japan threatened to end formal relations with the United States.

Carl saw war looming ever closer on the horizon.

His preparation for intelligence work began in 1926 when as a young officer he read in a military journal that Japan was building up its military might with aspirations to become a major power. He engaged a Japanese linguist and began a study of the language, starting with children's schoolbooks.

Like the American McGuffey Readers, the Japanese schoolbooks were full of history, legends, folk tales, and colloquial sayings. The books gave him his first insights into the Japanese character. Early on, he noted that their code of ethics was not based on truth or honor, but unwavering loyalty to one's superior.

After applying for a posting to Japan, Carl was assigned in 1927 to the American Embassy in Tokyo to begin a five-year assignment as a military attaché. His wife Margo moved with him. While stationed there, she gave birth to their son, Anders.

Within three years, Carl was completely fluent in conversational Japanese. Earlier in his career, Carl served a stint as a coastal artillery officer, and a Japanese staff officer asked if he would critique the effectiveness of a Japanese coastal artillery regiment near Nagoya. Seeing an opportunity to gauge their military readiness, he received approval for the assignment from the American ambassador.

The Japanese colonel in command of the artillery regiment was very impressed with Carl's knowledge of the language, complimenting him on his "Tokyo accent." At an evening sake party, the colonel confided that the Japanese high command considered even a bayonet a secret weapon. He told Carl that he could take all the photographs he wanted of his artillery units, but to hide his camera when "brass hats" visited the base.

During his time there, Carl came to learn a great deal about the Japanese military culture. The night before he went back to Tokyo, the Japanese colonel staged a farewell party for him. Carl was a bit apprehensive about receiving the honor because he knew the ritual required that he drink a half-pint cup of sake wine with every Japanese officer in the regiment, and there were thirty-five of them.

In his time in Japan, Carl had learned that sake lost alcohol content as it cooled. He devised a plan that he hoped would allow him to survive the evening's festivities.

Young kimono-wrapped geisha girls served each small carafe of sake wrapped in a steaming towel. When he received the first one, the kneeling Carl slipped it behind his back on the straw-mat floor. The next geisha assumed he hadn't been served and gave him another bottle. He placed that one behind him as well, eventually secreting away four of the half-pints to cool.

When the ritual marathon toasting began, each Japanese officer would squat in front of him with his own steaming bottle and cup. They exchanged carafes in order to serve one another. Carl would fill the other officer's cup with their hot sake and the Japanese filled Carl's cup with his cooler sake.

To the amazement of the Japanese, he still appeared sober at the end of the evening.

———

Returning with Margo and Anders to the United States, Carl was assigned to the submarine mine depot at Fort Monroe, Virginia. In 1937, Margo gave birth to a baby girl they named Karen.

In preparation for any future war, the army needed to make plans for the deployment of electronically controlled minefields to protect American shipping from attack while in harbor. Carl was responsible for testing and selecting the mine control system that would be standardized for use throughout the army, and was assigned to oversee its installation at American ports in both the Atlantic and Pacific. It was an important assignment, but as a career officer he had his eyes on Europe and the Pacific.

He was appalled when England and France signed the Munich Pact with Germany in 1938, allowing the Germans to dismember Czechoslovakia. In September 1939, England and France finally declared war against Germany after the invasion of Poland. Germany struck an alliance with the Soviet Union, then invaded France in May 1940. France was defeated in just six weeks, leaving England to fight alone.

Carl believed the United States would enter the war at some point, regardless of England's fate, because Hitler was committed to enslaving the rest of the world. His principal worry was that the Germans would join forces with Japan. Together, he thought they had a real chance to conquer the remaining global democracies.

Since his five-year tour in Tokyo, Carl continued to monitor the changes in the Japanese government and military. He had personally met a number of the military figures who were now in senior command roles. They were tough and seasoned warriors looking to expand Japanese influence through conquest.

In 1940 Carl was assigned to become a deputy chief of intelligence for the Philippines. As the tensions in the Pacific continued to mount, he noticed that his married counterparts in the Office of Naval Intelligence started evacuating their wives and children back to the United States. He sent Margo, thirteen-year-old Anders, and three-year-old Karen back to California aboard the transport USS *Grant*.

Shortly after, he began working with a British Commonwealth intelligence agent operating out of Manila, who had a network of spies scattered across the Far East. Together, Carl and the British officer assimilated the isolated scraps of information being sent back from Formosa, Japan, Manchuria, Korea, and China that signaled the Japanese military's war preparations. Carl translated the Japanese documents and attempted to make sense of them in regular intelligence reports.

He also made a practice of interviewing the people deported by Japanese authorities in the Far East as they arrived in Manila. The Japanese suspected many of them of being spies. All were loyal to the United States.

Occasionally, they provided valuable information about new Japanese military installations and troop deployments.

Carl discovered that the Japanese were training army units for a new type of warfare involving the dropping by airplane of combat troops wearing parachutes. In writing his summary, Carl coined the term *paratroops*, and Colonel Jones, his commander, predicted that the word would become standard terminology in the future.

As his work continued to draw praise, Carl drafted detailed briefs based on the information collected by the British agents in the Far East. These assessments were not only sent to British intelligence in London, but to Army Intelligence headquarters in Washington, DC, as well.

He was especially gratified when his British counterpart gave him a communication from his headquarters in London. It read, "Convey to your American opposite number the appreciation of the highest authority here." That authority was Prime Minister Winston Churchill.

When Carl's administrative secretary, the wife of a fellow officer, was sent back to the States, he needed a replacement to help with his ever-increasing paperwork. He asked for recommendations both in his own office as well as the Office of Naval Intelligence, which had a suite across the hall.

Learning of the position, Bing spoke to Florence about it. She was excited at the idea of working in an important role defending the Philippines. She and Bing were now seeing each other regularly and she asked him to submit her résumé for consideration.

When she arrived for her interview, Carl liked Florence right away. For someone so young, she was professionally poised and possessed a high level of self-confidence reflected in her bearing and demeanor. A clerical test revealed that her typing and dictation skills were superb. Her English usage in a brief paper he asked her to draft was better written than papers from some of the staff officers. He asked her if she could work nights and weekends. She said she would stay as long as it took to complete the assignments he gave her.

Since she would be handling highly classified information, he told her it was necessary to do a thorough background check. Florence assured him there was nothing detrimental in her background. Carl knew H. J. Scofield, the general manager at the YMCA. When Carl called him after the interview to ask about her, Scofield told him she was worth her weight in gold. The background check came back clean and Florence started her new job a few weeks later.

SIX

After her first lunch date with Bing, Florence's chief worry was that he might see her as "easy" because she was a mestiza. For many of the Americans living in the Philippines, mestizas were tolerated but not embraced as equals. Many other mestizas Florence knew ended up living with men who eventually discarded them.

When they began dating, she told Bing it was traditional in the Philippines for a girl of good upbringing to be chaperoned, but that she currently had no family members living in Manila. From the start he treated Florence respectfully and after they had been dating a month, Florence felt completely comfortable going out with him.

After dating Bing for several months, Florence still wasn't sure they would last. Bing was thirty-six. She was twenty-four. It was clear he had a lot of experience with women. When it came to dating and romance, she had very little. They had different interests as well.

Baseball was one of Bing's passions. He tried to explain how hard he could throw the ball and what he could make it do before it reached the plate. Florence knew nothing about baseball, but after All-Fleet games the players would get together with their wives and girlfriends. That part was fun and Florence saw Bing's natural popularity with his teammates.

Bing was also a gifted poker player and supplemented his pay with his winnings. Florence wasn't interested in card games or gambling. She enjoyed reading and for her part encouraged Bing to read some novels and

27

nonfiction so they could discuss them together. The effort didn't meet with much success.

He loved to go out and she liked to stay home. He took her to concerts, live theater, and fine restaurants. Over the many years of being on her own, she had become a good cook and enjoyed preparing him her favorite meals, including pancit noodles and adobo, empanadas, pork chicharrón, Philippine curry, and leche flan.

Bing remained a perfect gentleman and she felt a growing chemistry between them. At the same time she wasn't sure if he was equally serious about her, or even capable of a marriage commitment.

"Sailors are like turtles," Bing told her one evening after dinner. "Our shells are the ships that carry us all over the world."

"Are you ready to build a life with me?" she finally asked.

"I've made a lot of mistakes," he told her. "Probably the biggest was getting married to a woman I met on leave in San Diego ten years ago. We rushed into it without knowing one another and it ended quickly. I felt badly about the sadness I caused her. I don't want to make the same mistake twice."

"I suppose turtles need more time for everything," she told him. "I'll give it to you."

When another three months passed with no indication that he was seriously considering marriage, Florence confided her feelings to Carl Engelhart. By then, she was a valued member of his intelligence team. Initially, her role had been to take dictation, type orders, and review personnel documents. Soon, she was helping to collate intelligence provided by the American and British agents across Southeast Asia, including from Singapore, Jakarta, and Phnom Penh.

Carl's own feelings toward Florence evolved from being her professional superior to that of a close friend and self-appointed protector. He found her lovely and intelligent and trusted her fully. For her part, Florence viewed Engelhart as a brilliant and principled man as well as a father figure.

Carl proposed a strategy to draw out Bing's true intentions.

"Stop going out with him," he said. "See how he responds to that."

Florence took his advice, gently telling Bing she couldn't see him anymore.

Faced with the fact that their relationship was in jeopardy, he thought about what life without Florence would be like and realized he wanted her as his life partner to share everything going forward.

After purchasing a diamond engagement ring, he proposed to her on a moonlight cruise in Manila Bay and Florence happily accepted. They were married at the Central Student Church on Taft Avenue, which Florence attended through her years at Union Church Hall. Reverend Don Holter, the minister of the church, presided over the ceremony. Bing's friend Harry Glass stood up for him. Frances Dyson, one of her former bosses at the YMCA, witnessed for Florence.

She wore a simple white linen knee-length dress that accentuated her slender figure. Her only adornment was a white orchid corsage. Bing wore a matching white linen suit with a navy blue and white striped tie. He couldn't stop smiling.

They honeymooned for a week in Baguio, the mountain resort built near the army base where Field Marshal Douglas MacArthur and his Philippine Army staff spent the hottest weeks of the summer season.

It was bracingly cool in Baguio, which was surrounded by a tropical pine forest. The place held special memories for Florence. As a little girl, she temporarily escaped the family carnage at home to spend part of the summer there with the family of a friend of her father's from his army days.

Returning to Manila, she moved into Bing's house at 533 Pennsylvania Avenue. It was comfortable and stylish, with a large living room, dining area, three bedrooms, a terraced patio, and a garage for Bing's green Chevrolet.

He employed a Filipino chef called Old Clem and a house boy named Mariano. Clem was bent over with age but did the food shopping and prepared their meals now that Florence was working full-time. Mariano was Clem's nephew. He maintained the plantings in the garden and kept the house spotlessly clean. The two of them shared an apartment over the garage.

Florence was never happier. Bing began their family by giving her a puppy, but she hoped she was already pregnant with his child, and conveyed her thoughts in a letter to her Aunt Mabelle in Buffalo. After recalling the difficult times that she and her siblings had endured through the years, she wrote, *I am actually living the story of Sleeping Beauty that I read as a little girl.*

Since Bing's ONI office was across the hall from hers in Fort Santiago, they commuted to work, came home for a two-hour lunch break and siesta, and then went back to work until six before savoring another night together.

She made a number of good friends on Engelhart's intelligence team. One was Lucy Hoffman, a Swiss national married to an American. Fluent in Japanese, she was one of Carl's trusted intelligence interpreters. Lucy had a precocious five-year-old daughter named Lily who Florence also found delightful.

Another friend was Angelita Alvarez Sobral, who worked as the secretary for another officer. Florence's favorite companion was Lieutenant Ray Bibee, who had a folksy charm like a young version of Will Rogers, America's favorite humorist.

Her social friends included Dolores Gardner, who was also a mestiza. Dolores's father was a sergeant in the 33rd Infantry during the Spanish-American War and, like Charlie Ebersole, decided to make his life in the Philippines.

Florence was excited to meet Dolores's older brother Marvin, who was a famous movie star known as the "Rudy Valentino of the Philippines." His stage name was Eduardo de Castro, and Florence often read about his amorous exploits in the newspapers.

In September 1941, she received a letter from Flaviana, her stepsister turned stepmother, asking if Florence would consider allowing her youngest daughter, Olive (Florence's half sister), to live with her and Bing. Olive was fifteen years old and planning to attend Manila Central High School, the same institution Florence attended after leaving Union Church Hall.

Florence spoke to Bing and he agreed to let her stay in one of the two spare bedrooms. Olive would be able to walk to and from the high school on Taft Avenue and take her meals at home.

After Olive joined them, Norma arrived for a visit with her one-year-old son, Jerry. She told Florence that she had lost her job as a kindergarten teacher at the Peter Paul candy company in Candelaria. With the threat of war chronicled every day in the newspapers, the executives repatriated their children to the United States.

Jerry's father, Manuel Castro, hadn't asked Norma to marry him yet, and she thought her absence for a few months might bring him around. Noting that Florence still had a spare bedroom, she asked if she and Jerry could move in too.

When Florence suggested the idea to Bing, he grew angry. They had only been married for a few months, he told her, and he wanted to live with her as man and wife, not man and wife and wife's whole family.

Florence was upset, but Carl Engelhart assured her that Bing was absolutely right, and that as newlyweds, the two of them deserved at least some privacy in the first year of their marriage.

In a letter to her Aunt Mabelle in Buffalo, Florence wrote, *I now realize that my husband's wishes must come into the picture too and that I must not let my relatives spoil our life for us. I think Norma understands.*

Norma didn't understand, but she saw that the decision was clearly final and told Florence she would return to her apartment in Candelaria and to the man she hoped to marry.

SEVEN

Carl Engelhart suddenly found himself in serious trouble. It stemmed from a major shakeup in the command structure of the US Army in the Philippines. After leaving the US Army in 1935, Douglas MacArthur had come out of retirement at the behest of his friend, Philippine president Manuel Quezon, to serve as the Field Marshal of the Philippine Army. The force had grown to eighty thousand soldiers, although most were untrained for battle.

With war clouds looming, President Franklin Roosevelt recalled MacArthur to active duty in July and gave him command of a new military organization called the United States Army Forces in the Far East (USAFFE), which combined the Filipino and American forces. If war did come, Roosevelt wanted the troops in the Philippines to be unified under one commander, one who knew the land. MacArthur had commanded the American forces in the Philippines from 1929 to 1930.

The creation of USAFFE resulted in Engelhart's Office of Army Intelligence being reduced to a subordinate role. All war planning and intelligence gathering came under the control of MacArthur's personal staff.

MacArthur moved to quickly eliminate any possible rivals to his authority, beginning with Major General George Grunert, who commanded the American forces in the Philippines. MacArthur wrote to General George Marshall, the army's chief of staff in Washington, DC, to reassign Grunert immediately as "his services were no longer needed."

32

For USAFFE's new intelligence chief, MacArthur chose Colonel Charles Andrew Willoughby, who had served in the same capacity under him during his years as Field Marshal of the Philippine Army. Willoughby was born in Heidelberg, Germany. His birth name was Adolph Karl Tscheppe-Weidenbach, but after moving with his parents to the United States, he Americanized his name. General MacArthur privately referred to him as "my pet fascist," as Willoughby was an early admirer of Italian dictator Benito Mussolini.

Engelhart's daily intelligence reports now went directly to Willoughby's office, although copies were still sent to Washington, DC. Soon after Willoughby took over, Engelhart was personally commended by Washington for an intelligence breakthrough that accurately predicted the location of a Japanese army command being assembled at the port city of Takao on the island of Formosa.

The techniques Engelhart used to make the breakthrough were typically unorthodox. With his knowledge of Japanese military culture, Engelhart looked for clues that would have been meaningless to most intelligence analysts. He pursued a number of different sources, but the clinching evidence came from Japanese naval shipping manifests that revealed that a shipload of geisha and comfort women was sent to the port assembly area in Takao to service the military force.

Colonel Willoughby called Engelhart into his office and berated him in front of his staff. In spite of his commendation, Willoughby threatened to officially reprimand him for going outside approved channels and submitting intelligence reports to Washington, DC, that involved countries beyond the Philippines. If he continued disobeying orders, Willoughby said he would have him recalled to the United States.

Carl noticed that whenever the volatile Willoughby lost control, his native German accent came out more strongly. His amusement helped him endure the tongue-lashing, which finally ended after Willoughby ordered that all intelligence reports now be funneled through his office and that no independent assessments were to be forwarded by Engelhart to Washington, DC.

Knowing he was on thin ice, Engelhart complied. By late November, however, his agents were sending him increasingly alarming reports of unusual Japanese air activity over the Philippines, including aerial reconnaissance flights over the beaches at Lingayen Gulf, a natural invasion site. An American fighter pilot at Clark Field north of Manila reported that he was suddenly surrounded by Japanese Zero fighter planes and that one of the pilots waved at him before their flight broke away.

Engelhart passed the reports up the chain of command to Willoughby along with his view that a Japanese invasion could be imminent. His assessments elicited no response. Willoughby told his staff that he believed an attack by the Japanese against American territory was suicidal and therefore out of the realm of possibility, at least for the present.

For his part, Bing Smith and his fellow agents with the Office of Naval Intelligence noticed a surge in political activities within the Japanese community in Manila. One of his Japanese-speaking agents attended a gathering of Japanese businessmen to hear a talk delivered by an imperial messenger from Tokyo. At one point, the messenger told the group that any foreigner who could speak Japanese was an enemy of the empire and would eventually be hanged or shot. Knowing that Engelhart was fluent in the language, Bing passed along the information.

At night, Florence and Bing listened to the latest news on the shortwave radio in the kitchen before going to bed. Much of it was focused on the titanic battle taking place in Russia between the German and Soviet armies. The Germans were battling through blizzards and had reached the outskirts of Moscow. The newscaster predicted that the Soviet government was about to fall.

In Europe, war had been raging for more than two years, with tremendous bloodshed on both sides. If the Soviet Union was knocked out of the war, only England would remain to oppose the Nazi regime.

President Roosevelt decided to up the ante again on the Japanese when they still refused to withdraw from China and moved even deeper into Indochina. In response, the United States froze Japanese assets in the United States and embargoed all oil and gasoline exports to Japan. This hit the Japanese particularly hard since more than 80 percent of its oil came from the United States.

Bing read every intelligence assessment shared with the ONI. It was all coming to a head, he confided to Florence. Like Carl Engelhart, he worried that Japan and Germany would join forces and fight together to enslave the world.

Florence was encouraged by at least one news bulletin. On December 4, it was announced that two senior Japanese diplomats were on their way to the United States to try to negotiate a peaceful resolution to the crisis between their two countries.

EIGHT

DECEMBER 8, 1941
533 PENNSYLVANIA AVENUE
MANILA

It was still dark when Florence awoke to the ringing of the telephone in the downstairs living room. Glancing at the alarm clock on the bedside table, she saw it was only four in the morning. Bing had worked late the previous night at Fort Santiago and hadn't been asleep more than a few hours. Florence moved quickly in the darkness to the downstairs phone.

"Yes?" she said.

"This is Commander Cheek, Florence. I'm sorry to disturb you, but it's important."

Marion "Sam" Cheek was Bing's superior officer at the Office of Naval Intelligence. In all the time Florence had known him, he was always calm and unruffled. Now, his voice was clearly tense.

"Tell Bing to report to the office immediately. The Japanese have bombed our fleet at Pearl Harbor and we're at war."

The words stunned her. Even though Carl Engelhart told her that war with Japan was almost a certainty, she had retained hope that President Roosevelt would find a way to prevent it.

"And tell Bing to bring his .45," added Cheek. "There may be Japanese saboteurs and snipers roaming the city."

Before going back upstairs to wake Bing, Florence telephoned Carl Engelhart to make sure he had heard the news. He picked up the phone after only one ring and Florence repeated what Commander Cheek had just told her. Carl thanked her, saying he would see her at the office later in the morning.

Engelhart had been awake when she called because ten minutes earlier he had received a phone call from Colonel Willoughby. He had sounded agitated and his German accent was front and center.

"How long would it take you to start rounding up the Japs in the event of war?" Willoughby demanded.

"Five minutes after I contact the chief of the Philippine Constabulary," Engelhart told him. "We have a priority list and are ready to go."

Willoughby hung up without saying another word. He had to have known about the Japanese attack on Hawaii, and it was obvious he was trying to keep Carl out of the loop. Now that he knew for certain, Carl was furious and called Willoughby back at MacArthur's headquarters.

"Is it true the Japanese have bombed Pearl Harbor?" he asked.

Willoughby put him on hold and made him wait before coming back to say they had.

"Then what are we waiting for?" asked Engelhart.

"All right, go get the Japs," said Willoughby.

Carl immediately phoned Colonel Guido, the chief of the Philippine Constabulary, and ordered him to begin the roundup of Japanese nationals with suspected allegiance to their mother country. He then woke his housemates and gave them the news. Both served on his staff and neither acted surprised as they dressed.

Driving in their staff car to Fort Santiago, Ray Bibee asked the question that was on all their minds. "What do you think our chances are, Carl?"

"Ask me again after El Supremo—General MacArthur—decides what we're going to do," said Engelhart.

At 533 Pennsylvania Avenue, an anxious Florence awakened Bing and he rushed to get into his uniform. Grabbing his .45 Colt 1911 from the desk in their bedroom, he headed downstairs. Stopping, he turned and walked back.

Embracing her, he said, "Don't worry. Whatever happens, we'll be all right."

Although December was well past the rainy season, the early morning air was chilly as Florence stood shivering on the balcony off their bedroom and watched Bing back his Chevrolet out of the garage. Ever since moving into the house, Florence enjoyed starting each day on the balcony, savoring the fragrance of the jasmine, bougainvillea, and frangipani in the side yard. The combined scents reminded her of her father's plantation along the Calao River.

As Bing sped off down Pennsylvania Avenue, a golden dawn paled the eastern sky above Manila. Florence wondered how many more mornings she and Bing would have to share their safe haven.

When she went downstairs, Old Clem was in the kitchen making coffee. The radio was on and an announcer was warning everyone to remain in their homes until city officials declared it was safe. Florence didn't plan to comply with the order herself. Carl would need her at Fort Santiago. She told Olive to stay home from school.

Through the open window, Florence heard the wail of an air-raid siren. It quickly built to a loud, piercing whine and was soon joined by others across the city. The reality of a world war made her shudder.

"Are the Japanese coming here?" asked Clem. He was old enough to remember when the Filipino resistance fought and died in the insurrections against Spain and the United States, and she could see the fear in his eyes.

She gently took his hand in hers and said, "Don't worry, Clem. Whatever happens, we'll be all right." Even as she repeated Bing's words, she wasn't at all sure she believed them.

Sunshine lit the blue sky as she set out to walk to the bus stop an hour later. On a typical weekday morning, Pennsylvania Avenue teemed with people, but because of the ongoing sirens and radio broadcasts, it was eerily free of traffic. Reaching Taft Avenue, she saw that the buses weren't running and that she would have to walk to Fort Santiago.

Taft Avenue divided the two halves of the city and she began walking north toward the Pasig River. Most of the stores she passed were still shuttered. Reaching the river, she walked west to Fort Santiago.

Inside, she stopped in Bing's office long enough to let him know she was safe. Looking up from his phone, he gave her a thumbs up. She walked across the hall to the Office of Army Intelligence.

Florence could feel the tension and excitement in the air. The large, high-ceilinged rooms were packed with staff as reports flooded in from all over the country on enemy actions. Florence fielded one of the telephones and began writing down the agents' reports in shorthand.

At 10 a.m., a call came in to Carl from Lieutenant Colonel John Horan, the commanding officer at Camp John Hay in Baguio, where Florence and Bing had honeymooned in August. He reported that at least fifty Japanese fighter planes had machine-gunned the base and dive-bombers delivered a follow-up attack, causing serious damage and many casualties.

Another report revealed that Japanese naval and transport vessels had been sighted off the coast near Aparri, and a landing had already taken place on an island north of Luzon. To Carl, it all pointed to an impending invasion from the north. He knew that under the provisions of Rainbow Five—the war plan approved by the Joint Chiefs in Washington, DC, in the event of war with Japan—immediate air attacks were to be launched by the US Far East Air Force against the Japanese bases and staging areas on Formosa that the intelligence staff had already identified.

Intelligence data Carl had personally sent up to Willoughby confirmed that at least one hundred Japanese troop transports were anchored in Takao Harbor on the southwest coast of Formosa. He could only hope that precision bombing attacks by the force of B-17 bombers based at Clark Field north of Manila might eliminate their invasion ships before they were even underway.

NINE

Major General Lewis Brereton, the commander of the US Far East Air Force, sat seething in one of General MacArthur's outer offices at No. 1 Calle Victoria in the Intramuros.

Right after he had been awakened at 4 a.m. with the news about Pearl Harbor, he rushed to MacArthur's headquarters. There, he told Major General Richard Sutherland, MacArthur's chief of staff, that he needed MacArthur's immediate approval for launching the precision bombing attacks against the enemy staging areas in Formosa in accordance with Rainbow Five. Sutherland told Brereton that MacArthur was too busy to see him.

Brereton was still waiting outside the office at 5:30 a.m. when Sutherland received an urgent cable from General George Marshall, the chairman of the Joint Chiefs in Washington, DC, to immediately execute Rainbow Five. Sutherland took the cable to MacArthur's office, but didn't return for almost an hour.

When he came back, Brereton again asked to meet with MacArthur, telling Sutherland that they needed to hit the Japanese troop ships while they were still anchored in the ports. Sutherland again repeated that MacArthur was too busy to see him and urged him to go back to his headquarters at Nielsen Field and prepare a strike plan for possible approval later that day.

40

Brereton angrily responded that his staff already had the strike plan. Leaving the headquarters, he reached Nielsen Field at around 8 a.m. and briefed his staff on the current situation. Lieutenant Colonel Gene Eubank, who commanded the bombing group at Clark Field, assured Brereton that his B-17 crews were trained for the mission, knew their targets, and were ready to go.

"My orders from MacArthur are that we can't attack till we're fired on," responded Brereton.

His words were met by shock and disbelief. "How could the attack on Pearl Harbor not be considered an act of war?" Eubank demanded.

At 8:15 a.m., Brereton took a transoceanic call on his secure line from General H. H. "Hap" Arnold, the commanding general of the US Army Air Corps in Washington, DC. Arnold told him that at Pearl Harbor most of their planes were destroyed as they sat lined up on the ground at Hickam Field. He warned Brereton not to allow it to happen in the Philippines.

At 8:30 a.m., all the operational B-17s at Clark Field were launched into the air after reports of a Japanese army incursion in northern Luzon, although none carried bombs. They were ordered to circle around in the sky within thirty miles of the base. Two squadrons of P-40 pursuit planes were launched to provide fighter cover.

At 9:30 a.m., an increasingly anxious Brereton was informed that Japanese warplanes had bombed Camp John Hay at Baguio. He immediately called General Sutherland and gave him the news before again requesting authority to launch an attack against the Japanese invasion force.

When Sutherland again refused, Brereton blew up, but his angry words made no difference. Brereton asked an aide who had listened to the call on another line to make written notes of what was said.

At 10:15 a.m., approval finally came from MacArthur's headquarters for an attack against the Japanese staging bases in Formosa. However, the orders were that Brereton must wait until the early evening to launch the B-17s.

The new orders were met with more incredulity and anger. What was the point of waiting until sunset? It would only give the Japanese time to make more of their own air attacks unopposed.

At 10:30 a.m., the B-17s circling Clark Field had been in the air for two hours and they were ordered back to the base. After landing, they were dispersed to their sandbagged revetments for refueling and servicing. The fighter planes that had been escorting them were sent for ground servicing. The air crews went to breakfast.

At 11:30 a.m., the radar installation at nearby Iba Field reported a massive flight of incoming aircraft heading south in their direction, about 130 miles out. The signals officer alerted the command post at Clark Field, which had no radar facility of its own, but the sighting alert was somehow mislaid by the signals clerk.

At 12:30 p.m., the Japanese attack force arrived at Clark Field to find the bomber force of B-17s sitting on the ground at their revetments. The first waves of planes were Japanese Mitsubishi bombers. They began hitting the revetments and fuel tanks, also destroying a squadron of P-40 fighters that was preparing to take off.

As the bombers departed, thirty-four Zero fighters strafed the B-17s and the rest of the base for thirty minutes. A third wave of Japanese bombers followed the Zeros and obliterated the remaining planes on the ground.

When the last Japanese aircraft disappeared to the north, Clark Field no longer existed as an air base. Two hundred thirty men had been killed or wounded, the field's fuel tanks had been blown up, the hangars and repair facilities were demolished, one-third of the fighter strength was eliminated, and twelve B-17 bombers reduced to burned-out steel skeletons. Three more were no longer operational. A massive funnel of greasy smoke rose high above the field into the cloudless sky. It could be seen as far away as Manila.

Nearby Iba Field was bombed by a separate wing of Japanese bombers, followed by strafing attacks from fifty-one Zeros. The only operating American radar station in the Philippines was destroyed. Nearly 50 percent of the American pilots, air crews, ground crews, and defenders at Iba were killed or wounded.

In a little over an hour, the US Far East Air Force ceased to exist as a fighting unit. General Brereton laid the blame for the disaster at the feet of MacArthur and his staff.

———

At 1:30 p.m., Carl Engelhart was still fielding reports in Fort Santiago when the first devastating accounts of the carnage came in from Clark and Iba Fields. He gathered his immediate staff together, including Florence, and gave them the shocking news.

When asked about their chances, Carl was characteristically blunt but also tried to project optimism he didn't really feel. Reinforcements of air, naval, and ground forces were hopefully on their way from Hawaii, he said. He didn't add that without them, the battle for the Philippines was already lost.

TEN

Kiyoshi Osawa swung his golf club and watched the lofted ball sail true toward the green. The Japanese businessman was slender and athletic, with a crown of graying hair over an oval face and prominent nose.

Osawa was a fine tennis player, but golf was his true passion. He loved the sport so much that he had bought his home overlooking the Wack Wack Club so that he could play there almost every day. His golfing partners included the international elite of Manila society.

Golf was one of his few pleasures after sending his wife Katsuko and their young daughter Yachiyo back to Japan when he felt sure that war was coming. Katsuko didn't want to leave him, but she was pregnant with their second child and he wanted to be certain they were in a safe place when the baby came.

Osawa and his caddie were walking toward the next tee box when he saw the rotund manager of the Wack Wack Club coming toward him at a run.

"It's on the radio," he shouted. "The Japanese are bombing the Americans."

The news filled Osawa with excitement as the Filipino manager told him of the attacks on American military installations in Hawaii and the Philippines. He felt great pride in his people and what they had set out to accomplish. The time had finally arrived for the empire to bare its strength to the world.

Osawa knew that most Filipinos were loyal to the Americans, particularly after the Roosevelt administration spearheaded a law through Congress in

44

1934 that approved full independence for the Philippines in 1944. At the same time, he was confident they could be brought around to full cooperation with the Japanese Empire.

The Japanese employed dozens of paid Filipino spies, and through one at the Interior Ministry, Osawa knew of the planned roundup of Japanese nationals if hostilities broke out. As one of the most prominent Japanese businessmen in Manila, he was at the top of the list.

Osawa had prepared his own contingency plan for what to do when this day arrived, and he knew he would have to execute it quickly. Back at the clubhouse, his Filipino chauffer was waiting for him in the parking lot. Osawa told him to drive home.

Five minutes later, they were rolling up the long driveway to the Osawa family compound. In the middle of the circular courtyard, a fountain shot a column of water up as high as the peak of the three-story house.

Telling the chauffer to wait, Osawa unlocked the front door of his home and walked through the oak-paneled great room where an oil painting of Katsuko hung over the fireplace. It depicted the exact moment she finished the 800-meter track race at the Women's World Games in London in 1934.

Upstairs in his bedroom, Osawa removed the knapsack he kept in the rear of the closet. It contained several pounds of rice, jars of *umeboshi*—his favorite pickled plums—two changes of clothing, and toilet articles. Going to the wall safe, he removed three thousand American dollars in cash.

Carrying the knapsack downstairs, he relocked the front door and walked back to his car. His plan was to go straight to his safe house near the Daido Trading Company in Manila to hide until the Japanese took control.

He was climbing into the rear seat of his Packard when a green-painted truck roared up the driveway and came to a halt in front of him. Men wearing the uniform of the Philippine Constabulary jumped down from the truck's freight bed and surrounded the car.

After a quick body search, they found the cash. At rifle point, Osawa was marched down the driveway. Parked in the road below his house was an old bus. Through its dusty windows he could see a group of forlorn figures sitting inside, all Japanese. A soldier stood by the open door holding a submachine gun. As the bus pulled away with Osawa aboard, he saw his chauffer at the side of the road, watching impassively.

Over the next few hours, the bus stopped at a succession of homes and businesses. At most of the locations, Japanese nationals were arrested. When the bus was full, they were driven to a guarded stockade in Manila and herded into an open compound, where hundreds more stood or sat on the ground. Filipino soldiers with rifles stood guard above them on the parapets.

The sun was setting when Osawa and a group of other prisoners were summoned from the ranks of internees and ordered aboard another bus. Osawa recognized most of them: they were among the most powerful Japanese businessmen in Manila.

As the bus drove north out of the city into the countryside, he heard the approaching roar of engines and looked up through the window at a formation of fighter planes flying south toward Manila, their silver fuselages shining brightly. One passenger cheered when he saw the red circles painted on the wings.

Osawa was deeply moved. He was fiercely proud of his Japanese heritage and the brave young warriors from his fatherland who were challenging the vast might of the Americans and the other arrogant colonial powers. For months he had listened in bitter silence as American and British members of the Wack Wack Club gathered for drinks after their rounds of golf. The conversation always turned to the latest war news and derisive comments about the Japanese fighting abilities. The club members would laughingly ask how the Japanese could possibly fight when they were all bowlegged and wore Coke-bottle eyeglasses.

It was late at night when the bus finally reached its destination, the infamous Muntinlupa Prison Camp, where the country's most hardened criminals were housed. Inside its walls, Osawa and the others were led across the prison compound into a rundown wooden building. Iron folding cots had been erected on the plank floor. There were no pillows or blankets and the only light came from a few bare bulbs hanging from the ceiling. A Filipino guard who spoke Japanese called them to attention and declared that any prisoner who attempted to open one of the windows would be shot.

When the lights were turned off, Osawa lay down on one of the cots. His body was foul with dried sweat and he desperately wanted a bath, but he was a practical man. Since there was no way to change his fate, he determined to leave it to heaven and the young warriors of the empire. Soon he was fast asleep.

———

In Manila, Florence lay awake in the darkness, overwhelmed by the enormity of everything that had happened that day. Bing had sent her home in a staff car after telling her he would be working late.

The ride was a nightmare. People seemed to have lost their minds and were driving crazily, honking their horns and cutting each other off in their rush. Parts of the city were being blacked out, but as they rode through the streets, Florence saw that many shops were still open to a spree of panic buying.

When she arrived home, her half sister, fifteen-year-old Olive, told her that the schools were closed until further notice. She peppered Florence with questions about what it all meant for them.

Old Clem was so frightened of the Japanese that he asked if he should move back to his family home in the mountains. Florence tried to reassure him by saying that nothing would happen right away and to wait until they knew more.

Mariano tacked fabric covers on all the windows in compliance with the directives for a blackout. Filipino soldiers patrolled the streets and she could hear them shouting at neighbors whose lights still shone through their windows. None of it felt like reality.

After a hurried meal, she urged Olive and the others to go to sleep early so they would be ready for whatever came in the morning, but Florence found it impossible to rest. Across the city, air-raid sirens kept sounding their long, mournful wails. They would fall silent for a brief time only to go off again.

Bing came home around midnight and told her that President Roosevelt was about to address a joint session of Congress. With the different time zones, it was still midday in Washington, DC, on December 8.

Bing turned on his shortwave radio and they sat together in the breakfast nook as Roosevelt spoke to the bereaved nation and the frightened world.

No matter how long it may take us to overcome this premeditated invasion, the American people in their righteous might will win through to absolute victory... With confidence in our armed forces, with the unbounding determination of our people, we will gain the inevitable triumph so help us God.

To Florence, the president sounded so confident, his voice so self-assured and powerful, that she found herself crying tears of hope and relief.

"He almost makes you think we have a chance here," said Bing.

After the address, Bing quickly fell asleep but Florence was still in too much turmoil to drop off. Near dawn, she heard the bumblebee-like drone of aircraft over the city, followed a little later by the distant boom of explosions.

ELEVEN

Before leaving for Fort Santiago in the morning, Bing brought together Mariano and Old Clem. Aware of the level of panic buying that had taken place the previous day, he told them to make a round of the food markets with their pull cart to buy basic essentials like rice, powdered milk, tinned meat, and vegetables. Anticipating that gasoline would be rationed at some point, he asked them to purchase two bicycles.

Florence and Bing rode to work together in Bing's Chevrolet. Unlike the previous evening, the streets were relatively clear of traffic, as if the virus of fear had temporarily abated. At the office, Florence spent the morning collating updates on enemy activity from the intelligence agents in the field and typing reports for Carl. She took a short break for lunch and returned to the office early in the afternoon.

There had been no air attacks yet on the city of Manila, but the Japanese air force struck again at the American airfields across Luzon, further reducing the number of pursuit aircraft at Brereton's command. Most of the airfields were no longer serviceable even if there had been planes to take off and land.

Late in the afternoon, Carl learned of another ominous development. Admiral Thomas Hart, who commanded the US Asiatic Fleet, informed MacArthur that he was pulling all his surface warships from Philippine waters. Without air protection, he would not allow them to suffer the same fate as the battleships at Pearl Harbor and the bombers at Clark Field.

That evening, Carl climbed to the roof of Fort Santiago. Looking out at what had been a crowded anchorage of battleships, cruisers, and destroyers in the bay, he saw it was empty. He wondered how the Philippines could be resupplied if unarmed civilian transport ships weren't protected by the fleet. They would have to run a Japanese naval gauntlet without escort. It was suicidal.

The same night, General MacArthur's public relations staff put out a bulletin that the battle against the Japanese was going well and the general was promising complete victory. *Help is on the way*, the message stated.

Carl knew from the communications arriving every hour from Washington, DC, that no reinforcements of ships, planes, soldiers, or equipment were being readied for immediate movement to the Philippines. They were cut off and alone.

On December 10, Florence was walking back to Fort Santiago after lunch at the Army-Navy YMCA when she heard the distant roar of engines. She turned and looked back down the Pasig River to see dozens of silver dots in the sky. The dots soon became formations of planes. They flew three abreast up the river, with many more coming behind them.

Some of the planes had what looked like canisters under their wings and she suddenly realized they were bombs. As the first wave thundered over her, she stood transfixed, powerless to move. The roar of the engines swelled and engulfed her like booming surf.

The following wave of aircraft headed toward the Intramuros. These were single-engine planes flying lower than the first wave. As she watched, a bomb fell away from one and sailed downward through the sunny sky, striking somewhere inside the Intramuros across the river. The ground shook under her feet and the explosion sent a curtain of flame and dense smoke high into the sky.

She ran toward the fort. A stone bridge led over the double moat to the massive entrance gate. Two American military policemen armed with rifles were standing behind a ten-foot-high pile of sandbags. One of them recognized her and waved her through.

Once inside the twenty-five-foot-thick stone walls, it took her a few minutes to recover from the shock of seeing the attacking warplanes massed over her. She watched as a group of female staffers was shepherded down the stone steps to the safety of the ancient Spanish dungeon.

"They're bombing Cavite," she heard someone say.

Cavite was the massive naval base south of Manila. She could now hear the muffled explosions reverberating in the distance. A military policeman ordered Florence to follow the other women down into the dungeon.

As the bombing continued, a few of the women couldn't stop crying. Others stared vacantly in shock at the stone ceiling as they listened to the continued explosions. One woman made the sign of the cross after each new tremor.

The attack went on for almost two hours. Florence was surprised to discover that she was calm and felt no fear as the earth continued to rumble and the air became heavy with the smell of cordite.

When it was finally quiet again, a military policeman came down and said it was safe to return to their jobs. Florence climbed the stone staircase to her office and met with Carl. He had spent much of the attack on the roof of the fort, watching the destruction of Cavite Navy Yard. Carl said he hadn't seen a single American warplane.

When the first estimates of damage to the naval base came in, they were devastating. Most of the buildings and dock facilities at Cavite were wrecked and hundreds of men had been killed or wounded. Sixty percent of the navy's torpedoes were destroyed.

Japanese planes began bombing Manila day and night. From their office window, Florence could see the fires burning out of control at the piers and warehouses along the Pasig River.

Fear and panic were contagious. When a city official interviewed on the radio suggested that Manila's citizens should consider evacuating until the bombing ended, the roads to the north and south quickly choked with thousands of cars, trucks, and horse-drawn wagons, bringing vital military traffic to a standstill.

Florence grew accustomed to the constant wail of the air-raid sirens, along with the small mountains of sandbags stacked in front of the entrances to government buildings, and the constant sight and sound of ambulances carrying wounded civilians to the hospitals.

Leaving work one evening, she passed the headquarters of the 31st Infantry Division as the post personnel were conducting the daily retreat and flag-lowering ceremony at the end of the day. When the bugler performed "To the Colors," she put her hand over her heart and watched as the American flag was slowly lowered into the waiting arms of the color guard. When the last notes ended, she found herself silently sobbing.

TWELVE

Three days after the bombing of the airfields, General Lewis Brereton received another transoceanic call from General Hap Arnold, the commanding general of the US Army Air Corps in Washington. Arnold was livid.

"How in hell could all your planes have been caught on the ground at Clark Field?" he shouted over the phone.

Brereton told him he had done everything in his power to get MacArthur's approval to attack Formosa but had been rebuffed again and again. The still furious Arnold demanded definitive answers.

Later that day, Brereton met with MacArthur. The meeting lasted just long enough for Brereton to ask for MacArthur's "assistance in setting the facts straight" for Hap Arnold about what had happened to his bombers.

"Just go back and fight the war," said MacArthur icily.

It was all happening so fast. With each new report of enemy action flowing into the office, it was clear that the Japanese were winning stunning victories across the Pacific. In just the first week following Pearl Harbor, they captured the American possession of Guam, invaded British-held Malaya, and were routing the British army as it retreated toward the fortress of Singapore.

Another huge blow fell when Japanese warplanes in the South China Sea bombed and sank the newest English battleship, *Prince of Wales*, and the battle cruiser *Repulse*, the two most powerful warships England had deployed to the Far East.

General MacArthur was well aware that most of his 120,000 American and Filipino troops were poorly trained and equipped. He needed to buy time to prepare them for the invasion he knew was coming.

On December 14, he cabled General Marshall in Washington that he needed ten squadrons of pursuit aircraft and 250 dive-bombers to rebuild his depleted air force. He suggested they be flown into the Philippines from the navy's aircraft carriers based in Hawaii.

Upon receiving the cable, Marshall summoned his senior staff officer, Brigadier General Dwight D. Eisenhower, to ask him his views. Eisenhower informed him that the navy's current position on reinforcing the Philippines was that it lacked the capability after Pearl Harbor to conduct offensive operations and it would not venture into Philippine waters at the risk of losing its remaining surface ships.

Eisenhower told Marshall it would be a long time before major reinforcements could reach the Philippines, and probably longer than MacArthur's garrison could hold out if the Japanese invaded with sufficient forces.

Marshall eventually cabled MacArthur that due to the current situation it was impractical for the navy to deliver the requested aircraft by the direct route from Hawaii. Instead, he stated that a plan would be expedited to transport unassembled pursuit planes and bombers aboard cargo vessels being routed to Australia. It meant a delay of months and infuriated MacArthur, but there was nothing he could do about it.

On December 22, the principal Japanese invasion force arrived at Lingayen Gulf in North Luzon. One hundred Japanese transport ships began unloading the first forty-three thousand troops. Three elite army divisions were assigned to the invasion under the command of General Masaharu Homma. Two of the divisions had been combat-tested in China. All of them were superbly trained.

Major General Jonathan Wainwright IV commanded the twenty-eight thousand American and Filipino troops defending North Luzon. Only three thousand of his men were trained for combat and properly equipped.

Lanky, hawk-nosed, hard-drinking, and tough, Wainwright was a brilliant soldier who as a senior at West Point had been the First Captain of the Corps of Cadets. After thirty-six years in the army, he was admired by his peers as well as the men who served under him.

Wainwright had already received his orders from MacArthur: *In the event of a landing, attack and destroy the landing force.*

A day after the invasion force arrived, Wainwright received the first set of air reconnaissance photos revealing the vast assemblage of Japanese invasion ships off the beaches. If he had still possessed an air force, Wainwright thought the destruction of the troop transports might have been achievable, but the single American plane in the area was the photo reconnaissance aircraft.

The two armies collided on the coastal plain along Route 3, a cobblestone highway that led directly south from the Lingayen Gulf toward Manila. When Homma's advance elements came up against the American and Filipino defense lines, they were temporarily stopped by Wainwright's artillery.

General Homma immediately ordered his fighter planes and light bombers to maul the defense lines. Japanese tanks followed the air strikes and the defenders were quickly routed, with hundreds of American and Filipino soldiers killed or wounded.

Knowing that his untrained troops could not hold back the Japanese, Wainwright telephoned MacArthur in Manila on the afternoon of December 23 and requested that he be allowed to withdraw his forces farther south behind the Agno River.

MacArthur considered his options. He could reinforce Wainwright and make a stand at the Agno River or implement a war plan code-named Orange, formulated by the war department in the event of war sixteen years earlier. It called for all American forces to fall back to the Bataan Peninsula. The peninsula featured a number of natural obstacles to defend against enemy attacks, and if properly equipped and supplied, MacArthur thought Bataan could be held long enough until reinforcements arrived.

He notified his force commanders that he was implementing War Plan Orange.

THIRTEEN

It was like no Christmas Eve Florence had ever known. Instead of wrapping gifts and preparing dinner, she worked another twelve-hour shift, just as she had done every day since the catastrophic news from Pearl Harbor. Bing was working even longer hours and hadn't been home for several nights.

Looting had broken out in the city. The looters were mostly targeting stores and businesses owned by Japanese, but the scope of the looting was growing every night. Bing was in charge of the navy's shore patrol night detail again to help keep order and protect public property.

Carl Engelhart and Ray Bibee left the office in the morning to attend briefings and didn't return until late in the afternoon. Carl's face was ashen as he called the support staff together, including Florence, Lucy Hoffman, Angelita Alvarez Sobral, and Marcie Evans, who worked for Ray Bibee.

Carl had just been promoted to lieutenant colonel, but this wasn't the time to celebrate. He told the four women that MacArthur was implementing War Plan Orange and the Army and Naval Intelligence offices were being shut down later that day. He and the rest of the permanent intelligence staff had been ordered to conduct future operations from the island fortress of Corregidor and the Bataan Peninsula. Naval Intelligence would be going too, he said to Florence.

He told them the army was now consolidating on Bataan. General MacArthur was about to publicly declare Manila an undefended "open city" in the hope that the Japanese would stop bombing civilian targets. Carl estimated the Japanese army would be in Manila within two weeks, and the women would be on their own.

The news that Bing was going to Corregidor left Florence reeling.

Carl thanked the women for all their good work and then apologized, saying there was no way to pay their salaries since all the personnel records were being destroyed to keep them out of Japanese hands.

"For your own safety, say nothing to the Japanese about your past work for the American army," he told them.

Still stunned, Florence went across the hall to Bing's office. He was in the middle of preparations for the move and told her he would come home that evening before leaving for Corregidor. For the rest of the afternoon, she helped the other women take the top secret military files outside in cardboard boxes to throw them on a massive burn pile.

While they worked, Florence could hear thunderous explosions as fuel tank facilities around the city were blown up by army combat engineers. Although her eyes were tearing from the smoke of the fire, she saw the same fear and confusion in the other women's faces that she was feeling herself.

When it was time to leave, Carl took Florence aside for the last time. Holding her hands in his, he told her to do whatever she felt necessary to survive until the American forces could return.

"Promise me that every single morning you will say to yourself, 'I will survive this war.'" She promised him.

On her way home, Florence saw long military convoys of cars, jeeps, and trucks carrying Filipino and American troops north on Admiral Dewey Boulevard. They were on their way to Bataan to make their stand. People on the sidewalks stood silently, many in tears, watching the men go and knowing they would soon be at the mercy of the Japanese army.

Florence hadn't had time to decorate the house for Christmas, although Mariano hung some colored balls on the rubber fig plants in the living room. Old Clem cooked a special dinner. Olive put on her best dress and looked radiant in spite of the terrible news.

When Bing got home, he said that he didn't have time for dinner, but there were things he needed to tell Florence. They went upstairs to their bedroom and he began to pack what he needed in a navy duffel bag.

"You and Olive must stay inside the house after the Japanese army gets here," he said. "Have Mariano and Old Clem do the shopping for food and other things you need."

"I understand," said Florence.

"Never go out at night. We know how their army behaved in China. You can bet some of their soldiers will be roaming the streets drunk on victory and liquor."

It was really happening, she thought, he was really going. His words came more quickly.

"I don't think you and Olive should live here alone," he said. "With the extra bedroom, you could invite Margaret or one of your other friends to stay here until I get back."

Like Florence, Margaret Cirstens was a mestiza and they had been friends since their days at Union Church Hall. She was single and lived alone, running a local bookstore.

"I'll reach out to her," Florence told him.

Bing gave her a thick envelope filled with American cash.

"This is all the cash in our bank account. Try to make it last until I get back," he said. "Hide it in the secret place under the closet floor with my spare pistols and ammunition."

"I'll do it," she assured him, still trying to absorb the enormity of it all. "How do you think the Japanese will treat us?"

"They'll come down hard on the Americans and the British," he said, "and they'll all be put in internment camps."

"What if they find out I have an American passport?" she said, feeling dizzy and sitting down on their bed.

"At some point, they will come to the house to see who lives here. Put your passport and military ID card in the hiding place with the money, and only use your Philippine identification. And get rid of my spare uniforms and military gear."

Florence had promised herself she wouldn't cry at their parting, but when he took her in his arms and kissed her, she couldn't stop the tears flowing down her cheeks.

"Being with you has been the happiest time in my life," she said.

"Mine too," he told her before turning to go. "It's probably being repeated a million times by people all over the world tonight," he said with a careful smile, "but I'll come back to you, Florencia."

FOURTEEN

On Christmas Day, Florence told Mariano to hide the metal trunk with Bing's spare uniforms in the crawl space under the garage. As she waited for him to finish, she saw he had forgotten to take in the washing from the clothesline the previous evening. The sheets and towels were coated with black soot from the fuel dump fires and the air was still harshly pungent from its acrid smell.

Mariano called it his first "black" Christmas.

As promised, General MacArthur publicly declared Manila an open city, but it didn't seem to matter to the Japanese. Their bombers came over on Christmas Day and every day afterward to deliver more bombs.

With Bing gone, Olive said she wanted to go out in the evening to be with her friends. Fun-loving and spirited, she chafed at staying home. When Florence refused, Olive threw a fit and told Florence to stop acting like her mother. Florence told her she was free to go back to Isabela Province to live with her real mother and siblings where it was safer.

That night, Florence lay in bed, her mind spinning. Bing had only been gone one day and she already missed him terribly. He had such natural confidence and strength that it infused everyone around him.

She was alone and responsible for three other people. Aside from her issues with Olive, Clem and Mariano's wages had to be paid in January along with the rent, and she no longer had a job or income.

For the next few days, Florence only ventured out during the day to get a few needed supplies. The people in the streets turned increasingly silent, walking quickly to their destinations as if desperate to escape the reality of what was about to happen.

It was different at night. Legal order disappeared. Looters no longer concentrated on Japanese stores and businesses. Their targets were indiscriminate, with marauding gangs breaking into stores and cleaning out everything on the shelves. Saboteurs began setting fires in public buildings to sow further chaos, and the sirens from fire engines and police cars echoed through the night.

On December 29, Florence and Olive listened on the kitchen radio as General MacArthur spoke from Corregidor to the people of the Philippines. He sounded confident, but his words were increasingly worrisome. In preparing for the arrival of the Japanese army, he urged people who had worked for the US military to destroy any papers that revealed their involvement. At another point, he recommended that they pour all intoxicating beverages down the sink to prevent them from getting in the hands of the soldiers.

"May God be with you . . . I shall return," he proclaimed.

Florence's US Army identification card was already safely hidden under the floorboards, along with the money Bing had given her and his two pistols. But he also had a fully stocked liquor cabinet.

She remembered Bing's warnings about how Japanese soldiers ran amok in China while drunk. Her compromise was to have Mariano bury the bottles alongside Bing's uniforms under the garage.

During Christmas week, Florence received a letter from Norma in Candelaria. She and Jerry were fine. She still wasn't married but she was sure it was only a matter of time. Manuel Castro was a good man and a patriot, and he planned to join the resistance.

On New Year's Day, Florence's friend Dolores Gardner called to say that Philippine officials in control of the few remaining military warehouses had announced they were opening them to the public, and citizens were free to take what they wanted.

They drove together in Dolores's car to the heavily bombed warehouse district. When they reached it, a mob of several thousand people was swarming through the streets, some battling over the supplies they had dragged outside. Deciding it was too dangerous to go farther, Florence and Dolores returned home empty-handed.

Florence desperately hoped for a message or phone call from Bing to let her know he was safe, but there was only continued silence. With nothing to do but wait, the days and nights dragged on.

On January 2, Florence spent most of the day at home knitting a blouse for Lucy Hoffman's daughter, Lily. Late in the afternoon, Clem complained about having stomach pain and Florence walked with the now six-month-old puppy Bing had given her to a drugstore on Taft Avenue to buy Clem a tonic.

She was returning on the sidewalk with the medicine when she suddenly heard a deep rumbling noise coming from the far end of Taft Avenue. She turned to look back and there they were, filling the avenue as far as she could see: the advance elements of the Japanese army.

Mechanized tanks thundered past first, followed by a long convoy of trucks filled with soldiers. Behind the trucks came soldiers riding bicycles. Seeing her standing alone on the sidewalk with the little dog, some of them shouted at her in Japanese.

Behind the bicycles came seemingly endless ranks of soldiers on foot led by officers on horseback, the men walking in loose formation. They wore olive-colored uniforms and visored cloth caps with pieces of cloth hanging from the back to protect their necks from the sun. Every minute or two, one of them would scream out, "BANZAI! BANZAI! BANZAI!" and be joined by the rest.

Even without understanding Japanese, she knew it was a battle cry of victory.

Two thoughts ran through her mind as the procession continued to roll past. Their red-balled Japanese flag reminded her of a fried egg. The other was that most of the men were small, the size of American boys before their final growth spurt to manhood. It gave her a momentary dose of confidence until she realized something else: the little men had driven the Americans out of Manila.

FIFTEEN

It was already dark on Christmas Eve when the intercoastal steamer carrying Bing, Carl, and hundreds of other officers left the Manila docks and began the twenty-six-mile trip to Corregidor. Most were still standing at the deck railings when the night sky behind them lit up with huge explosions. The bitter truth of defeat was evident to them all as they watched tons of ammunition and gasoline erupt in towers of flame along with military warehouses full of food and medical supplies.

Three hours later, the steamer landed at Corregidor and Bing and Carl filed ashore to join the ten thousand sailors and soldiers already deployed on the island. With the island blacked out, a beleaguered group of military policemen attempted to help the new arrivals find their way to their units or to temporary housing.

Carl knew Corregidor well and had flown over it numerous times. From the air, he thought the island resembled an immense tadpole swimming west away from the southern tip of the Bataan peninsula.

The head of the tadpole was more than a mile across and the rest of its body stretched out almost four miles to the tail. The section at the head was called Topside and it rose about five hundred feet above sea level. Topside was where most of the fifty-six heavy guns of the coastal artillery guarded the entrance to Manila Bay.

The fortress had been constructed to be impregnable from an attack by sea, and the heavy guns were all pointed in that direction. The southern tip of the Bataan Peninsula was only two miles away. None of the guns pointed there because the war planners never considered the possibility that Bataan might end up in the hands of an enemy.

About halfway to the tadpole's tail was Middleside, a phalanx of warehouses, barracks, workshops, fuel storage tanks, and the power station. The north and south tips of Middleside held the deepwater piers and docks.

The command headquarters on Corregidor was located in Malinta Tunnel, a massive bombproof, underground cavern nine hundred feet long and almost thirty feet wide. The tunnel had been augmented with twenty-five lateral tunnels. One housed a fully equipped hospital with a thousand beds, and others contained sleeping quarters for several thousand men, field kitchens, refrigerated food storage, and ammunition lockers.

Leaving the dock area in the blackout, Carl led Bing to the three-story military barracks at Middleside. It had been constructed to house two thousand officers and enlisted men, but now the corridors and meeting rooms were crammed with folding cots to accommodate thousands more.

A makeshift canteen next to the lodging office was offering sandwiches, doughnuts, and coffee under a hand-painted sign that read MERRY CHRISTMAS 1941. It didn't feel like Christmas as Carl and Bing sank into their cots well after midnight. Carl fell asleep grateful that he had sent his wife and son back home. Bing was already worried about Florence.

On Christmas morning, the men went their separate ways. Bing headed for the headquarters of the Office of Naval Intelligence, which was established in one of the side tunnels. When he arrived, Commander Cheek told him he wasn't sure what work they would be doing going forward. All the ships in the American naval surface fleet had left Philippine waters and weren't coming back anytime soon. Aside from a handful of submarines and a flotilla of the small but fast and heavily armed PT (patrol, torpedo) craft, there was no American naval presence left. Cheek told Bing to stand by until things were sorted out.

That same morning, Carl walked from the Middleside barracks to the main defense headquarters commanded by Major General George Moore. There, he learned that the Army Intelligence staff had already moved to Bataan and he should follow them.

As Carl was leaving the tunnel, he encountered a member of General Moore's staff who had been Carl's commanding officer years earlier at the submarine mine depot in Fort Monroe, Virginia. While serving there, Carl had earned several commendations for developing advanced electronic firing mechanisms to detonate the mines.

The officer told Carl to wait and went directly to General MacArthur to countermand Carl's orders to go to Bataan. That afternoon Carl was put in command of all the minefields around Corregidor.

At the motor pool, Carl was given a small Crosley automobile and he set out to survey the minefields' state of readiness. The fields were all controlled electronically from concrete bunkers called casemates that were positioned around the shoreline. Each casemate controlled about two hundred mines.

He quickly discovered that much of the electronic equipment they were using was obsolete and needed major upgrades to function properly. Offshore, many of the cables to the mines were also inoperative and needed replacement. His first challenge was to find the necessary parts.

On the other end of the rock, Bing Smith was not the kind of man who found it easy to "stand by." Sam Cheek told him that a handful of submarines were still operational, and Bing knew they were being serviced and supplied by the big submarine tender USS *Canopus*. Bing served aboard the *Canopus* in 1938 and knew how vital a role it played in keeping the subs running.

After learning that the *Canopus* was anchored near Mariveles at the southern tip of Bataan, Bing hitched a ride to the ship on one of the launches ferrying men and supplies back and forth to the army.

The ship was in a small cove near the jungle's edge and the crew had spread green camouflage nets above the upper works, topped by hundreds of palm fronds to make it appear the ship was an extension of the land. Reporting aboard, Bing was welcomed by the officer he served under a few years earlier.

Valuing Bing's experience and resourcefulness, the officer immediately offered him a job. Bing sent a message to Commander Cheek to explain the situation and Cheek ordered him to remain there.

———

It was approaching noon on Monday, December 29, and Carl Engelhart was directing the replacement of obsolete wire cables from a mine-laying ship in Manila Bay when he heard the growing drone of approaching aircraft. He knew instantly they were Japanese. There was no American Far East Air Force left.

From his grandstand seat offshore, he watched wave after wave of Japanese light bombers blast Corregidor from head to tail in an attack that lasted more than two hours. As one of the planes finished its bombing run, the pilot turned to fly directly toward their mine-laying ship. He came over so low that Carl could see the pilot's face as Ed Rosenstock, the ship's captain, cut loose at the plane with a Browning automatic rifle.

Across Mariveles Bay, Bing and the rest of the crew watched the attacks from the deck of the *Canopus* as the bombers pummeled the northern part of the island, the explosions setting off innumerable fires. Hidden under its camouflage netting, the *Canopus* was ignored through most of the attack, but a pilot in the final wave of returning planes observed the anchored ship, and his squadron flew back to make an attack.

Only one of their bombs struck the ship, but it was armor-piercing and landed with deadly accuracy, penetrating each of the ship's lower decks until it exploded over the propeller shaft and blew open the hatches to the ammunition magazines.

A desperate struggle ensued to put out the raging inferno before it could detonate the tons of ammunition in the powder magazines. The lives of every man in the crew hung in the balance as the ship's firefighters fought against the odds and finally put it out. Six sailors were killed and twenty seriously wounded.

When the all clear sounded, Bing and the rest of the sailors began the vital job of repairing and rewiring the ship's electrical and communications systems.

———

After Carl brought his mine-laying ship back to the docks, he checked in at the command headquarters to find out the extent of the damage from the attack. Twenty-four men had been killed and ninety wounded. Power was cut in many parts of the island. A gasoline dump was burning out of control. He thought it could have been much worse.

General MacArthur had narrowly escaped death. He had just left the cottage where he was quartered when the first bombers attacked. Caught in the open, his Filipino orderly, Sergeant Domingo Adversario, sheltered MacArthur's body with his own as a bomb blew up MacArthur's cottage a hundred feet away. Bomb fragments wounded the orderly but MacArthur was unharmed.

Carl returned to his own new billet at Topside and found the building flattened. The nearby hospital had also been hit and the patients were being transported to the underground hospital in Malinta Tunnel.

With no place to stay, he set up a cot in his own headquarters, which was the principal mine casemate located at James Ravine. Many of the shore cables connecting the casemate bunkers to the submerged minefields had been destroyed, and he began directing the effort to splice new wiring to them.

Japanese bombers continued to pound the island and its defenses every day. Usually there were air-raid warnings but not always. Carl was standing near a casemate with two of his men when a bomb suddenly exploded in the road nearby. As they watched, a truck driver was blown out of his cab and landed a headless corpse.

At the same moment, Carl felt a blow to his right shoulder like he had been hit with a baseball bat. Blood began spurting from a deep shrapnel wound in his arm. After wrapping a tourniquet above it, one of his men helped him to the nearby first aid station of the 4th Marines, where the injury was dressed.

As the days passed, Carl began to wonder if he was being personally targeted by the Japanese. The engine in the little Crosley automobile he drove was so loud that he sometimes couldn't hear the bombers coming.

When another bomb landed near the car a few days later, Carl slammed on the brakes in a cloud of flying debris. A few moments later, he felt a stream of blood running down his neck and soaking his shirt. At the aid station, the same medic jokingly chided him about wanting to become a regular customer.

Awarded the Purple Heart for his first wound, he took his third shrapnel hit a week later and it required another dozen stitches. He concluded that the Crosley was unlucky and turned it back in at the motor pool. From then on, he walked to the casemates with his ear cocked for approaching aircraft.

———

Aboard the *Canopus*, Bing and the rest of its crew made the ship seaworthy again in less than a week. It was still needed to service and repair all the vessels supplying Bataan, and remained at anchor in the cove under a new set of camouflage screens.

Spotted again during another air raid, Japanese bombers attempted to deliver the coup de grace. At least a dozen bombs rained down on the ship, but once again, only one was a direct hit. This one was a fragmentation bomb that unleashed a torrent of metal splinters across the open decks, wounding fifteen sailors. Another bomb landed close enough to stove in the hull below the water line.

After the ship was again repaired, the captain devised an ingenious plan to convince the Japanese that they were now a derelict hulk. He had a number of the compartments belowdecks on one side flooded so that it listed heavily over. During the day, smoke pots were placed along the upper deck so that the ship appeared to be on fire. The Japanese never bombed at night, so he had the crew sleep ashore during the day. At dusk each evening, the ship came alive and the crew worked all night making repairs to the army and navy's support vessels.

At MacArthur's headquarters inside Malinta Tunnel, another portentous development threatened the army's future survival on Bataan. In pursuing War Plan Orange, MacArthur and his staff had failed to recognize that one key element of the plan required food supplies sufficient to feed the army for six months be stockpiled on Bataan and Corregidor. The army had failed to do so.

On January 6, MacArthur was informed that even on half rations, food would run out in less than ninety days. He immediately put the eighty thousand men on Bataan and the ten thousand on Corregidor on half rations, "effective immediately." Company cooks began to slaughter the army's remaining cavalry horses and pack mules to supplement a diet consisting largely of rice and canned vegetables. When their food ran out, MacArthur knew they would be forced to surrender.

SIXTEEN

Florence awoke to the noise of angry shouting in the street. From her bedroom window, she saw two Japanese soldiers at the front door of the family who lived across from them on Pennsylvania Avenue. They were an English couple and the husband had been a banking director in the city. His wife and two small daughters were standing on the sidewalk and the children were crying. He was trying to speak to one of the soldiers but was being shouted down. When the Englishman persisted, the soldier clubbed him in the face with his rifle butt. Florence watched in horror as the man was dragged onto a waiting bus, followed by his wife and children.

Many English and American families owned or rented homes in her neighborhood and the roundup continued over the next several days. If no one answered the door to the soldiers' knocking, they battered it open and went inside to search. Upon leaving, they pinned signs on the houses reading, *This is property of the Imperial Japanese government. Do not remove.*

Florence's friend Dolores Gardner told her that an internment camp had been set up on the campus of the University of Santo Tomas and that all the British and American civilians were being forced to live there. Florence could only wonder if the Japanese occupying authority knew that her house had originally been rented to Bing. If so, she would have to go too.

She kept every promise made to him on the night he left for Corregidor. Since the occupation, she and Olive rarely ventured outside during the day

71

and never at night. Although Old Clem was becoming more terrified of the Japanese every day, he and Mariano did the shopping for food and other necessities.

Olive begged to be allowed to go out with her friends, but Florence forbade it, and renewed the threat that if Olive disobeyed her, she would be sent back to live with Flaviana in Isabela Province.

Margaret Cirstens had agreed to live with them as well. She was in love with a Swiss national named Alfred Keller who worked for the Peter Paul candy company where Norma had taught the children of its expatriate executives. Since Switzerland was a neutral country, Alfred was allowed to keep his job.

Although Margaret hoped Alfred would ask her to marry him, she agreed to move in with Florence until he reached a decision. Margaret was older than Florence and had a strong, self-reliant personality. Having her in the house gave Florence a new sense of security.

One afternoon about a week after Margaret moved in, there was a loud knocking at the front door. When Florence answered, three Japanese soldiers were standing on the portico, each armed with a rifle. They immediately brushed past her into the living room.

The first soldier spoke a smattering of English and demanded to see everyone who lived in the house. Margaret and Olive joined her in the living room. Florence went out to the garage and brought back Old Clem and Mariano.

While two of the soldiers began searching the house, the first one asked where each of them had been born. Florence gave him her Philippine identity card that stated she had been born in Isabela Province in 1915. The others provided their own information.

"Do you have guns here?" the soldier asked Florence.

In her mind's eye she saw the two pistols under the floorboards.

"No," she told him.

"Do you have liquor here?" he demanded next. She pointed to the empty liquor cabinet and said no again.

The soldiers were making a thorough search, going into the closets in every room and poking the walls with their bayonets. One of them began tapping the floor in several places with his rifle butt, and she felt a surge of terror. What would they do if they found the hiding place and knew she'd lied?

The first soldier gave them back their identification cards, eyeing Olive for some time before handing Florence a single mimeographed page. The words were in English; instructions for how Philippine citizens were to act toward the men of the Japanese army. One line read, *Anyone who inflicts, or attempts to inflict, an injury upon Japanese soldiers or individuals, shall be shot to death.*

It also stated that a curfew would be in force between 8 p.m. and 6 a.m. People found on the street during curfew would be arrested. Anyone found looting would be immediately executed.

Old Clem was quaking with fear after they left. Apologizing to Florence, he told her that he could not stay in Manila and would make plans to return to his family in the north. Mariano was afraid too but agreed to stay.

One morning, Dolores Gardner called and asked if Florence would join her in a visit to the internees imprisoned at the University of Santo Tomas. Dolores had heard that the living conditions were terrible and wanted to find a way to help. They first drove to a wholesale food store to buy rice and canned goods. Florence was shocked to see that prices for the items had almost doubled since the Japanese arrived.

It was Florence's first time out of her neighborhood in weeks, and as they drove across the city, she was startled to see the many military checkpoints with armed soldiers deployed every few blocks along the principal avenues.

The scene at the gates of the university was utter chaos. Five thousand British and American civilians had been rounded up in the two weeks since the army had arrived and they had all been herded inside the sprawling campus, which was surrounded by a six-foot-high concrete wall with vertical iron bars embedded in the concrete. The Japanese topped it with barbed wire.

Peering through the bars near the gate, Florence saw hundreds of the internees outside in the merciless heat, lying or sitting on the ground next to their belongings. A few ventured close to the perimeter, where street peddlers were selling food and personal articles that they threw over the wall after receiving money through the bars.

Entering at the gate, Dolores bowed deeply to one of the guards and furtively bribed him for permission to allow her and Florence to bring their parcels of food to a "sick female friend."

Florence knew that Dolores had a close friend inside, but it wasn't a sick woman. His name was Bob Hendry, and he was in love with Dolores. Bob was married but his wife didn't like the Philippines and had returned to California with their daughter. Dolores and Bob hoped to get married but he had to wait for his wife to give him a divorce.

It took Florence and Dolores hours to find him. The men had been separated from the women and the early arrivals had been crammed into the former university classrooms, with fifty people to each room. Florence could hear the constant wailing of babies through the open windows of the women's wing. Traumatized children wandered everywhere.

There weren't enough toilets for even a fraction of the number of people held within the buildings. People waited in long lines to use one of the two toilets on each floor. Many suffered from dysentery and were forced to relieve themselves where they could. A terrible stench hung over the hallways and the fetid air drew clouds of mosquitoes.

Some people had been there for two weeks but the Japanese still hadn't supplied the internees with any food, instead allowing them to use their remaining money or tradable articles to purchase or barter food from the vendors.

When the two women finally located Bob Hendry, he was lying among a few dozen other men on the floor of a classroom. Each had been allotted a space about the size of a coffin. When Dolores called out to him, he happily joined them in the corridor.

Florence thought he had aged a year in the month since she had last seen him. His arms and wrists were covered with red welts. They had no mosquito netting and Bob told the women an army of fleas and bedbugs was overrunning the building.

He hadn't eaten for two days and was deeply grateful for the food they brought. Like so many others, he had an intestinal infection from tainted drinking water and was worried about contracting dysentery. There were no medical supplies.

"I'd like to move into the women's quarters so I can be closer to you," Dolores told Bob. "We can share these trials together."

"You can't," said Bob, appalled at the idea. "Your being free gives me something to look forward to after the Americans come back. It can only be a few more months."

Florence wasn't so sure it could happen that quickly, but didn't say anything to spoil his apparent optimism.

Driving home, Dolores said, "I'm going to do everything I can to help Bob and our friends."

"I'll help you," Florence promised.

The only question was how.

Florence's only other foray into the city resulted from needing a job. She knew that the money Bing left her would only carry so far, and she was responsible for Olive and Mariano. Margaret contributed a small amount each week to the household budget from her job at the bookstore of the Philippine Education Company.

Florence thought that H. J. Scofield, her former boss and the general manager of the Army-Navy YMCA, might still be at the club and could possibly offer her a job. Wearing a tropical business suit, she took the bus at Taft Avenue.

Along the way, the bus passed Fort Santiago and it brought back vivid memories of the time she had worked there with Carl and Bing. Like all the other military buildings, its entrance gate was now flanked by enormous Japanese flags.

The Army-Navy YMCA looked no different from the outside when the bus arrived. Inside, the changes were startling. The lobby was crowded with Japanese officers and at the front desk only one Japanese girl spoke English.

When she asked about Mr. Scofield, the girl had no idea who he was and told her the general manager was Japanese. Florence was on her way back across the lobby when a grinning officer intercepted her. Speaking in Japanese, he pointed toward the bar and motioned her to come along with him.

Bowing, she apologized in English for not understanding his language and politely told him she had to leave. Perhaps he had seen the wedding ring on her finger, but she doubted this made a difference. She was relieved when he didn't follow her.

SEVENTEEN

General Douglas MacArthur's headquarters on Corregidor was starkly different from the one he had left behind at No. 1 Calle Victoria in the Intramuros, with its conquistador furnishings, cathedral ceilings, and ornately carved staircases.

He now directed the defense of the Philippines from a one-hundred-foot-long lateral tunnel under Malinta Hill. The stone walls were newly excavated and dripped evil-smelling water. The uneven floors were bare concrete. The sole illumination came from a spider web of bare bulbs in individual sockets strung from the twelve-foot-high ceiling. The only furnishings in the headquarters were the desks and chairs for his staff officers and army clerks.

The final battered desk at the end of the passageway belonged to MacArthur.

On the surface, nothing in his demeanor appeared to have changed. He listened to the relentlessly depressing news from every front with the same calm fortitude he always displayed on the battlefield. It was a marvel to the men who served under him.

In a coded cable to General George Marshall, MacArthur laid out the stakes of their situation.

> The question of time is paramount. It is
> estimated that this garrison unsupported can
> survive serious attack for possibly three
> months at most . . . I have no resources except
> as provided from the United States . . . This
> immediately raises the question of the
> intention to effect relief and the rapidity of
> action. I believe there is time if the
> resources of Great Britain and the United
> States are exerted. England is safe from attack
> during the winter . . . It is vital to me in the
> conduct of this defense to be informed in the
> broadest terms of United States' plans.

There was no immediate reply.

On January 10, MacArthur made a personal inspection tour of his forces on Bataan. By then, he had reorganized the diverse Philippine and American divisions into two army corps. I Corps was commanded by General Jonathan Wainwright and II Corps by General George Parker.

The defense line on the Bataan Peninsula was divided between them, with I Corps holding the western half of the peninsula and II Corps the eastern half. MacArthur's defense line was now less than twenty-five miles from the southern tip of Bataan.

Located between the two corps in the center of the peninsula was Mount Silangan, a four-thousand-foot promontory covered with almost impenetrable jungle. The Japanese began infiltrating advance units through the jungle on both sides of the mountain, hoping to prevent coordination between the two corps.

On his inspection tour, General MacArthur first visited Parker's II Corps and then drove west in a small convoy of vehicles to meet with Wainwright and his staff. At one point the convoy was stopped by Japanese heavy artillery fire. MacArthur ordered his staff to seek shelter, but remained standing alone in the middle of the road without a helmet, aiming his binoculars in the direction of the enemy artillery battery. General Sutherland, his chief of staff, called out to him to please take cover, but he shouted back, "Don't worry. There is no Jap shell with MacArthur's name on it."

Reaching the lines of I Corps, MacArthur complimented Wainwright on the execution of his withdrawal down the peninsula.

"Your gallant fight has caught the imagination of the American people and plans for help from Australia are underway," he told the general.

He asked about the condition of the soldiers and Wainwright told him in no uncertain terms. His Filipino troops were largely untrained and they lacked basic equipment. They had begun the battle wearing conventional sneakers, but repeated withdrawals through razor sharp jungle grass left most of them barefoot. As for the Americans, they were doing poorly on half rations.

Regardless, Wainwright promised MacArthur that his men would all fight to the end. Returning to Corregidor, MacArthur publicly issued a general order to all the unit commanders serving under him.

```
Help is on the way from the United States,
thousands of troops and hundreds of planes are
being dispatched. The exact time of arrival of
reinforcements is unknown as they will have to
fight their way through Japanese attempts
against them. It is imperative that our troops
hold until these reinforcements arrive. No
further retreat is possible. We have more
troops in Bataan than the Japanese have thrown
against us; our supplies are ample; a
determined defense will defeat the enemy's
attacks. It is a question now of courage and
determination.
```

On January 17, a frustrated MacArthur sent another cable to Marshall, sensing that his command was being considered expendable.

```
The food situation here is becoming serious.
For some time I have been on half rations and
the result will soon become evident in the
exhausted condition of the men. Many medium-
sized or small ships should be loaded with
rations and dispatched along various
routes . . . Unquestionably ships can get through
but no attempt yet seems to have been made
along this line. This seems incredible to
me . . . The repeated statements from the United
States that Hitler is to be destroyed before an
effort is to be made here is causing dismay. I
repeat that if something is not done to meet
the general situation which is developing the
disastrous results will be monumental.
```

On January 21, General Wainwright reported to MacArthur that Japanese infiltrators captured the only road leading south from his defensive line. He personally led a counterattack to try to take back control of the road and had committed all his reserves, but the attack failed. The men who were cut off to the north had only one avenue of escape and it was on foot along the rocky coastline. Before retreating, they were forced to destroy all their mechanized transportation and artillery.

On January 22, Japanese advance units broke through the western flank of General Parker's II Corps, and MacArthur ordered a general retreat of both corps to a new line farther south. That night he sent another dire cable to Washington.

```
Heavy fighting has been raging all day . . . My
losses during the campaign have been very heavy
and are mounting. They now approximate 35%. My
diminishing strength will soon force me to a
shortened line on which I shall make my final
```

```
stand . . . I intend to fight it to complete
destruction. This will leave Corregidor.
```

On Bataan, a dispirited General Wainwright again took stock of the conditions his men were facing as the Japanese prepared to attack his new defense line. His soldiers were weak from constant hunger, their energy drained by the steaming heat, and many were on their backs with malaria.

Wainwright ordered all the horses of his beloved 26th Cavalry Regiment to be shot. The butchered meat was shared by his remaining troops. An aide tried to lighten Wainwright's spirits by showing him the lyrics of a new song written by Wainwright's friend, Frank Hewlett.

We're the battling bastards of Bataan:
No momma, no poppa, no Uncle Sam
No aunts, no uncles, no nephews, no nieces,
No rifles, no guns or artillery pieces,
And nobody gives a damn.

EIGHTEEN

Bing had to laugh after one of his crewmates came up with the name for the strange little vessel that they had fabricated from the *Canopus* scrap heap. The sailor christened it the *Mickey Mouse Battleship*. It was no battleship and might have been tiny, but Bing hoped it would prove deadly to the Japanese.

The little gunboat began life as one of the *Canopus*'s forty-four-foot motor launches, which ferried repair crews and replacement parts to the submarines it serviced. In turning it into a lethal weapon, Bing and his crewmates had mounted a 37 mm M3 anti-tank gun onto the bow. The cannon could fire high explosive rounds five hundred yards with great accuracy. Each round was a foot long and a trained gun crew could fire up to twenty rounds in a minute.

In addition to the cannon, they mounted stands for four heavy machine guns with rotating turrets, one at port and starboard amidships, and one each in the bow and the stern. They then welded iron boilerplate shields to protect the boat's engine and the new firing positions.

While the conversion was underway, the rest of the *Canopus*'s crew found new avenues for their own employment as the battle on Bataan continued. With the Japanese army less than 20 miles away from its southern tip, 130 crewmen from the ship volunteered to join the battle in a unit being formed by Navy Commander Frank Bridget.

Bridget led a separate force of 150 naval aviation crewmen who no longer had planes to service. Another 80 men who had worked at the destroyed Cavite ammunition depot also signed on. One hundred unassigned marines brought the number to over 450 men, and the marines were sprinkled throughout the untrained ranks to help the new recruits learn the rudiments of ground fighting.

Many of the men in Bridget's force had never fired a rifle, but even though they had no uniforms and were armed with a hodgepodge of guns begged from the army, Bridget took them straight across Mariveles Bay to join the battle.

On Bataan, they were assigned to I Corps under General Wainwright and ordered to undertake a field training exercise to toughen them up for real combat. Through a fluke of timing, real combat awaited them on the training ground.

Wainwright expected an attack from the north, but instead the Japanese launched four amphibious landings along the coast south of his lines. The daring move caught the Americans by surprise.

The first Japanese detachment of three hundred men landed on a beach below the cliffs at Longoskawayan Point, a barren finger of land off the southwest tip of the Bataan Peninsula, and nearly ten miles behind Wainwright's defense line. They were elite troops, expert at jungle fighting, and their goal was to sever the vital road link of Wainwright's supply line.

When the Japanese detachment began moving inland to reach the road, they ran into Bridget's naval irregulars. The irregulars had no knowledge of infantry tactics or jungle fighting, but they intrepidly held their ground in the face of a night attack with Japanese infiltrators crawling through the dense jungle into the American positions. The infiltrators tried to cause panic, but the men held.

The following morning, the irregulars were reinforced by a five-hundred-man Philippine Scout battalion and counterattacked the Japanese positions, pushing them all the way back to the cliffs above Longoskawayan Point. The cliffs contained a warren of caves and crevasses that the Japanese fortified with machine guns and mortars. Dug in, it proved impossible to dislodge them.

This stalemate led to the baptism of fire for Bing Smith and the *Mickey Mouse Battleship*. The men who manned it, including Bing, all volunteered. They were commanded by Lieutenant Commander "Hap" Goodall, the executive officer of the *Canopus*.

Goodall told them that their job would be to attack and destroy the Japanese machine gun and mortar positions in the caves under the cliffs. The following dawn, they set out for the target area.

As they traveled across Mariveles Bay, Goodall assigned Bing to direct the fire of the 37 mm cannon in the bow. Upon their arrival at Longoskawayan Point, Bing used his binoculars to target the first cave, hoping that after some ranging shots he would be able to zero in on the first position.

It didn't take any ranging shots. After Bing estimated the distance and elevation, the gun crew opened fire and the first two rounds of high-explosive shells blasted several Japanese soldiers out of the first cave.

The crew erupted in cheers.

One by one, Bing turned the cannon on the remaining caves and crevasses containing the machine guns and mortars. When the gun crew ran out of ammunition, they raced back to the *Canopus* for more and returned to the cliffs. With unerring accuracy, Bing eliminated the last elements of the Japanese detachment. Goodall sent a longboat into the beach to pick up the five dazed Japanese who survived.

The *Mickey Mouse Battleship* had scored its first victory.

NINETEEN

Carl was at a first aid station near his casemate to have the stitches removed from his shrapnel wound when he stepped onto a weight scale and saw that he had lost 15 pounds from his normal 165. With each new week on half rations, his khakis hung looser on his lean frame.

The defenders were down to two meals a day, usually a cup of boiled rice flavored with canned peas or corn. Drinking water became precious too. Carl and his men shaved every morning with seawater carried from the small inlet below the casemate.

Although Carl believed the garrison was ultimately doomed, he finally had a chance to hit back. Late one night while monitoring the electronic grid of the minefields, a contact signal began pinging out in Manila Bay.

Carl immediately detonated the closest mine. The following morning no wreckage was sighted in the bay, but he sent out a diver who thought the mine cable might be buried beneath the hull of a Japanese submarine. If true, it felt good to help even the score. He and his men celebrated by sharing a bowl of rice pudding with dried raisins.

Realizing he no longer had any use for money, Carl went to see the finance officer in Malinta Tunnel to change his pay allotment so it would go to his wife in San Diego. The officer told him that hundreds of applications preceded him and his would be processed in the order of its filing.

He was leaving the tunnel to return to the casemate when he ran into Bing Smith. They hadn't seen each other since arriving together two months earlier, on Christmas Eve, and Bing briefly recounted his adventures aboard the *Canopus* and the *Mickey Mouse Battleship*.

Bing told Carl they had just received orders for another mission and it was probably going to be hairier than the first. He asked if Carl had a "belly" gun he could lend him in case the fighting became hand to hand.

Carl had a .25 automatic and plenty of ammunition to give him, and Bing followed him back to the casemate to get it. During the walk, Bing spoke about his constant worry for Florence's safety under the Japanese occupation. If anything happened to him, he asked Carl to let her know how much he loved her and that he never stopped thinking about her. They shook hands and Carl wished him luck before Bing headed to the docks to catch a ride back.

At the mission briefing in the *Canopus* wardroom, Commander Goodall announced that the crew had just finished converting a second *Mickey Mouse Battleship*, which doubled their firepower for the second mission. Goodall updated the men on the four amphibious landings that the Japanese had carried out behind the American lines.

Their own successful attack had wiped out the Japanese elite regiment at Longoskawayan Point a week earlier. Two of the other three Japanese detachments had been eliminated since then as well.

The fourth detachment at Quinawan Point still represented a serious danger behind Wainwright's lines and threatened to cut off his supplies. The battle had been raging for twelve days and losses were severe. Four hundred Americans and Filipinos had already been killed or wounded.

The Japanese force numbered about six hundred men and they were holding a set of cliffs similar to the ones that Bing and the rest of the crew had successfully attacked the previous week. The Japanese were dug in with mortars and heavy machine guns and were being resupplied at night.

Goodall told them that their job was to destroy the detachment before it could be reinforced. In addition to the second gunboat, two of the *Canopus*'s longboats, each crammed with soldiers, would land on the beach to the north and south of the cliffs to mop up after the gunboats eliminated the fire from the caves.

An hour before dawn on February 8, the tiny armada from the *Canopus* set out across Mariveles Bay for their second battle. When they arrived at Quinawan Point, the morning sky was slowly illuminating the cliffs where the Japanese were dug in.

Unlike the previous mission, when Commander Goodall stayed out of range of the Japanese machine guns and allowed the cannon to reduce their positions, this time he brought the two gunboats within range to draw the enemy fire away from the unarmed longboats filled with soldiers as they ran in to the beach.

Bing saw that these cliffs were much higher than those at Longosk-awayan Point, with many more caves honeycombed into the rock. Moving to an exposed position beyond the iron gun shield, he directed the first rounds of cannon fire as enemy machine gun rounds slammed into the bow section of the boat and clanged into the iron shield protecting the cannon.

Once again, Bing pinpointed his targets with remarkable accuracy, and as with their previous attack at Longoskawayan, the high-explosive shells began blasting the Japanese and their weapons out of the caves.

Working in tandem, the two gunboats systematically reduced the number of targets until enemy fire finally ceased almost two hours later. Commander Goodall signaled the soldiers on the beach to move in and they reported that the surviving Japanese had either surrendered or committed suicide.

As the two *Mickey Mouse Battleships* headed back across Mariveles Bay, the crewmen were celebrating their second successful mission when they heard the roar of approaching aircraft over the drone of the boats' engines.

Four Japanese planes dove toward them from out of the sun. Two were Zero fighters and the other two were Aichi dive-bombers. The Japanese pilots split up into two formations, with one fighter and one dive-bomber attacking each gunboat.

Commander Goodall ordered the engineer to give him maximum revolutions and motioned to the skipper of the second boat to follow him as he began zigzagging, first to port, then to starboard, and then back again, desperately hoping to throw off the pilots' aim.

Bing manned one of the machine guns as the Zero made its first strafing run. Leading the plane as it came down, he poured out a stream of .50-caliber bullets in concert with the boat's other gunners and the Zero broke away before completing its strafing attack.

The dive-bomber attacked next, following the same path as the Zero. Again, Bing and the others put up a curtain of fire as the pilot held steady in his attack. Black smoke suddenly began to stream from his engine, quickly followed by bright orange flame from their mortal hits.

With his burning plane hurtling toward the sea, the pilot released his bombs. Seeing their trajectory, Bing knew they were going to land close and he ran to join the men in a protected position behind the iron gun shield. Glancing back, he saw a young seaman frozen with fear, standing alone in an exposed position on the deck. Giving up his spot, Bing ran to the seaman, pulled him forward, and shoved him into his own place behind the shield as the plane hit the sea and exploded.

One of the bombs blew a hole in the hull below the waterline and unleashed a torrent of shrapnel above the deck. Deadly steel splinters hit Commander Goodall and three other men behind the shields.

Standing unprotected on the deck, Bing was killed instantly along with two other sailors.

Wounded in the legs and unable to stand, Goodall ordered the crew in the second gunboat to return to the *Canopus*. With his own boat sinking, he told his crew to head for the nearest shoreline.

After running the boat onto the shore, the stunned survivors carried the wounded men up the beach inside a line of palm trees in case the Japanese planes returned for another attack. Goodall asked his men to go back to the boat and bring up Bing's body along with the other two dead crewmen.

Some of the men hadn't seen what Bing had done and Goodall told them how he had died saving the young crewman's life. Bing's body was carefully wrapped in a canvas tarpaulin. As it was lowered reverently into a hastily dug grave, those who could stand came to attention and saluted him. Before leaving, one of them marked the site of the graves with small piles of stones so that the bodies might eventually be recovered for internment in a military cemetery.

The crew improvised stretchers for Goodall and the other wounded men, and they slowly hacked their way through the dense jungle until they reached the main coast road. An army truck stopped to pick them up and the driver took them to the nearest aid station.

A few days later, Commander Sam Cheek, Bing's former boss at Naval Intelligence, sought Carl out at his mine casemate and gave him the news of Bing's death. Cheek said that Goodall was planning to write up a recommendation for Bing to receive a medal for his key role in eliminating the Japanese positions and for sacrificing his life to save his crewmate.

Carl could only think of how he might gently break the news to Florence—and how he could even get word to her, and when.

TWENTY

As each week dragged by, Florence became increasingly apprehensive of the growing menace from their occupiers.

She gave up the once pleasant task of walking her little dog and turned it over to Mariano. On the few occasions she was forced to venture out during the day, she couldn't walk more than a half-dozen blocks without being stopped at one of the military kiosks and asked for her identification. One morning she did not bow sufficiently deeply from the waist in the traditional Japanese way to a soldier, and he cuffed her on the side of the head. Over and over, she watched soldiers slap or punch people for no reason at all, sometimes kicking them into the street. Many obviously enjoyed the power.

At one of the military checkpoints, a soldier put his hands on her breasts while pretending to search for contraband. As much as his crude actions infuriated her, she could only endure them as part of the new reality of the occupation.

Japanese officers were now living in the homes in her neighborhood once owned by British and American residents. Often, she could hear them late into the night, drunkenly singing songs, or staggering down the avenue in the morning after an all-night party.

Much uglier was the proliferation of Japanese "service clubs" around the city. Margaret learned that Filipina women were being recruited or forced to work in them. Lines of soldiers often stretched down the block, waiting to enter.

There were also rumors of young Filipina women stalked by Japanese soldiers on their way home before curfew and found the next morning, wandering naked and disoriented.

Late one night, Florence heard men's raised voices outside the house followed by loud hammering at the front door. She hid with Margaret and Olive in one of the bedrooms until they finally went away.

Before going to bed each night, Florence sat at the kitchen table in the darkness and listened to the latest news on Bing's shortwave. The Voice of Freedom radio station was still broadcasting an hour-long program from Corregidor and its news reports indicated the battle was going well.

The radio stations in San Francisco and Australia delivered all the bad news. The fall of Hong Kong was followed by the collapse of the British and Australian armies in Malaya. The Japanese had driven the Allies all the way down the Malay Peninsula and the mighty fortress of Singapore was now under siege.

If help was coming to the Philippines, no one was talking about it.

Each day, Mariano came back from the markets to tell her that the price of staples like fish, milk, tinned meat, and rice was higher. Each week the cash in the envelope that Bing had given her continued to shrink.

Florence and Dolores Gardner were working hard to collect food and medicine they could bring to Bob Hendry and his friends in the Santo Tomas prison camp. Florence made her own small donations and asked other friends to help too. The combined results of their efforts were pitifully small.

Through long, mostly sleepless nights, she lay in bed and listened to the distant thunder of shell fire from Bataan, Cavite, and Corregidor. The depth of her loneliness was overwhelming, a constant ache. Mostly, she missed the treasured sanctuary of being held safe in Bing's arms.

He was only twenty-six miles away on Corregidor, but it might as well have been a million.

TWENTY-ONE

More than anyone, General Douglas MacArthur could see the writing on the wall for the Allied forces left in the western Pacific.

In what would come to be known as the most humiliating military disaster in British history, its fortress at Singapore, which was considered impregnable and nicknamed "the Gibraltar of the East," had fallen on February 15, and eighty-five thousand British, Indian, and Australian troops were driven like cattle into Japanese prisoner of war camps. British influence in the Far East had been eradicated in one blow.

Throughout February, MacArthur continued to press the War Department in Washington, DC, to send him more men, ammunition, and food supplies, or face the same consequences as the British.

```
The troops have sustained practically 50%
casualties from their original strength . . . Some
units have entirely disappeared. They are
desperately in need of rest and refitting. All
our supplies are scant and the command has been
on half rations for the past month . . . Since I
have no air or sea protection you must be
prepared at any time to figure on the complete
destruction of this command.
```

In Washington, DC, General George Marshall and his staff had already reached the tragic conclusion that the Philippine garrison was doomed. There was no avenue to get MacArthur's army resupplied in time to save them. Of more concern to Marshall was the impact on the country if MacArthur surrendered to the Japanese with his men or was killed leading them. More than anything, he symbolized America's power and prestige in the Far East.

When Marshall met with President Roosevelt in the White House to discuss the question, he recommended that MacArthur be ordered to go to Australia and assume command of all the troops in the Pacific theater from there. On the surface, it didn't make sense, since virtually all the American troops in the Pacific were in the Philippines, but logic had nothing to do with the decision.

The president agreed that MacArthur's death or capture would deal a huge psychological blow to the American people. The fight for Bataan was front-page news almost every day and people across the country were inspired by the valiant stand of MacArthur and his beleaguered men.

In the meeting, presidential adviser Robert E. Sherwood played devil's advocate. "It's like ordering the captain to be the first to leave the sinking ship," he told Roosevelt, but the president had already made his decision. Draw up the order for him to go, he told Marshall.

```
The President directs that you make
arrangements to leave Fort Mills and proceed to
Mindanao. You are directed to make this change
as quickly as possible. . . . From Mindanao you
will proceed to Australia where you will assume
command of all United States troops.
```

MacArthur bristled with rage as he read the words. He knew there were no troops in Australia, but if he disobeyed a direct order from the president, he could be court-martialed. If he obeyed the order, many would see him as a coward who abandoned his soldiers while victory or defeat was still in the balance.

He briefly considered the melodramatic idea of resigning his commission and joining the men on Bataan as a volunteer, but his staff was unanimous in urging him to comply with Roosevelt's order. They assured him that a large American army would almost certainly be assembled in Australia and once there, MacArthur could lead them back to save the Philippines. MacArthur finally acquiesced.

On March 10, General Jonathan Wainwright, who commanded I Corps, was summoned to Corregidor from his headquarters on Bataan. At Mariveles Bay, he boarded a small Elco cabin cruiser and made the run across the bay.

General Sutherland met him at the north docks and told him MacArthur was leaving the island on a PT boat, and that Wainwright was being put in command of the remaining troops on Luzon and Corregidor. He then escorted Wainwright to the small bungalow where the general was staying with his wife and son after his first cottage had been destroyed. MacArthur was waiting on the porch when Wainwright came up.

"Jonathan," he began, "I'm leaving for Australia pursuant to repeated orders of the president. I want you to make it known throughout all elements of your command that I'm leaving over my repeated protests."

Wainwright said he understood and promised to comply.

"If I get through to Australia," said MacArthur, "you know I'll come back as soon as I can with as much as I can. In the meantime, you've got to hold." Saying he had a few small gifts for him, MacArthur gave Wainwright a box of cigars and two jars of shaving cream.

"Goodbye, Jonathan," said MacArthur, and they shook hands for the last time.

As darkness fell on March 11, MacArthur boarded *PT-41* along with his wife, his four-year-old son, and the boy's Cantonese *amah*, Ah Cheu, to begin the long journey by sea to Mindanao. Three B-17 bombers were waiting to fly him to Australia.

Although he knew it would leave Wainwright without many experienced staff, MacArthur decided that most of his senior staff should accompany him to Australia. It reflected his private conclusion that Bataan would eventually fall and he would need them with him for his future campaigns.

When the bow and stern lines were cast off and *PT-41* left the dock, MacArthur remained standing on the stern, looking back at the doomed soldiers watching him from the pier. As the boat disappeared into the darkness, he raised his cap in a farewell salute.

TWENTY-TWO

General Jonathan Wainwright assembled his senior officers to take stock of the latest military situation and to tell them MacArthur would now be organizing the effort to bring new men and supplies from Australia. Hearing the latest updates from his officers, it was clear that the situation they faced was precarious.

II Corps under General Parker had less than thirty thousand men left to defend the eastern half of the peninsula, and I Corps had about twenty-five thousand. The physical condition of the troops was grim.

The Filipinos were enduring reasonably well on half rations of rice, since they were smaller and their regular diet consisted principally of rice. The Americans were not only perpetually hungry, but their health had been battered by continuous jungle fighting and the merciless heat. Three-quarters of the Americans had malaria and suffered from dysentery. There was very little quinine or other drugs left to treat them.

Ammunition was running low, particularly for the artillery pieces that were vital to stopping the Japanese offensive, and according to the latest intelligence, the Japanese had recently landed thousands of fresh troops at Lingayen Gulf. They were now moving south to strengthen their existing lines and were equipped with two hundred new artillery pieces.

Since most of the new Japanese units were massing in the eastern half of the peninsula in front of II Corps, it seemed certain that they would face the brunt of the next Japanese offensive. Enemy fighter planes were already strafing and bombing its lines.

Wainwright returned to Corregidor to prepare a report on the latest situation for General MacArthur in Australia. When he arrived at his headquarters in Malinta Tunnel, he was told that President Roosevelt had just awarded MacArthur the Congressional Medal of Honor.

DOUGLAS MACARTHUR, GENERAL, UNITED STATES ARMY.

FOR CONSPICUOUS LEADERSHIP IN PREPARING THE PHILIPPINE ISLANDS TO RESIST CONQUEST, FOR GALLANTRY AND INTREPIDITY ABOVE AND BEYOND THE CALL OF DUTY IN ACTION AGAINST INVADING JAPANESE FORCES, AND FOR HEROIC CONDUCT OF DEFENSIVE AND OFFENSIVE OPERATIONS ON THE BATAAN PENINSULA. HIS UTTER DISREGARD OF PERSONAL DANGER UNDER HEAVY FIRE AND AERIAL BOMBARDMENT, HIS CALM JUDGMENT IN EACH CRISIS, INSPIRED HIS TROOPS, GALVANIZED THE SPIRIT OF RESISTANCE OF THE FILIPINO PEOPLE AND CONFIRMED THE FAITH OF THE AMERICAN PEOPLE IN THEIR ARMED FORCES.

Wainwright cabled MacArthur a coded missive with his congratulations, then sent his accompanying encrypted report on their desperate situation, detailing the dwindling supplies and ammunition, as well as the deteriorating health of his men. Wainwright asked MacArthur for B-17 bombing attacks on the Japanese airfields on Luzon as well as the troop ships still landing at Lingayen Gulf ahead of the new Japanese offensive.

General MacArthur covertly cabled back that he would arrange the B-17 missions. In the meantime, he recommended that Wainwright launch a bold attack with both corps to seize the Japanese-held port on Subic Bay, which was a principal supply dump for the Japanese. Capturing the port would allow Wainwright to immediately resupply his men. MacArthur concluded by writing that "under no conditions should this command be surrendered."

Before the attack on the supply depot could be mounted, the Japanese began their new offensive. After a heavy artillery barrage, assault waves of infantry attacked General Parker's II Corps lines, supported by tanks and strafing fighter planes. By April 3, the Japanese penetrated almost half a mile behind his front line.

In a desperate attempt to stem the tide, Wainwright personally raced to Parker's headquarters and helped organize a counterattack to try to restore the line. After temporary gains, the Japanese broke through again and II Corps disintegrated.

General Edward P. King, who replaced Wainwright as the field commander on Bataan, was faced with a terrible decision. King was a seasoned commander decorated for bravery in World War I, and his brilliant use of artillery had halted the previous Japanese offensives. But to fight on meant sacrificing thousands of men without adequate supplies or ammunition in a battle they had no chance of winning.

King sent his chief of staff to Wainwright to tell him that the situation was hopeless and it was time to surrender. Wainwright responded that MacArthur's last cable was explicit: there could be no surrender.

"You go back and tell General King that he will not surrender. Tell him he will attack. Those are my orders," said Wainwright.

On April 8, the hundred female nurses still serving at the military hospitals on Bataan were withdrawn to Corregidor. While they were being towed across the bay on a barge, the night sky erupted with a series of shattering explosions. Combat engineers were blowing up all the fuel and ammunition dumps on Bataan.

In response to Wainwright's order, General King committed all his reserves to a final desperate infantry assault on the Japanese positions. It could not be sustained very long and the attack failed. At 6 a.m. on April 9, Wainwright was awakened by the news that General King was about to surrender his forces. Wainwright attempted to reach him to reverse the decision, but it was too late.

Only Corregidor now barred the door to the Japanese conquest of the Philippines.

TWENTY-THREE

The days passed slowly. The nights seemed interminable.

Racked by the uncertainty of Bing's fate, Florence's daily bouts with anxiety and depression were compounded by the awareness that there was nothing for her to do. She rarely ventured out of the house, but staying inside day and night, hour after hour, felt like being trapped in a cage. She had to do something.

In response to newspaper job listings, she submitted her résumé for clerical positions at public utilities and private companies. Only one application led to an interview. The conversation only lasted a few minutes because a long line of other women were being considered too.

With their shrinking savings, Mariano could only afford to buy the most basic food staples at the local markets, and Florence no longer found enjoyment in cooking her special meals as she once had for Bing.

Tempers continued to flare between Florence and Olive, who felt equally imprisoned and took out her frustration with regular tantrums. Flaviana wrote to her daughter, urging her to come home to the plantation in Santiago, where it was much safer than in the Japanese-occupied capital, but Olive wanted to stay in Manila so she could be with her friends.

The puppy Bing had given Florence was now almost a year old. It appeared to sense the constant tension in the air and spent most of each day curled up in her bedroom closet next to Bing's shoes. With her limited resources, Florence began to look at the dog as another hungry mouth to feed.

During the day, she tried to divert her mind from continual worry by mending clothes for the internees at Santo Tomas and continuing to collect small donations to bring to Bob Hendry. At night she listened to the latest war news from the stations in Australia and San Francisco on the shortwave radio in the kitchen. The updates were unrelentingly depressing, with the Japanese army and navy consolidating their conquests across the Pacific.

The Manila newspapers were Japanese-controlled, and every day saw more headlines about the Japanese army advancing on the Bataan Peninsula while its planes reduced Corregidor to a rubble pile. She wanted to believe it was all propaganda.

They were completely cut off from the United States. The only mail delivered was local to the Philippines. Florence could only wonder if Mabelle and the rest of the Ebersole family had any idea what was happening under the occupation.

Every time the phone rang, her heart began to pound, thinking it could be Bing. Even though she knew the men on Corregidor and Bataan had no way to contact anyone in Manila, she clung to the illusion that somehow he would get a message through to her.

At night in bed, when the city was relatively quiet, she could hear the boom of artillery on Bataan and Corregidor. It was reassuring, because it meant the battle was still joined and she could hope for news of an American-Filipino victory.

On the night of April 8, Florence was awakened by the sound of tremendous explosions from Bataan, even louder than the regular booms of cannon fire. She wondered about its significance until the following day, when Margaret burst into her bedroom carrying a newspaper with a banner headline proclaiming that the Americans on Bataan had surrendered.

Florence would have been inconsolable if not for the fact that Bing and Carl had been ordered to Corregidor back in December. It was an island fortress, and could presumably hold out until more troops and supplies arrived.

Bing was indestructible, and he had promised to come back. Like her, he would somehow survive.

TWENTY-FOUR

During a brief lull in the Japanese shelling, Carl encountered General Wainwright as he was leaving the tunnel to return to his casemate. The general was sitting in a hard-backed chair near the tunnel entrance, smoking a cigar and staring out across Manila Bay.

Carl had long admired the commander and gave a crisp salute before congratulating him on his recent promotion to lieutenant general. Wainwright casually flipped his hand in acknowledgment and growled, "Hell of a sop, Colonel, for having to end my career by surrendering."

Carl knew the end was drawing closer every day, and for the first time since the war began, he thought about what captivity might be like. In late April, a Filipino soldier who had escaped into the jungle after the Bataan surrender made his way to Corregidor in a small outrigger canoe. He reported that the thousands of Americans and Filipinos who surrendered had been forced to march fifty or sixty miles without food or water and many had died along the way. Although there was no way to confirm his account, Carl knew the Japanese had only contempt for soldiers who surrendered.

Within hours of Bataan falling, the Japanese began shelling Corregidor without pause. The tonnage of high-explosive shells increased even more after the Japanese put batteries of their long range 105 mm artillery pieces on Cavite and Batangas.

Even more terrifying were the 240 mm cannons that were deployed at the edge of the jungle along the Bataan Peninsula, only four miles from Corregidor. Each shell weighed 450 pounds and Japanese spotters with binoculars on Mount Mariveles directed their fire at important targets, including the American anti-aircraft batteries, the power plant, and the water works.

The shells arrived at a rate of one every six seconds.

Hidden in the dense jungle, the Japanese batteries used smokeless powder so there was no way for American spotters to pinpoint their location. The men on Corregidor heard the shrieking of the shells as they came over. Wherever they hit, thousands of deadly metal splinters flew in all directions. The landscape of the island began to resemble the craters of the moon.

There was no letup at night. Although the Japanese artillery batteries couldn't fire with the same accuracy, it was impossible for the defenders to know where they might land, and the continuous detonations spread fear among the men holding the beaches.

To add to the general misery, Japanese bombers came over every day at high altitude to drop incendiary bombs. The rapidly diminishing number of functioning American anti-aircraft batteries could no longer do anything more than harass the planes.

The only place on Corregidor immune to the concussion of shells and bombs was the Malinta Tunnel complex, and it could hold only a fraction of the eleven thousand men defending the island.

Inside its cavernous gloom, life was little better than outside. Newly opened cracks and fissures in the limestone leaked steady rivulets of what the soldiers called acid rain and their living quarters reeked of dampness and mildew. The electrical lines from the power plant were repeatedly cut and the tunnel would suddenly plunge into blackness until backup generators could restore a few lights to the lateral tunnels.

One morning, Carl was in his casemate in James Ravine when the surrounding area was hit by a rolling wave of artillery fire. He felt the shockwave through the concrete floor and heard the shrapnel flaying the casemate's concrete walls.

When the air cleared, he could hear people screaming and he ran out to find that a 240 mm shell had made a direct hit on the anti-aircraft gun battery by the ravine. A few weeks earlier, its gun crews had dug a deep cave into the hillside as a shelter and shored it up with timbers.

When Carl got there, he was shocked to see that although the shell had not destroyed the cave, every man inside was dead, even though there were no wounds or signs of concussion. A medical officer arrived to examine the bodies and told Carl they were killed by anoxia when the shell blast burned up all the oxygen in the air.

During the third week into the siege, Carl reported to General Moore, who still commanded the island defense force under Wainwright. After congratulating Carl on his management of the minefields, he asked if Carl would volunteer for a dangerous assignment. Without knowing what it was, Carl said yes.

"We've got to bury some treasure," the general told him.

The Philippine gold bullion reserves had already been transported to the United States from Corregidor by submarine, but before leaving Manila, the Philippine government had moved tons of silver specie coins in wooden crates to Corregidor worth $20 million. From Australia, General MacArthur ordered Moore to keep the silver out of Japanese hands by sinking the crates in the deepest part of Manila Bay.

At night, barges were going to be towed over to the chosen location, but someone needed to mark the exact spot for the captains to find. Giving Carl a paper with the two intersecting compass bearings, Moore asked if he would go out in his mine-laying yawl and place a spherical mine case there as a buoy. Hopefully, the Japanese spotters would assume Carl was just dropping another mine.

Studying a map, Carl saw that the yawl would be under artillery fire from Bataan all the way to the tail of the island and once he was around the tail, he would be an inviting target for the big guns at Cavite and Batangas.

Moore gave him the option of backing out, but Carl said no. Late that afternoon, he and two crewmen cast off from the north docks. Soon after they were underway, the field guns on Bataan opened fire on him. It quickly became a game of cat and mouse.

Each time he heard a shell blast, Carl would vary his speed, sometimes slowing down, sometimes speeding up. There were two near misses but no hits as he finally approached the tip of the island. Once he cleared it, he was able to lock on to the first of the two compass bearings and set out across South Bay.

The big guns at Batangas were ranging in on him when he reached the exact intersection of the second bearing. He ordered the crew to dump the mine buoy overboard with its anchor and then hit the throttle for the return journey.

The next minutes seemed to last an hour as the slow-moving yawl crept back the way it had come. From the steering compartment, Carl could see the explosions landing closer and closer as the Japanese gunners finally found the range.

Two shells straddled the yawl and nearly swamped it when a small mountain of seawater poured in belowdecks to the keel. With its bilge pumps clanking away, the yawl barely made headway, chugging along with Carl zigzagging to port and starboard to throw off their aim.

Thankfully, darkness fell quickly in the tropics, and it finally cloaked them from the gun spotters. Carl navigated safely back to the north docks, where General Moore was waiting to congratulate him.

———

On May 5, twenty-seven days after the beginning of the siege, General Wainwright ordered the garrison's code books and secret intelligence documents destroyed. The end had arrived.

Carl was on his way back to tell his men the news when he heard the shriek of an incoming artillery shell. Hitting the ground, he covered his head with his arms and prayed for survival.

When the debris stopped falling, he tried to stand up and saw that his left trouser leg was a deep, wet scarlet. Carried once more to the first aid station of the 4th Marines, he was examined by a young medic. "The Japs damn near made a soprano out of you, Colonel," he said, after cutting away his pants. "You're a lucky man."

Carl glanced down at the deep, jagged gash on the inside of his left thigh. It started an inch below his genitals. The medic put a tight compress on before Carl was put in an ambulance and rushed to the hospital in Malinta Tunnel. While a doctor sutured the wound, Carl tried to remember the number of stitches sewn into him since he had arrived on the rock, and finally gave up.

After the doctor finished, he warned Carl to leave the stitches in place because the wound would take some time to heal without the benefit of penicillin or sulfa drugs. Carl fell asleep in the hospital to the heavy thump of shells landing on top of Malinta Hill.

He awoke to eerie silence.

Carl asked a nurse what was happening and she told him that General Moore had announced the surrender and the Japanese had landed on Corregidor. Wondering if Moore might need an interpreter, Carl got out of bed and asked for a pair of pants. He had reached the eastern end of the tunnel when he saw a squad of Japanese soldiers approaching the entrance. A young lieutenant was leading them and behind him was a soldier carrying a flamethrower, its tip spouting a short tongue of fire in readiness.

Carl could see the lieutenant was nervous. As Carl limped toward the group, the lieutenant raised his automatic pistol. When Carl opened his mouth and began speaking in fluent Japanese, the lieutenant's face creased in astonishment. He holstered his pistol and told Carl he wanted the tunnel cleared immediately. Everyone inside should exit at the other end, he said. Carl passed the message to some officers at the entrance and they began ordering the men to head for the west entrance of the tunnel.

Carl asked the Japanese lieutenant what he wanted next.

"Coca-Cola! For my men!" he said.

Stifling his surprise, Carl led him to the lateral tunnel where the soft drinks had been stored on pallets, and showed him there was nothing left but soda water. At that moment, he heard someone yell from farther down the tunnel that the Japanese would not let anyone leave at the other end.

Carl translated this to the lieutenant. The two separated Japanese units had issued conflicting orders.

"Everybody sit down and leave an open path in the middle," the lieutenant ordered.

At that point, Carl received a message from General Moore asking if he would accompany him to a meeting with the Japanese commander to discuss the surrender terms. They were driven to a bombed-out building where the Japanese colonel had established his headquarters.

The meeting proved futile. With Carl interpreting, Moore asked what orders the Japanese wanted carried out. The reply to that and to every other question was that the colonel was waiting for instructions. He told an infuriated Moore to go back to his own quarters and wait.

The following day, a Japanese naval officer arrived at Malinta Tunnel, asking for Carl to show a naval delegation the location of all the minefields. Still in pain from his wound, Carl accompanied him to the north docks, where a dozen Japanese officers waited in one of the few undamaged buildings. They sat in folding chairs in a semicircle behind a table covered with maps and charts.

One of the officers asked him his name and rank.

"Ee. Karu Engeruhahto, Chu-sa, Kai-gan-joo-hoh-hei, Bei-koku riku-sun," said Carl. It translated to "E. Carl Engelhart, Lieutenant Colonel, Coast Artillery Corps, United States Army."

The officer asked where he had learned to speak Japanese. Carl told him about his assignment at the American embassy in Tokyo.

One officer handed Carl a small book. It was the *Gunner's Manual* for submarine mining. The officer asked if the information in the book was accurate and Carl answered that it was.

"How do you know?" he demanded.

"I wrote this edition of the book," he answered in Japanese, "and it is the latest information."

He did not tell them that the book was worthless, since he had edited out all the detailed descriptions of mine devices and apparatus from the previous editions that should have been classified secret.

He was then asked about the specific locations of the minefields and Carl offered to show them exactly where they were, although due to the heavy shelling, many of the firing mechanisms for the mines were destroyed.

"Have you fired a mine that might have destroyed a Japanese submarine?" another officer asked him.

Carl vividly recalled his probable destruction of their patrolling sub.

"It's possible," he responded, and they did not pursue it further.

When word spread among the Japanese officers that one of the Americans was fluent in their language, he was recruited on the following day to give a VIP tour of Corregidor to a group of senior army staff.

While conducting the tour, Carl noticed that great deference was being shown to a young Japanese lieutenant by the most senior officers. When he heard a colonel address the lieutenant as "Kakka," which meant "Your Excellency," he knew the lieutenant was nobility.

When the lieutenant asked Carl a question, Carl made sure to add "Your Excellency" to his reply.

The young man smiled and said, "Never mind that. You're a lieutenant colonel and I am just a lieutenant."

They chatted for the rest of the tour, and the lieutenant stayed behind when the other officers left. Knowing that Carl was headed into captivity, he asked if there was anything he could do for him.

Carl said that a close friend had gotten married just before the war and was then killed in action. His young wife lived in Manila and Carl said he was concerned that she would not learn she was a widow until after the war ended.

The lieutenant understood and said he would inform her of her husband's death, but that he was not fluent in English. Removing a notebook from his breast pocket, he tore out a page and handed it to Carl with a pen, telling him to write down her name and address and a short message.

In his musette bag, Carl carried a carbon of the award citation Bing received posthumously for his gallantry off Bataan. General MacArthur approved the citation on April 9, the same day Bataan fell, and Commander Cheek gave Carl one of the copies.

Carl handed the folded citation to the lieutenant, with Florence's name and address written on the outside. The lieutenant nodded and said, "Yoroshi"—"Good." Pocketing the pages, he saluted and left.

The wound in Carl's leg became more painful, and he limped back to the hospital to have the dressing changed. There, he received the word that all the officers under the rank of full colonel were being transferred that night to another location on the island.

Before leaving the hospital, Carl acquired a small spiral steno pad and a handful of pencils to put in his musette bag. He hoped to keep a journal and record his experiences under Japanese captivity.

In a driving rainstorm, the officers—many, like Carl, still recovering from wounds—were herded across the island and into an open hangar with a bomb-damaged roof. Hundreds were already there. They all spent the rest of the night trying to sleep on the wet concrete floor.

No food had been issued since the surrender, and their only drinking water came from a single spigot. While younger officers dug latrine pits inside the wire, small foraging parties were permitted to go out and dig in the rubble of the demolished warehouses to bring back any food they could find.

One group returned with a few cases of tinned abalone, and Carl shared the soggy shellfish in one of the cans with two other men. In his desperate hunger, he thought it tasted like the finest lobster from the Gulf of Maine.

After three days and nights, the foraging parties began to come back empty-handed and the men in the hangar became ravenous. Many lapsed into unconsciousness before the Japanese finally announced that the men would be transferred to Manila.

On Saturday, May 23, they marched in ranks to the south docks, where they were joined by thousands of enlisted men. Like the officers, none had been fed and they were in poor physical condition. At the docks, the Americans were separated from the Filipinos.

All day, the vanquished defenders were ferried in small launches out to Japanese freighters anchored offshore. The Americans were packed into one group of ships and the Filipinos another. Still unfed, they endured a long night crammed into the reeking holds without water or sanitary facilities.

The next morning, the ships raised anchor and steamed the twenty-six miles across the bay to Manila. When they arrived offshore, the ships holding the Filipinos were disembarked at the Manila docks, where they boarded trains to carry them north to their prison camps. The ships holding the Americans anchored near a section of beach south of the Manila Yacht Club.

As the men were brought up from the holds and began climbing down the rope nets hanging from the hulls of the freighters, Carl suddenly realized what the Japanese had planned for them. The starving Americans in their ragged uniforms would be forced to wade ashore and would then be paraded through the streets of Manila so that the Filipino civilians could see what defeat truly looked like and what conquest meant.

On the long stretch of beach, the Japanese formed the Americans into a single, ragged column four men wide. By the time Carl came ashore, hundreds of men were already wending their way up the beach in the four caterpillar-like lines toward Admiral Dewey Boulevard.

When he trudged past the entrance to the boulevard, Carl saw that a large crowd of Filipinos and Japanese lined both sidewalks. The buildings behind them were adorned with huge Japanese flags, and many of the Japanese on the sidewalks were cheering and waving smaller ones. Most of the Filipinos stood silently as the Americans staggered past.

The sun beat down mercilessly and like all the others, Carl was faint from hunger. Before he finished the first long block, the wound in his thigh began to throb painfully in time with each beat of his heart. He felt an odd swelling under his khaki shirt, and pulled up the hem to reveal an egg-sized bulge emerging between his ribs. He had no idea what it was or why it was happening.

Up ahead, weaker officers began to fall out of line, some dropping unconscious. As Japanese guards shouted at them to get up and march, Carl wondered how long it would be before he joined them on the pavement.

TWENTY-FIVE

Florence awoke to the shouts of newsboys hawking papers on Pennsylvania Avenue. She ran out to the sidewalk to buy the extra edition of the *Manila Star*. The headline read CORREGIDOR SURRENDERS. The story provided few details aside from the fact that the American forces on Corregidor, numbering more than eleven thousand officers and enlisted men, had capitulated to the Imperial Japanese Army.

The next few days passed without further word, and Japanese troops celebrated their latest victory with parades and public events in which their handpicked Filipino collaborators hailed the Japanese defeat of the colonial powers and their creation of the "Greater East Asia Co-Prosperity Sphere."

What had they done with the men on Corregidor? Florence wondered. She heard rumors that thousands of the soldiers who surrendered on Bataan died while marching without food or water to prison camps far north of Manila.

Her apprehension about Bing's fate had further frayed her relationship with sixteen-year-old Olive, who was adjusting to the new reality of the Japanese occupation and always wanted to be with her friends. Schools had reopened and after school she began going out to visit at their homes. This only added to Florence's anxiety.

A news bulletin on the Japanese-controlled radio station finally provided an answer: the prisoners from Corregidor were being transported by ship to Manila, and the Japanese occupying authority encouraged the city's residents of Manila to come out to witness the Americans being paraded in defeat. A street map in the morning newspaper showed the route.

Knowing that Bing had been sent to Corregidor, Florence could only pray that he was one of the survivors. She decided to watch for him from the corner of Taft Avenue near their house on Pennsylvania. Bing would be looking for her along that patch of sidewalk.

Margaret and Olive accompanied her to the parade route. Both adored Bing and Margaret was a good friend of Carl Engelhart from the days when she had managed his favorite bookstore in Manila. Working together, the women hoped to spot both men in the ranks of prisoners.

The sidewalks were packed with people when the three women took their places on the corner of Taft Avenue. The crowd was mostly women, children, and old men. They spoke in whispers to avoid attracting the attention of the armed Japanese soldiers who stood every ten feet along both sides of the street.

Someone whispered, "They're coming," and Florence watched as the first ranks of Americans emerged from the corner of San Luis Avenue and slowly came toward them up Taft. She saw there were four separate columns of men spread out across the road. They no longer resembled soldiers. Although a few attempted to march with some degree of military precision, most looked like beggars or scarecrows. Many were barefoot.

A Japanese officer was sitting on a horse near the sidewalk, watching the prisoners come. It might have been comical under other circumstances, but he had placed a straw plantation hat on the horse's head to shield it from the sun.

Only a few of the Americans had any headgear at all.

Florence scanned the face of every man going past. The four columns seemed endless and there were a number of tall men who under their beards might have been Bing, but they didn't look her way as he would have done. Occasionally, she heard a person gasp or sob as someone they knew staggered past.

Hundreds of men had passed by when one in the far rank began to wobble in the clutch of exhaustion. When he dropped to his hands and knees, a Japanese soldier quickly went to the spot and shouted at him to get up and march. The American didn't move and the soldier kicked him hard in the backside, driving him forward onto his stomach. When he failed to react to two more kicks, the guard drove his bayonet into the man's back.

There was a shocked gasp from the onlookers as the dead man was dragged to the side of the road, leaving a trail of blood, but no one spoke.

The lines of prisoners continued in a steady flood, and it became impossible for the three women to keep track of all the faces as they lurched by. The avenue was completely silent aside from the tramping of their feet.

"It's Carl Engelhart," Margaret whispered at last.

Florence's eyes found Carl's gray and unshaven face as he limped toward them. He was almost a walking skeleton. He had always been very fastidious about his appearance, but he was now wearing stained and mismatched khakis. The three women began waving.

"He sees us," whispered Margaret, as Carl's eyes focused on them until he was past.

The women remained on the sidewalk until the last Americans went by. None had caught a glimpse of Bing. As they walked home, Margaret suggested that they might have missed him or he had come ashore too late to join the procession. The anguish of not knowing led to another sleepless night.

———

The following afternoon, there was a knock at the front door and Florence opened it to find a young Japanese lieutenant standing on the portico. She bowed deeply to him as she now did to every Japanese soldier. He gave her a piece of paper with her name and address on it. Below her address was scrawled *E. C. Engelhart* in Carl's handwriting.

"You know name?" the lieutenant asked, and she nodded yes.

"Very sorry," he said, bowing his head in response.

The officer saluted her and left.

Walking back inside, Florence met Margaret and Olive, who were both nervous at the unusual visit. Florence unfolded the document. It was a carbon of a citation. She read the first words at the top of the page.

*SMITH, CHARLES EDWARD (KIA)

CITATION:

THE PRESIDENT OF THE UNITED STATES TAKES PRIDE IN PRESENTING THE DISTINGUISHED SERVICE CROSS (POSTHUMOUSLY) TO CHARLES EDWARD SMITH (3205576), CHIEF ELECTRICIAN'S MATE, U.S. NAVY, FOR EXTRAORDINARY HEROISM IN CONNECTION WITH MILITARY OPERATIONS AGAINST AN ARMED ENEMY WHILE DETACHED FOR SERVICE WITH THE UNITED FORCES IN THE PHILIPPINES, IN THE VICINITY OF QUINAWAN POINT, BATAAN, PHILIPPINE ISLANDS, ON FEBRUARY 8, 1942.

WHEN IT BECAME NECESSARY TO COORDINATE AN ATTACK FROM SEAWARD WITH THE OPERATIONS OF GROUND FORCES IN BREAKING THE RESISTANCE OF A DEFILADED AND STRONGLY HELD ENEMY POSITION, CHIEF ELECTRICIAN'S MATE SMITH WAS CHARGED WITH DIRECTING THE FIRE OF THE BOW GUNS FROM ACROSS AN EXPOSED POSITION OUTSIDE THE GUN SHIELDS. DURING THE ENTIRE OPERATION THIS INTREPID BLUEJACKET MAINTAINED ACCURATE AND VOLUMINOUS FIRE FROM HIS EXPOSED POST IN THE BOW OF THE BOAT DESPITE HEAVY ENEMY FIRE FROM THE BEACH, AND SEVERAL HOSTILE DIVE BOMBING ATTACKS.

ON THE RETURN TRIP, AFTER COMPLETION OF THE MISSION, CHIEF ELECTRICIAN'S MATE SMITH TOOK A MACHINE GUN POSITION IN AN OPEN PART OF THE BOAT WHERE HE IGNORED CONSIDERATIONS OF PERSONAL SAFETY IN FIRING AT DIVE BOMBERS AS THEY CAME IN TO ATTACK, THEREBY DRIVING OFF TWO SUCH ATTACKS. ON ONE OCCASION, SEEING BOMBS FALLING TOWARD THE BOAT, CHIEF ELECTRICIAN'S MATE SMITH PUSHED A CREW MEMBER INTO A PROTECTED SPOT WHICH WAS AVAILABLE TO HIM,

THEREBY SAVING HIS COMPANION'S LIFE AT THE EXPENSE OF HIS OWN. THIS VALIANT BLUEJACKET WAS KILLED ONLY AFTER HAVING CONTRIBUTED IN LARGE MEASURE TO THE SUCCESS OF THIS VITAL ENTERPRISE.

Headquarters: Allied Forces in the Philippines, General Orders No. 20 (April 9, 1942)
Born: Cedar Rapids, Iowa
Home Town: Cedar Rapids, Iowa

In shock, Florence handed the citation to Margaret and Olive. When Olive read it, she began to cry. Margaret told Florence that the Distinguished Service Cross was the second-highest award for personal valor after the Medal of Honor.

Florence didn't care about the medal. She wanted Bing. When the other two women attempted to comfort her, she left the house and began walking blindly along the streets. Oblivious to other people, she attempted to absorb the enormity of it all. Perhaps it was the pain etched in her face, but no one accosted her.

She knew that young women all over the world were receiving the same tragic news every day. The world was at war. Bing had been a warrior, and warriors died. She tried to find comfort in the fact that he sacrificed his life to save a crewmate. That was Bing. But by doing it, he gave up their life together. They had only been married for six months. It was only just beginning for them. Now it was over.

As evening turned into night, she kept walking. Her eyes would fill with tears, but she didn't cry. At one point, she sat on a park bench in the darkness and gazed up at the stars. It was so hard to take in the finality of it.

She grieved for him all that night and for the long nights afterward.

As the days passed, life continued as it had before, but there was no longer any uncertainty about the future. She was alone again. As with every other challenge she encountered in life, she would persevere facing forward, and not look back. She wouldn't burden anyone else with her grief.

Margaret and Olive tried to comfort her, but she rebuffed their attempts at sympathy, determined to begin the work of healing by taking action. She decided that the best way to honor Bing's memory would be to somehow help defeat the Japanese. She wasn't sure what that meant but silently vowed that she would try. Florence also forced herself to face the hard realities of what lay ahead. She no longer had a job or career, and the money Bing had left for her would soon run out. She needed a plan to survive.

As much as she had loved Bing, she had never been dependent on him. She made her own way in life to become who she was now. It had been a hard journey. She had left home at the age of seven after enduring the traumatic disintegration of her family. She overcame the doubters at Union Church Hall who viewed mestizas as racially inferior. She earned her every accomplishment at school and the commendations in her professional work since.

She would survive.

TWENTY-SIX

It felt good to Japanese businessman Kiyoshi Osawa to be shaving down his golf handicap again. The weeks he spent in the prison at Muntinlupa and then a second internment camp in Manila were already becoming a distant memory. Now it was the Americans' turn to enjoy the hospitality of prison camps.

The food in his two camps was execrable but there had been a lot of it, and there were few punishments for the inmates. During the day, they were allowed to exercise and one morning during a soccer match, they were treated to a marvelous spectacle.

Osawa was running down the ball when he heard the sound of aircraft and looked up to see a Japanese Zero fighter plane dogfighting with an American warplane. Moments later, the American plane fell from the sky. When it hit the ground and blew up, Osawa and the other prisoners cheered wildly.

After word spread that a Japanese invasion force had landed near Lingayen Gulf, tension mounted between the prisoners and the guards. Rumors began circulating that the prisoners would face reprisals if the Japanese won. Secretly, they began collecting flattened cans and sharp-edged rocks to fight back if necessary.

Osawa had been moved to his second camp at an abandoned school in Manila when the Filipino guards came inside their compound and told the prisoners that the Japanese army was about to enter the city. A number of the guards said they wanted to switch sides.

When they were released, Osawa and the other prisoners surged through the gates in time to hail the first arriving soldiers. "Banzai!" Osawa shouted in exultation as he hugged one of the liberators.

A few weeks later, the new occupying authority recruited Osawa to join a group of Japanese business executives to confiscate all the assets owned by the British and Americans in the Philippines. Osawa was assigned responsibility for the restructuring of Manila Railways, the Manila Electric Company, the Bank of New York, and the San Miguel Brewery, and to appoint the new Japanese managers.

After completing his assignments, one of his friends in the occupying authority confided to Osawa that he would shortly be hearing exciting news about his next position. When it was officially announced, Osawa was stunned.

Under Ordinance Number One of its new occupation mandate, the Imperial Japanese Army created the Philippine Liquid Fuel Distribution Union to establish military control over all the energy resources in the country. The board of directors of the new organization comprised the general managers of the top trading companies in Japan, including Mitsui & Co., Mitsubishi, and Daiken Sangyo. They appointed Kiyoshi Osawa as the first managing director.

It was a testament to his success in building several successful businesses in the Philippines, as well as the warm relationships he had honed with Japanese business leaders in Tokyo. Most of all, it was a testament to his loyalty to the Emperor.

The scale of the new organization required him to hire hundreds of people to carry out its mandate of providing all the liquid fuel needs of the Japanese army, including gasoline, diesel fuel, lubricating oil, alcohol, and heavy fuel oil for Japanese shipping. The remaining fuel stocks were to be rationed to the Philippine people based on a distribution system he needed to devise.

His principal administrative offices would be in Manila, with subsidiary offices in each major city in the country. He also had to establish a network of fuel stations to dispense the fuel under his new rationing system. Osawa staffed the most senior positions in the company with Japanese businessmen.

Osawa decided that his rationing plan would employ a priority system based on the applicant's relative contribution and importance to the Philippine economy. At the lowest rung were individual citizens seeking fuel for personal use.

He moved quickly. For his new company headquarters, Osawa requisitioned the offices of the American-owned Standard Oil Company, which was located in the iconic Metropolitan Theater Building on Ayala Boulevard. The building had expansive grounds and was in the center of the Manila commercial district.

Osawa felt proud as he settled into the corner office previously occupied by the president of Standard Oil. It was on the ground floor and looked out onto a beautiful park. The building was equipped with central air conditioning, which was a rarity in the city and would be an asset for his employees during the hot season.

Over the ensuing months, he interviewed and hired hundreds of Japanese for each branch of the organization, including accounting, production, and distribution. At one point, he hired all twenty-four engineering graduates from the University of the Philippines for field positions outside Manila, even though they were Filipino and not Japanese. This led to hard questioning from the Japanese general overseeing the civilian-run company. He came to Osawa's office and demanded to know his reasoning.

"Setting these brilliant graduates free in the streets will only contribute to the downfall of our occupational policy," Osawa told the general.

"How?" he demanded.

Osawa explained that unlike their Spanish predecessors, the Americans had built schools, hospitals, and roads across the country to improve the lives of the Filipino people. A large percentage of the population was loyal to them. With the fall of Bataan, hundreds of Filipino soldiers had refused to surrender and melted into the mountains to organize bands of guerrillas.

There was little coordination between them, and Osawa said he was sure the Japanese army could crush the disorganized groups so long as young men like his engineers didn't leave their families and jobs to go off and fight alongside them.

The general gave Osawa permission to retain the Filipino engineers in the field.

On the first day that applications for fuel from the general public were accepted, several hundred Filipinos joined the line outside the entrance to the building and patiently waited for the chance to acquire what they needed.

For Osawa, the moment was the fulfillment of everything he aspired to in his life: faithfully serving his Emperor and at the same time assisting the Philippine people to improve their living conditions. He had only one nagging concern. It related to behavior he was observing almost every day.

He fully understood the need for harshness in punishing the Americans who had finally surrendered on Corregidor; they were the enemy. What concerned him was the brutal way in which some of the Japanese soldiers were treating their new Filipino partners. Many clearly did not understand the people or their culture, and were not interested in learning.

Through the windows of his corner office, Osawa regularly witnessed casual cruelty. People simply enjoying a walk in the park were accosted by soldiers, and if they didn't bow deeply enough or show appropriate deference, they were beaten or kicked.

Osawa was sure most Filipinos would cooperate with the Japanese occupying authority if they were treated with respect, but too often they were treated as conquered subjects. They were fiercely proud people, and Osawa knew that cruel treatment would only turn them against the authority.

TWENTY-SEVEN

Margaret Cirstens came home one evening in May and told Florence she was planning to move out of the house. Alfred Keller, the Swiss business-man she was in love with, had asked her to live with him. Although he still hadn't promised to marry her, Margaret felt confident he eventually would.

She had been contributing a small amount to the monthly household budget, and after she moved out, Florence took stock of her situation again. The cash Bing had left her in December was nearly gone. She would need to earn money to cover the rent as well as the expense of supporting Olive and Mariano.

With Margaret gone as a controlling influence, Olive began to assert herself once more, demanding more freedom. Matters came to a head one evening when she told Florence she was going out and would be home by their agreed curfew time of 10 p.m.

When ten o'clock came and went, Florence initially thought Olive was just being inconsiderate. By midnight, her irritation turned to anxiety. Many Japanese officers lived in the neighborhood, and Olive was a known presence.

Florence had no idea which friends Olive was visiting or where her friends even lived. There was no one she could call, and the last thing she wanted to do was alert the military police that Olive was missing.

Florence remembered Bing's warnings of what might happen to them at night, and now she was sure that something terrible had happened to

Olive. What could she possibly tell Flaviana about the failure to protect her daughter?

It felt like deliverance when she heard the sound of a key moving in the front door lock. The door opened and she was elated to see Olive standing on the landing. Her sense of relief quickly dissipated when Olive acted as if nothing was out of the ordinary. She told Florence she had lost track of time at the party, and asked her why she was so agitated.

Florence slapped her across the face.

"I'm no longer a child," Olive shouted at her.

"No, but you're spoiled and ungrateful," said Florence.

Morning brought no cease-fire. When Olive threatened to return home to Isabela Province, a still angry Florence said that decision would make her very happy.

Olive left a few days later.

Since March, Florence had been sending money each week to Norma in Candelaria. She was raising Jerry on her own after the baby's father, Manuel Castro, told her he was joining the resistance. Months went by with no further word until a man in the Candelaria underground related that Manuel had been captured with several others and probably executed by the Kempeitai. Florence wrote and invited Norma and Jerry to come live on Pennsylvania Avenue. Norma gratefully accepted.

Florence's friend Dolores Gardner still worked every day to gather food and medicine for Bob Hendry and his friends at the Santo Tomas internment camp. Florence tried to help too, asking friends for donations and collecting small supplies of rice and other staples.

She and Dolores visited the camp every few days to deliver what they had gathered. With gas rationing, Dolores no longer used her car, and they now traveled by bus. The guards knew them both and allowed them to bring in their supplies without always receiving a bribe. At the end of each visit, the women gathered the men's soiled clothing and took it home for laundering.

Bob Hendry and his friends constructed a small shanty on the grounds of the complex with canvas and tar paper walls and a palm thatched roof.

It was one of hundreds constructed by prisoners who did not want to live in the bug-infested classrooms. The only sanitation was a chamber pot. The shanty had no running water, and there was no source of heat for cooking, but there was a semblance of privacy and Bob and his roommates had worked hard to make it insect-free.

Each morning at home, Florence read the classifieds in the newspaper. One day she saw an opening for a position as a bookkeeper with the Philippine Liquid Fuel Distribution Union. It required a person with an accounting background and excellent writing skills in English.

Florence typed up a résumé that included her educational background and her years working at the Army-Navy YMCA, but leaving out her time at the Office of Army Intelligence. She mailed the application letter to the main office on Ayala Boulevard.

When Norma and Jerry arrived at the house on Pennsylvania Avenue, Florence revealed her financial situation, and Norma found a job almost immediately as a waitress in a restaurant within walking distance of the house. It required her to work nights, so Florence began taking care of Jerry after Norma left for work.

A few days later, she received a letter from Mr. Oka, an executive at the Philippine Liquid Fuel Distribution Union. He wrote that he had reviewed her qualifications and wanted to schedule an interview. At the appointed day and time she went to the address on Ayala Boulevard.

The grand entrance to the Metropolitan Theater Building was crowded with people, many waiting on a long line to get inside. She saw that most were in a line to apply for fuel ration coupons.

Two Japanese guards flanked the entrance, and before allowing her to go in, one searched her purse. When he nodded his approval, she was ushered into the office of Mr. Oka, a slight Japanese man in his forties. He spoke fluent English and spent a few minutes asking about her experience at the YMCA before telling her she would need to take a written English proficiency test for the bookkeeping position. He explained that the work of the fuel union required regular written interaction with the public and as she already knew, very few Filipinos understood Japanese. Accordingly, all the financial ledgers were recorded in English. After Florence completed the written tests, Mr. Oka thanked her for coming in and said she might be hearing from him again.

One morning, she received a message from Angelita Alvarez Sobral, who had worked with Florence at the intelligence office in Fort Santiago. The last time Florence had seen her was on Christmas Eve of 1941 when they burned all the secret documents, the same evening Bing left for Corregidor.

Florence returned the call, and Angelita invited her to come to her apartment one evening later that week. She didn't specify a reason and Florence sensed she didn't want to provide it over the phone.

Born to former Spanish nobility, Angelita was intelligent, lovely, and well respected in the Army Intelligence office, although Florence found her a bit prim and prudish.

At her apartment, Angelita revealed that she had made a trip north to learn the condition of the American prisoners of war. Prior to the trip, Angelita bought a small supply of drugs and medicines. Dressed as a nurse for the International Red Cross, she made the long journey to the camp in a horse-drawn *calesa* wagon. At several of the traffic checkpoints along the highway, Japanese soldiers stopped the cart. After checking her papers, they subjected her to an unpleasant body search.

As Angelita described the soldiers' crudity, it reminded Florence of an incident that occurred when they were working together at Fort Santiago. It was during the rainy season, and Carl Engelhart had taken Angelita's arm when they were about to descend some slippery steps. She pulled away, saying, "Please don't touch me."

It left Carl feeling embarrassed and upset until he learned from another officer that in her Spanish Catholic family, an unmarried woman was not to be touched by a man under any circumstances until she was married to him. Yet now Angelita endured the soldiers' behavior to complete her mercy mission.

"I was horrified at the condition of the prisoners when I arrived at the camp," she told Florence. "Between hunger and disease, they are dying by the hundreds. One of the prisoners I saw there was Ray Bibee, although there was no chance to talk."

Florence asked about Carl. Angelita hadn't seen him, but thought it likely he was at Cabanatuan with the thousands of other men from Corregidor. She told Florence that the prisoners had somehow set up a courier system under the noses of the Japanese and that it would soon be possible to send messages to the prisoners.

"I'm starting a small network to try to smuggle food and medicine into the camp," she said, "and I was hoping you could be part of it."

Stirred by the once reticent Angelita's bravery, Florence agreed to help.

TWENTY-EIGHT

The airlessness and heat in the dusty cattle car were pitiless. Dozens of American prisoners took turns standing near the partially opened door as the train rumbled slowly north to Cabanatuan prison camp. There was no room to sit down and no place to relieve themselves or defecate, except where they stood. It took the entire day to reach their destination, and the Japanese gave them no food or water.

Arriving at a deserted railroad siding, the men were herded on foot to the entrance gate.

Carl saw that the newly built camp was bordered by an eight-foot-high barbed wire fence. Wooden guard towers loomed above the perimeter, manned by soldiers with machine guns. Stepping inside the gate, he breathed in the stink of death, sickness, and misery.

Near the front gate, scores of prisoners who had survived the Bataan death march were standing in line under the blazing sun to draw water from a single faucet. Most were bare-chested and without uniforms. They stood silently, too lethargic to even speak to one another.

Beyond them, row after row of crudely constructed barracks stretched into the distance of a vast compound, separated by narrow strips of sunbaked clay. The latrines consisted of shallow slits in the ground, covered by thick clouds of flies. By then, the camp held about seven thousand prisoners, with more arriving every day from the Corregidor garrison.

Just outside the camp entrance, Carl observed a small roadside food market with wooden bins containing fresh fruit and vegetables. On their first night in the camp, some of the men who had arrived with him snuck out under the barbed wire to buy food. Tipped off by an informant, the Japanese captured six Americans along with the four Filipinos running the stand. The following morning, the ten men were marched into camp and shot in front of the assembled prisoners.

The Japanese divided the newly arrived officers into ten- or twelve-man squads, depending on the size of their quarters. Carl was assigned to a wooden shack with eleven other lieutenant colonels and majors. The large single room was devoid of furniture, pillows, or blankets. The men slept on the floor. There was no electricity, and at night the only illumination came from the floodlights set up along the perimeter of the barbed wire fences.

The reason for dividing the prisoners into squads became clear when the Japanese announced that if one or more of the men in a squad attempted to escape, the remaining prisoners would be executed. The Americans began referring to their groups as firing squads.

Carl picked out an alcove in the shack that was just deep and long enough for him to lie down. After settling in, the officers introduced themselves and described how they had come to Cabanatuan. The subject of escape came up pretty quickly. The stark truth was that although it was the duty of a POW to try to escape and rejoin their forces, there were no organized forces left to rejoin in the Philippines.

Even if one cut through the perimeter fence to escape at night, there was no place to go and the physical size of the Americans would immediately give them away. They unanimously agreed that to try to escape under the current conditions was suicidal.

That first night, swarms of mosquitoes attacked in droves. Carl had managed to retain an eighteen-inch-square piece of netting that kept the insects out of his eyes but, like the others, was bitten everywhere else. He fell asleep to the constant sound of the men slapping themselves.

In the morning, he was thrilled to encounter Ray Bibee, whose easy sense of humor made him a boon companion. Ray told Carl that about a week earlier he had seen Angelita Alvarez Sobral dressed in a nurse's uniform and unloading some boxes from a wagon near his camp's gate. He thought she recognized him but there was no way to know for sure.

Ray had been on Bataan with the rest of Carl's Army Intelligence staff when the surrender took place, and he had survived the Bataan death march. He laconically described the daily torture of being driven on foot for sixty-five miles in the tropical heat without food or water. Every man who fell out along the way was bayoneted, clubbed to death, decapitated, or shot.

The end results of the march were immediately evident in the daily death toll inside the camp. Through the month of June, there was only one regular work detail inside Cabanatuan, and that was to carry the bodies of Americans who died the night before to the mass gravesite south of the camp. The Japanese used a small bulldozer to excavate pits large enough to entomb forty men at a time. The covered burial mounds already contained hundreds of corpses.

The death march survivors were among the first to succumb, with many having suppurating wounds, malaria, dysentery, and beriberi, a disease causing inflammation of the nerves and heart failure. Five hundred or more died each week. Before they were placed in the burial carts to be carried to the gravesite, uniforms and shoes were stripped and distributed to those prisoners reduced to wearing rags.

A few days after his arrival, Carl was summoned to appear before a guard officer who had been informed that Carl spoke fluent Japanese. When he arrived at the office, the captain was already furious. An unsheathed samurai sword lay on the table between them.

In Japanese, the captain told Carl that American warplanes had bombed Tokyo and had machine-gunned women and children in the streets. He screamed that if another terror attack took place on Japanese soil he would personally kill every American prisoner under his command. At the end of his tirade, he picked up an armband from the table. It had the word "tsuyaku" printed on it in Japanese, and he ordered Carl to wear it at all times. In English, the word meant "interpreter."

His first interpreting job occurred the morning after several shots rang out in the middle of the night near the camp hospital. Carl was summoned to the guardhouse, where the body of an American lay outside on the ground. A guard told Carl that he had been found crawling under the perimeter wire.

Carl translated the news to the senior American officer in the camp. Another prisoner said the Japanese were lying and that the dead man was racked with dysentery and trying to make it to the hospital. It was the first of scores of murders.

All the prisoners were starving. The only food the American cooks received each day was rice. Anything else had to be provided themselves. At first, the rice was only supplemented with hogwort, a fibrous weed that grew in abundance in the dusty soil of the camp.

To add scraps of meat to their diet, the campgrounds were relentlessly searched for iguanas, rats, snakes, worms, and even the large bats that sometimes sought refuge in the outbuildings. Rumors circulated that a dead prisoner had been cannibalized.

A possible long-term solution to their survival was found when an army lieutenant named Henry Jones managed to acquire vegetable seeds from the Japanese and with their approval planted a garden outside the prison compound. At first, he and his men could only till the dusty earth with sharpened sticks and tools made from scrap metal, but they persevered.

As primitive as the effort was, Jones convinced Carl and some of the other senior officers that the garden could eventually enhance their rice diet with fruits and vegetables. When the Japanese agreed to give Jones additional tools, most of the American officers resented being asked to do menial labor. Carl made the case that their future survival might rest with the food they grew, but his views yielded little initial cooperation or support. In their weakened state, most of the officers were simply trying to regain their strength.

An underground courier service sprang up to connect the prisoners to friends in Manila. It was started by a man named Kliatchko who had worked in a civilian capacity for the American army before the war and was now a POW in the camp. He began it by making friends with the Filipinos who worked at the prison freight shed, where supplies were brought to Cabanatuan. Kliatchko promised to pay them to smuggle letters and small articles in and out of the camp. They agreed to help.

Carl was stunned one day to receive a bar of soap through the courier service. Inside the soapbox was a note from Florence Smith, whom he'd last seen as the prisoners from Corregidor were paraded through the streets of Manila. She wrote to thank Carl for sending the Japanese officer with news of Bing's death. She also informed him that she was being considered for a job working for a Japanese government agency and asked his approval to take the position.

Reading between the lines, Carl realized that she had no source of income since Bing had been killed and didn't want to be considered a collaborator by her American friends. He talked it over with Ray Bibee and then wrote back, urging her to accept the position. "Tell your friends I approve," he wrote.

The deaths from wounds, disease, and starvation continued without pause, and Carl often awoke to the creaking and groaning of the burial cart as it meandered between the rows of barracks, picking up the withered and shrunken bodies.

He noticed that along with the men who made the death march, the oldest officers were among the first to die, as their limited stamina simply wore out and they gave up the will to live. The biggest and tallest men had to survive on the same pitiful rations as the smaller men, and more of them went too.

Carl was thankful he was lean and wiry, although that wasn't his only survival advantage. Whenever a prisoner was being beaten or a POW was having trouble with a guard, the call went out for Carl. He had little time to worry about his personal condition.

On Corregidor, he had lost 30 pounds from his prewar weight of 165. At Cabanatuan, his weight continued to fall and his hair and fingernails stopped growing. With the loss of subcutaneous fatty tissue, there were now ugly folds of sagging skin at his waist. Only a thin layer of flaccid skin covered his buttocks, and he was no longer able to sit down without pain. Malnutrition caused his ankles to swell over his shoes, and a camp doctor informed him he had beriberi.

Around this time, he had a very disturbing dream that he recorded in his spiral steno pad.

I awoke in the middle of a night in utter and complete darkness. I could see nothing and the darkness was so black and intense, it felt like it was pressing upon my face and body. I did not know where I was. Horror descended on me when I realized I did not know who I was. I was an entity afloat in blackness.

I lay there trying to hold against creeping panic. Then I felt an odd sensation high up on the inner side of my left thigh. I cautiously felt the spot and my fingers told me I was feeling the thread ends and knot of a suture. Reality flooded back to me. I was Lt. Colonel Carl Engelhart in the POW camp at Cabanatuan and I was fingering the stitches in my thigh wound.

It was a tremendous relief to be in control of myself again, and I told myself to get one of our doctors to pull those stitches for me. I went back to sleep.

Carl worried that as his physical condition continued to deteriorate, the disembodiment of his soul and spirit would only worsen and accelerate his end.

The new and unsettling symptoms were ongoing. Unable to sit without pain, he would usually squat on the ground. When attempting to regain his feet, he would sometimes black out. A blood pressure test put him at 88 over 58. More repulsive was the fact that he often couldn't control his sphincter muscle. His energy was diminishing by the day, his mind gradually more logy and unfocused.

At night in the blackness, Carl thought he might be close to the end, foreseeing the day when his own desiccated corpse would be carted down the road to join the thousands in the mass graves south of the camp.

TWENTY-NINE

JULY 1942
PHILIPPINE LIQUID FUEL DISTRIBUTION UNION (PLFDU)
METROPOLITAN THEATER BUILDING, MANILA

A few weeks after her first interview with Mr. Oka at the PLFDU, Florence received another letter from him requesting that she return to the offices for a final interview. This one would be with the managing director, Kiyoshi Osawa.

Mr. Oka greeted her at the accounting office and escorted her to meet the director in his large corner suite on the first floor. Florence's pulse began to race when she saw that Japanese military officers in full uniform occupied many of the nearby offices. The thought that she might have to work alongside them was deeply unsettling.

Her first impressions of Kiyoshi Osawa were positive as he welcomed her to a chair. Tall for a Japanese man, he had a kindly face and an almost courtly manner, which quickly put her at ease.

"Please call me Ken," he said. "You should know I have lived in the Philippines for twenty-two years and greatly admire the Philippine customs and traditions. I have already hired many Filipinos to work with us. You have good qualifications but I only want people who are competent and eager."

"I have always worked hard and done my best," said Florence.

Osawa repeated what Mr. Oka had said about the financial records of the fuel union being kept in English. Her job would be to help maintain the official ledgers and fill out the approved ration coupons and warehouse orders.

When Florence told him she was eager to get started, he proposed to hire her on a provisional basis. If her work was satisfactory after three months, the job would become permanent.

He was escorting her out of the office when he stopped and smiled at her.

"Do you play badminton?" he asked.

The question struck her as very strange, but she replied that she didn't.

"I will teach you," he said. "Sports is a path to relaxation. I encourage all our civilian employees to participate."

Florence promised to try to learn, and her first immersion into the sport began a few days after she started the job.

Osawa had constructed a badminton court under a gigantic acacia tree on the grounds of the Metropolitan Theater Building. The tree's umbrella of branches and leaves provided full shade during every part of the day for those competing underneath it. White tape marked the court's boundary lines and beach sand coated the playing surface.

Although not particularly athletic, Florence participated in the badminton games organized by Osawa during the midday breaks and after work. Cool refreshments were always provided and the games ended early enough for her to catch a bus home.

At work, she shared the responsibility for cataloging the vouchers, invoices, shipping tickets, and warehouse release orders with two other women in the bookkeeping department, who all reported to Mr. Oka. She and the other clerks had excellent handwriting. They recorded the names on the coupons of the individuals and companies approved to receive fuel as well as the amounts allotted to each.

After her first month on the job, Florence was familiar with every facet of the process. In the close quarters of the accounting office, she also learned a good deal about the working atmosphere, along with the building tension between some of the Japanese officers and the female employees. Too many of the officers maintained an attitude that the young women working in the PLFDU were there to service their needs both professionally and personally. It made many of the women frightened and uncomfortable, including

Florence. One clerk had already rebuffed the sexual advances of a drunken officer who caught her alone one evening in the office. She reported it to Mr. Oka but was concerned about possible retribution.

At one of the badminton games, Florence met a Filipino employee who worked in the distribution department. His name was Ricardo de Castro, and he had been formerly employed as a civilian worker at the Cavite Navy Yard. When they were alone, he confided his resentment at being forced to work for the Japanese in order to support his family.

She was surprised at his candor in expressing his true feelings about the Japanese to someone he had just met, and wondered if he was simply trying to draw her out in order to trap her. He seemed honest, but she didn't respond in kind.

When she received her first paycheck, she sent a quarter of it to Carl Engelhart.

THIRTY

When he received the first packet of money from Florence through the courier service, Carl was deeply moved. If she could continue sending the gifts, it would mean survival. He vowed that if he could stop the weight loss that was slowly killing him, he would work to save as many men in the prison camp as he could.

In Manila, the pesos Florence sent were sufficient to buy food for a week. Inside the camp, it was barely enough to bribe a guard to purchase some scraps of meat and a few fish heads, but it meant the difference between life and death.

Carl already knew he could make a difference on behalf of his fellow prisoners by using his fluency in Japanese and his knowledge of their culture to help make the lives of the prisoners better. To do that, he needed to be able to walk.

Over the next few weeks, the scrapings of additional food he and his hut mates acquired to supplement their rice ration stopped their weight loss. Pipe-stem arms and legs slowly began to fill out again.

Carl was pathetically grateful to recover control of his sphincter muscle and he could feel his energy returning a little at a time. He thought in some part it might be because his sense of hope was restored. He wrote back to Florence to thank her for saving their lives.

Other prisoners began receiving small gifts of money, food, and medicine through the underground courier service and it slowly reduced the daily death toll. Then, a potentially deadly epidemic threatened to kill every prisoner in the camp. It began with the hospitalization of two men who appeared to have tonsillitis. A medical examination by American camp doctors led to a diagnosis of diphtheria, a highly infectious disease that in the tropics often led to irreversible nerve damage, heart failure, and death.

Diphtheria usually began with a sore throat and desperate coughing followed by a buildup of thick mucus in the air passage, which often caused suffocation or paralysis of the heart. The two prisoners with diphtheria were immediately quarantined, and they soon died.

By then, dozens more had been infected and brought to an isolation ward. The sounds coming from the hospital ward sounded to Carl like a kennel full of barking dogs as the men desperately tried to cough up the deadly mucus.

Every prisoner in the camp suffered from malnutrition and their weakened immunity to disease made it inevitable that the epidemic would spread. Without an antitoxin to vaccinate the rest, most of the men would die.

Lieutenant Colonel Jack Schwartz, the senior American doctor in the camp, went to Lieutenant Colonel Mori, the camp commandant, and told him the situation. Fearing that his own men would become infected, Mori immediately placed a call to Manila. In a few days, enough serum arrived to inoculate all the Japanese guards and several thousand prisoners. Thousands more remained unprotected.

A frantic plea went out to the underground networks to help find the resources to purchase enough diphtheria antitoxin to inoculate the rest of the POWs.

It seemed like an impossible task, but a supply was tracked down at a pharmaceutical facility operating secretly on the island of Mindanao. Underground operatives from Manila made the dangerous journey by boat to the island. Evading Japanese patrols, they reached the facility and acquired the serum.

Returning across the Sulu Sea, they arrived at Cabanatuan and smuggled the antitoxin into the camp. By then, more than a hundred prisoners had died. Doctors administered injections to every remaining POW and the disease only claimed a handful of additional men.

The first opportunity for a rejuvenated Carl to serve the other prisoners occurred when he was summoned to appear before a new officer of the guard, Lieutenant Hayoshi.* Coming to attention, Carl saluted and congratulated him.

"What for?" demanded Hayoshi.

"You earned the kinshi-kunsho," replied Carl—the highest Japanese combat decoration for valor.

"Who told you that?" asked Hayoshi.

"No one," said Carl. "I saw the ribbon on your chest."

Intrigued, the lieutenant asked him to sit down and explain his facility with Japanese. He was fascinated to learn that Carl's son Anders had been born in Tokyo and that he learned the language from children's schoolbooks. Hayoshi told Carl that since they were both professional soldiers, he looked forward to talking privately with him about the war.

After the two men spent several evenings together, it was clear that the camp guards noticed. They began treating Carl with a politeness bordering on deference. This was put to the test when an American officer who supervised prisoners working on Lieutenant Jones's farm told Carl that a sadistic Japanese guard was beating his men.

Carl went out the next morning after the farm detail began its work. The guard in charge was a private named Aihara but the prisoners called him Air Raid since he enjoyed hitting them on the head with a pick handle he called his "vitamin stick." When Carl arrived, two prisoners were lying on the ground after being hit and the guard was screaming at them to get

---

* In the text of Carl Engelhart's memoir, he put an asterisk next to the name of Lieutenant "Hayoshi," one of the Japanese officers at Cabanatuan who had been commended for bravery. Carl then wrote that Hayoshi was not his real name but offered no explanation for why he had changed it.

up. Carl took a long-shot chance. He strode up to the group and with the snarl of a Japanese officer ordered Aihara to shut up. Continuing to rant, Carl threatened to report him to Lieutenant Hayoshi. Incredibly, the guard walked away.

Carl made another dangerous decision when a young American officer approached him to say that he had been a ham radio enthusiast before the war and had built numerous small radios from spare parts. If Carl could provide him with flashlight batteries, a telephone receiver, and a few other parts, he thought he could make a shortwave receiver.

Lieutenant Colonel Mori had decreed that anyone found in possession of a radio would be executed. Carl knew that if the young officer were ever caught with the radio and tortured, he would probably reveal who got the parts for him. Yet the lure of having genuine war news outweighed the concern.

Carl sought out one of the enlisted prisoners who worked as a janitor in the Japanese barracks. After telling the man he did not want him to take any undue risks, he described what he needed. A few weeks later, the radio was functioning and the officer who built it was bringing in the KGEI station in San Francisco.

Dozens of men were still dying every day from malnutrition and disease, compounded by overwork. One group of enlisted men was assigned to Jones's quickly expanding farm. There was no natural irrigation at the site and the exhausted prisoners were forced to carry water all day in five-gallon cans from a stream a quarter mile away.

Carl suggested to Lieutenant Hayoshi that an electric pump be procured to pipe the water to a water tank at the garden, and a few days later a Japanese corporal brought him a motor and pump. Carl saw that it was a DC motor and told the guard it wouldn't be able to power the pump. Carl explained the difference between DC current and AC current and that an AC motor was needed to handle the electrical load.

Furious, the guard accused him of lying and ordered his men to hook up the motor. When it ran perfectly, he threatened to send Carl to the confinement hut. However, when the motor was connected to the pump, it died.

An AC motor was appropriated from a Filipino machine shop. It worked perfectly and water began flowing from the stream to the storage tank. Carl's satisfaction came from knowing that the malnourished prisoners no longer had to lug the five-gallon cans.

He returned to his shack one evening to find his hut mates embroiled in an angry argument over the Japanese attack at Pearl Harbor. Lieutenant Colonel Howard Breitung, a West Pointer like Carl, angrily condemned the Japanese treachery while someone else responded by accusing President Roosevelt of baiting the Japanese into attacking. Another officer, Lieutenant Colonel Briggs, sided with Breitung.

Breitung wouldn't let the argument lie, and the others felt a growing concern about his mental stability when he began loudly repeating the same tirade several times a day. Malnutrition affected every man differently, and even though their diet improved with the additional food Carl was purchasing, the hut mates agreed that Breitung was becoming disturbed.

Late one night, the officers in the shack were awakened by an American captain who served as the adjutant for the POW camp leader. He anxiously told them that Lieutenant Colonel Breitung and Lieutenant Colonel Briggs had been caught trying to escape. A quick search of the shack revealed the men were gone.

When Carl arrived at the POW camp leader's hut, he got a full account of what happened: Breitung and Briggs, along with a navy lieutenant named Gilbert, had been lying in a drainage ditch near the perimeter wire, waiting for a sentry to reach the other end of his patrol section before cutting their way out.

An American prisoner with dysentery had run out of his hut to try to reach the latrine and couldn't make it. Squatting over the drainage ditch, he spewed out a liquid mass of feces onto Briggs.

Enraged, Briggs climbed out of the ditch and attacked the ill prisoner, yelling obscenities at the top of his lungs. Men began pouring out of nearby huts to try to stop the fight, but Briggs battled like a madman, struggling to break free and yelling that it was their duty to help him escape.

After dragging him inside the camp leader's headquarters, the men tried to quiet him to no avail. Hearing the ongoing racket, Japanese sentries rushed in and took Briggs, Breitung, and Gilbert to the guardhouse. Briggs then began ranting at the Japanese officer in charge.

His outburst ended when the three men were separated and each subjected to brutal beatings for the rest of the night. In the morning, guards were posted outside Carl's shack. None of the ten remaining squad members were allowed to enter or leave except under guard and only to go to the latrine.

Their apprehension grew with the passing of each day. Mori, the Japanese commandant, had been clear on the shooting squad policy from the start. Any attempt to escape by one would lead to the execution of all. This would be the chance to make an example of them to the thousands of other prisoners thinking about escape.

The brutal beatings of Briggs, Breitung, and Gilbert continued for three days. On the fourth day, the three men were taken out and beheaded. The lives of the ten men remaining in their squad hung in the balance.

THIRTY-ONE

OCTOBER 1942
PHILIPPINE LIQUID FUEL DISTRIBUTION UNION
METROPOLITAN THEATER BUILDING, MANILA

The idea came to Florence while she was reading the weekly company newsletter circulated to all the departments in the fuel union. It included announcements of job promotions, new facility openings, and future company events.

What caught her eye was a story about the arrest of a man who attempted to acquire gasoline at one of the company's fuel stations by using a forged ration coupon. As a result, employees at the fuel stations were warned to be vigilant in closely examining each coupon before dispensing fuel.

That got her thinking about the company coupon system. Each one of the hundreds of coupons processed weekly were officially stamped by Florence or her fellow clerks, Imelda de Asis and Soledad Javier, after they had handwritten the name of the person or the company approved for receiving the fuel and the amount that could be purchased.

The ration coupons were printed with the fuel union's colorful logo and seal. Florence and the other clerks hand-recorded the transaction number on the coupon and then recorded it with the other information in the company's ledgers so that a monthly tally could be made of exactly how much fuel of each type had been distributed.

Theoretically, an officially stamped genuine coupon could be filled out with a false name of an individual or company. Approved purchasers were not required to show identity cards at the fuel station since the officially stamped coupon itself was the sole medium of exchange.

For a diversion plan to work, there were two additional steps that would have to be undertaken to avoid getting caught. At the end of each week, the fuel stations sent in their weekly tallies as well as the actual coupons used to acquire the different fuels. Florence would need to alter the weekly tallies in the ledger, and she would have to destroy the false coupons when they came back to the office.

Florence felt a thrill of excitement at the possibilities. It compensated for the shudder of fear when she imagined what the Japanese would do to her if she were caught. But for the first time, she realized there was a chance to help more of the American POWs in Cabanatuan along with her friends interned at Santo Tomas. She could acquire the fuel, sell it, and use the profit to buy supplies that could be smuggled into Cabanatuan.

Very few coupons were approved for individuals seeking to acquire gasoline for personal use because they were at the lowest end of Ken Osawa's priority list. This led to a steep decline in vehicular traffic in the city. The people of Manila now rode buses, bicycles, and horse-drawn carts.

Most of the approved coupons were for larger quantities of fuel since the successful applicants were typically individuals and businesses that made or delivered important commodities to the general population. Gasoline was dispensed largely for use in trucks and other delivery vehicles, while diesel fuel was utilized to run equipment and machinery in mills, factories, and other commercial enterprises.

Every month, hundreds of blank ration coupons were printed. They were lying on the storeroom shelves. If she was careful, she could imprint the official stamp on blank coupons in the storeroom and smuggle them out of the building at the end of the day. They could then be filled out with false names at home.

Japanese soldiers guarded each entrance and they routinely searched handbags, briefcases, or carryalls brought into the building. From her observation, however, they didn't ordinarily search bags or items carried out of the building, at least by the employees.

Florence concluded she would need to recruit others to help her. A woman did not fit the profile of a typical customer at the fuel stations. Customers were Japanese and Filipino businessmen or the men who worked for them. A man would have to be recruited who was trustworthy and not afraid to take a risk. And he would need to have access to a truck or other large vehicle to transport the fuel. A typical coupon for commercial purposes totaled twenty gallons or more, far larger than the reservoir in a car's gas tank.

She thought about what might be done with the fuel once it was in safe hands. There was a thriving black market in Manila where one could purchase just about anything for the right price, but she knew no one involved and many were part of the criminal underground, out for themselves. She had read that the price of fuel on the black market was much higher than the amount being paid for it through the fuel union. The same was true of drugs and medicines. If she were to acquire these critical supplies for the POWs and internees, the sale of the fuel would have to be brokered by someone and the cash used to purchase what she needed. The first step would be to identify a person to work with her on the plan. In the meantime, she would speak to no one about it.

When she made another visit to Santo Tomas with Dolores to deliver a small supply of food, clean laundry, and personal items, she saw a demonstration of the pluck and determination of the thousands of British and Americans imprisoned there and their will to survive. New camp leaders had been elected by the other prisoners and were now in charge of running the prison under the authority of the Japanese. Healthy internees were assigned jobs, everything from kitchen chores to cleaning the buildings and landscaping the grounds. Athletic events were organized and there were soccer and basketball teams.

After eight months, the Japanese were still not providing food, clothing, or other supplies to the internees, but they allowed the International Red Cross to do so in their place. Unfortunately, there was never enough food for everyone.

Primitive kitchens were installed along with new latrines, but each classroom still housed fifty people with only a few inches of space to walk between bedrolls. Most went to sleep hungry, battling clouds of insects.

Bob Hendry told Florence and Dolores that a contest had been arranged by the camp leaders in which a prize was offered to the child who could kill the most flies in a week. A twelve-year-old boy earned the money for eliminating fifteen thousand.

Bob and his hut mates further improved their outdoor shanty so that each man had a cot and a mosquito net supplied by friends. Partitions made of bamboo matting allowed a minimal level of privacy, but Florence recognized that their continued existence would only come through help from outside the walls.

THIRTY-TWO

The ten condemned men waited in the shack to learn their fate.

After the beheadings, Carl found himself surprisingly calm. He had become a fatalist about the war after narrowly escaping death on Corregidor. He had been wounded four times and a few inches difference in any of those locations would have left him buried there. Surrendering to fate allowed him to face death with stoic calm.

It didn't lessen the apprehension for the others. The hot, sweaty nights seemed interminable, with each man alone in his thoughts. The ones who couldn't sleep spent hours discussing the odds of their making it.

Several days after the beheadings, they were visited by a Marine Corps major named Frank "Pete" Pyzick, who gave them an update on their precarious situation. He spoke enough Japanese to plead their case to Lieutenant Colonel Mori. He based his plea on the fact that the three prisoners hadn't escaped, and that this was due to their being blocked from getting through the perimeter fence by American POWs who'd come out to stop the fight.

A Japanese officer at the proceeding made the case that if the hut mates weren't executed, it would only lead to more escape attempts. For the future security of the camp, it was necessary to impose the preordained punishment so that the prisoners would not question Japanese strength of character.

Pyzick told the men in the shack he thought they had a fifty-fifty chance to survive. Mori owned a bicycle shop in Manila before the war, he said. He did not seem to have a hatred of Americans.

Lieutenant Colonel Mori finally made his decision. He conceded to Major Pyzick, but punished the hut mates by sentencing them to thirty days additional confinement in their shack.

Expecting the worst, the reprieve was like a rebirth. They were all already confined behind barbed wire and would remain Japanese prisoners as long as the war lasted anyway.

With nothing to do, Carl removed a four-foot strip of wood from one of the joints and began to whittle it with his penknife. Although he had never done so before, he soon completed two sets of simple chessmen. A hut mate used a fountain pen and ink mixed with water to dye one of the sets. A wedge of cardboard too thick for toilet paper became the game board and a round robin chess marathon began.

While they were still serving their sentence, Carl was summoned to the main guardhouse. When he arrived, he immediately sensed something serious was taking place. In addition to the guard officers, a Japanese man in a white tropical suit was there, along with two officers from the Japanese Imperial Staff.

"How many Jews are there among the American prisoners of war?" the Japanese civilian demanded in a Tokyo accent.

Carl concluded that Japan's German allies were pressuring them to adopt the Nazis' own policies of persecuting the Jews. He had no idea how many Jewish officers were in the camp, but there were probably several hundred.

"There are no Jews in the American armed forces," he responded in Japanese, "only Americans."

Attempting to find a Japanese parallel, he said that the only original Americans were the natives, who were like the indigenous Ainu tribe in northern Japan, and that all the others in America came from other countries. He told them his father came from Denmark, his wife's father from Germany, and that his son had been born in Tokyo.

"What does that make my son?" he concluded by asking them.

One officer laughed and said, "Japanese."

"No Jews here?" repeated one of the staff officers from the high command.

"No Jews," Carl assured them.

"Then we have no problem," said the staff officer.

At the POW leader's hut, Carl called together the senior American prisoners and told them what had happened. They were all shocked at the development and agreed to pass the word through the camp that if a POW was asked the same question, he should adopt the same line.

As the weeks passed, at least some of the POWs retained their sense of humor. One posted a cartoon on the bulletin board outside the camp leader's hut. It depicted a likeness of General MacArthur addressing a radio microphone.

"My father took the Philippines. I lost the Philippines. Do not lose hope; I have a son!"

MacArthur's son, Arthur, was four years old.

In October, rumors began circulating through the camp that the war had reached a stalemate in the Pacific and that President Roosevelt was considering a proposal to exchange the American POWs in the Philippines for Japanese soldiers captured elsewhere.

Wishful thinking, Carl believed. As a cadet at West Point, he had read about the Union soldiers imprisoned at Andersonville, Georgia, during the Civil War. All they dreamed about was a prisoner exchange with the Confederates until the day they died. And as far as he knew, the Japanese army hadn't surrendered anywhere.

Carl went to see the officer who had built the shortwave radio and asked if he could listen to the latest news for the first time. Security was very tight, the officer told him, and he only risked listening when circumstances allowed. A few nights later, Carl and a few other officers were invited to the shack where the radio was hidden. At the top of the hour the officer tuned it to KGEI San Francisco.

War news led the broadcast, although most of the update was focused on the European theater. The Germans were locked in battle with the

Soviet army at Stalingrad. Rommel's Afrika Korps was retreating in North Africa. In the Pacific, American marines invaded an island called Guadalcanal and defeated a heavy counterattack there while sinking many Japanese ships attempting to resupply their forces.

One of the officers whispered that he felt like cheering, because it meant the Americans were on their way. His enthusiasm was blunted when Carl told him that Guadalcanal was in the Solomon Islands, about three thousand miles from the Philippines.

THIRTY-THREE

Florence came home from work one evening to find Norma in a state of shock. Earlier that afternoon, Japanese soldiers had come to the door and stormed inside. They ordered her, Jerry, and Mariano into the bathroom while they searched the house.

The soldiers left after an hour. They had been very thorough and the scattered articles from open drawers and closets still lay on the floors in every room. Norma said the one thing they had taken with them were samples of the typeface on Florence's typewriter.

Florence learned at work the next day that neighborhoods all over the city were being searched without warning. They were looking for guns, radio transmitters, and anything else that would indicate participation in the resistance. Presumably, they had taken the sample from her typewriter to match against anti-Japanese leaflets. New pamphlets appeared around the city every week by different underground networks, urging the people to resist the occupation. Florence knew none of the people involved.

Norma quickly calmed down, but Mariano said he could no longer remain in Manila and that he planned to rejoin his family in the north. He packed his things and left on a bus the following day.

Florence and Norma settled into a regular routine. With Mariano gone, they shared the marketing, housekeeping, and cooking chores. Florence took care of Jerry at night until Norma returned from her job at the restaurant. Norma had Jerry during the day while Florence was at work.

The unanticipated search by the Japanese reinforced for Florence that she had to be very careful moving forward with her fuel diversion plan to help the POWs and internees. She decided not to tell Norma about it, believing there was no reason to put her and Jerry at risk in case anything went wrong.

She met again with Angelita Alvarez Sobral, who now operated a small network of couriers to deliver supplies to Cabanatuan. Without saying how she planned to do it, Florence told her she hoped to provide substantial assistance in the future.

Angelita did not press her for details. She had already counseled Florence that it was safer for all of them if a leader in one network didn't know the people involved in another, in case they were captured and tortured.

Florence went over and over in her mind who she might recruit as an ally. After observing several of the fuel stations to see how they operated, she confirmed her assumption that the ration coupons were redeemed almost entirely by men.

There was one person she worked with at the fuel union who might be a possibility: Ricardo de Castro, the Filipino who had worked for the Americans at the Cavite Navy Yard. In their brief conversations during Osawa's badminton tournaments, he made derogatory comments about the Japanese occupation authority. Her only concern was that he might have been equally indiscreet with people loyal to the Japanese, and therefore already under suspicion.

There was only one way to find out. She asked de Castro to meet her one evening after work. They spent some time talking about their families. He had a lot to lose.

Florence asked him his feelings about the Japanese occupation. Without reservation, he expressed his bitterness over what they were doing to his country, and how hard it was to report to work every day, but knew he needed to do it to support his family. He assured her that he had not expressed his feelings to anyone he thought was possibly loyal to the Japanese.

Florence told de Castro about Bing and his valiant death and why she was committed to hurting the occupying authority in every way possible. It would be a long time before the Americans came back, she said, but in the meantime she would try to make a difference.

She described to him the condition of the American POWs at Cabanatuan and also brought up helping the internees at Santo Tomas. De Castro said he already knew their situation and had friends imprisoned there.

Finally, Florence told him about her work for Army Intelligence before the Japanese invasion and showed him the note Carl Engelhart had sent in support of her taking the job at the fuel union.

De Castro asked how he could help.

She briefly outlined her plan for smuggling officially stamped coupons out of the office and filling them out with falsified names of individuals and companies. When the coupons were returned from the fuel stations at the end of the week, she would alter the supporting documents from a station where they had used the coupons and then enter the adjusted tallies in the ledger. The final step would be to destroy the coupons.

"Could you organize the rest of the operation?" Florence asked, explaining he would need to convert the fuel into cash to buy the needed supplies for Cabanatuan and Santo Tomas, or barter with the fuel to get them.

De Castro said he had several close friends in the resistance, and they were already working with black marketers to acquire weapons and ammunition. He promised to find out more.

The two agreed that the first step would be to make a test run to see if the plan worked.

They had at least one advantage, added de Castro. Most of the Japanese had so little respect for women that it would be hard for them to believe a young female bookkeeper in the fuel union could damage them in any serious way.

"If they catch us," he said to her, "the Japanese will show no mercy."

THIRTY-FOUR

NOVEMBER 1942
PHILIPPINE LIQUID FUEL DISTRIBUTION UNION
METROPOLITAN THEATER BUILDING, MANILA

Kiyoshi Osawa was facing his first serious crisis, and his Japanese military superiors were demanding a solution. In October, the stocks of liquid fuels in the Philippines, particularly gasoline, diesel fuel, and lubricating oil, began to dwindle. New shipments from Japan and the Dutch East Indies slowed down after the Japanese high command in Tokyo shifted its fuel priorities to meet demand from every corner of its far-flung new empire.

The Imperial Navy required more oil for its warships as they contended with growing American naval power in the south Pacific. Land battles raged at Guadalcanal in the Solomon Islands and on Papua New Guinea, and local army commanders needed their share of gasoline and diesel fuel.

Osawa's most immediate challenge was the rapid depletion of his remaining supply of lubricating oil. Without it, machinery couldn't run. In the first days of the occupation, Japanese troops entering Manila had found massive stocks of lubricating oil stored in fifty-gallon drums, which American combat engineers had failed to destroy. The drums were now nearly empty.

Japanese scientists in the Philippines spent months trying to create a lubrication substitute using castor oil seeds and pili nuts, without success. In desperation, the occupying authority turned to Osawa and ordered him to find a solution.

After consulting every person he knew with a technical and scientific background, Osawa was directed to a Philippine University chemistry professor named Luzurriaga. The professor was a researcher without political leanings, and he claimed to have developed a viable alternative to lubricating oil. Osawa went to his laboratory with the Japanese technicians to learn if the process produced genuine results. As Osawa watched, Luzurriaga mixed a very small measure of lubricating oil with much larger quantities of his new additive and then put the mixture through a fusion heating process. In examining the results, the Japanese technicians confirmed that the lubricant was of sufficient quality to operate machinery and engines.

Osawa wasn't sure it could be produced on a large enough scale, but he took the risk of immediately putting the process into mass production under the direction of Luzurriaga. A factory site was found and a construction team worked around the clock in three shifts to build the infrastructure for producing the new additive mixture. Within a month of the factory being operational, substantial new supplies of the lubricant were delivered to the military. There was even a surplus that went to the business sector.

Major General Yokoo, the commander of the principal Japanese weapons depot, traveled to Manila to personally congratulate Osawa on his vital contribution to the war effort. Osawa told General Yokoo he had also implemented a plan to address the dwindling supplies of gasoline. He planned to manufacture butanol as a substitute for the army's trucks and tanks. The first quantities were being produced biologically through a fermentation process using a culture of raw sugar and cow manure. Osawa felt sure that butanol could meet the army's needs in spite of reduced imports.

The reward for his contributions became clear in October when the occupying authority announced a new dictate. All civilian Japanese males in the Philippines below the age of forty-six were conscripted into the army for the duration of the war. There were no exceptions.

A few days before his own physical examination in Manila, Osawa went to watch the friends he had served with on the property confiscation board as they stood naked or in underwear for their medical examinations as martial music blared from loudspeakers.

Osawa was thirty-nine and prepared to do his duty, but was secretly thrilled when he received an official notification from army headquarters the day before his examination: *Kiyoshi Osawa is hereby exempted from the conscription examination.*

The privileges did not stop there. Along with his position as managing director of the PLFDU, he was appointed to be one of the twelve councillors overseeing all Japanese civilian activities in the Philippines, and given the rank of a nonregular military officer.

While he continued to fulfill his duties with fervent dedication, Osawa desperately missed his wife Katsuko, his daughter, and his new son Ichiro, whom he hadn't yet seen. Although he maintained a brave face during the day, each night he fell into deep melancholy.

His good friend Tokuji Sakamoto, the general manager of the Manila Hotel and his frequent golf partner at the Wack Wack Club, had sent his family back on the same ship as Osawa. They both cried at the parting. After the fall of Corregidor, Sakamoto arranged for the return of his family, and he seemed on top of the world.

Osawa knew he could bring home his own family with a simple request to the military governor in Manila. Katsuko had written repeatedly that she wanted to return to the Philippines, yet a shadowy foreboding led him to wait. Although Japanese radio broadcasts proclaimed victory after victory by the Japanese army and navy, a friend who secretly listened to news broadcasts from Australia told him that the Americans defeated the Japanese fleet in two major battles in the north Pacific.

Something else troubled him. In the months since the humiliating defeat of the Americans, Osawa witnessed a slow change in the prevailing attitude of Filipinos toward the Japanese occupiers.

Over the many years he had lived and worked in the Philippines, he had contributed time and money to enhance the Filipino way of life. Before the war, he earned a reputation for being honest, polite, and civic-minded. At the time of the American surrender, he was sure that most Filipinos would have an open mind about the future. They simply wanted to be treated with respect. But that hadn't happened. Too many of the Japanese still treated them as subjects. And it was hard for Osawa to ignore the vulgarity that accompanied the proliferation of whorehouses and the casual brutality of so many soldiers. The worst injustices were imposed by the Kempeitai.

One evening, Osawa was asked to come to the Kempeitai headquarters in Fort Santiago. There he was shocked to find one of his closest friends, a Filipino businessman whom the military police suspected of disloyalty. He was held for two months in prison before being released. When told he could telephone someone to come for him, he called Osawa.

As a young man, Osawa's friend had been an amateur heavyweight boxing champion weighing in at two hundred pounds. Now hunched over in the waiting room, his clothing hung on him in folds. When he saw Osawa, he began crying and said he hoped he hadn't gotten him into trouble. Osawa drove him to the hospital, but it was too late. The man died a few days later.

Osawa attended his friend's funeral, and there he witnessed the rage and hatred in the eyes of many of the mourners, much of it directed toward him because of his race. He felt deep shame at the conduct of many of his countrymen. They were simply too ignorant to realize they were sowing the seeds of rebellion. According to his friends in the Interior Ministry, more Filipinos were joining the guerrillas each month.

For his part, Osawa vowed to maintain a good relationship with all his Filipino friends and his Filipina employees at the fuel union. He would try to ensure their well-being as they served the empire.

As to the idea of reuniting his family, he sent a letter to Katsuko. "We need to wait and see," he wrote. "We must be patient."

THIRTY-FIVE

The food shortages in Manila were becoming more severe every week. Prior to the invasion, a one-hundred-pound sack of rice cost less than ten Philippine pesos. Now, the price was nearly forty if it could even be found, because the Japanese army was confiscating much of the rice crop and shipping it to its threatened army garrisons across the Pacific.

At the beginning of the occupation, the Japanese created their own military currency and demanded that all Philippine pesos be turned in to the banks and replaced with Japanese military pesos. Knowing the new money had no intrinsic value, most Filipinos refused to do it despite the punitive threats for hoarding the native currency.

Acts Punishable by Death: (13) Any person who counterfeits military notes; refuses to accept them or in any way hinders the free circulation of military notes by slanderous or seditious utterances.

For those like Florence who had not hoarded the pesos, buying power was significantly diminished. Both she and Norma were paid in Japanese pesos, and the money now had one quarter the value of the Philippine pesos. When they went shopping for staples, there were two prices for every

155

item: the official price using military pesos and the much lower, under-the-table price with original ones.

Illegal money changers made fortunes while those at the lowest rung of society faced starvation. For many in the city, particularly in the poorer neighborhoods, it had become the law of the jungle. The murder rate sky-rocketed. Armed robberies of stores and businesses became endemic, and physical assaults on women and the elderly took place daily.

As the violence and lawlessness accelerated, Florence and Ricardo de Castro decided to execute their trial run. Florence took the first step. After waiting until her coworkers in the clerk's office left for the day, she went to the locked cabinet where the official stamps were stored. Each of the clerks had a key.

Florence removed the appropriate stamp and carried it into the store-room where the ration coupons were kept. No one kept a daily tally of the papers. When the stack began running low, they simply ordered more to be printed.

Taking a single ration coupon from the pile, she stamped it. After slipping the coupon inside the pages of that day's newspaper, she returned to the office, replaced the stamp in the cabinet, and locked it again. Putting the folded newspaper in her handbag, she left the office. At the entrance of the building, the guards didn't give her a second glance as she left and walked to her bus stop a few blocks away.

For the test run, Florence decided to approve a coupon for twenty-five gallons of gasoline, a very common amount. She filled out the coupon with the same pen she used in the office and with the same neat block letters. She created a false company name that was very similar to a gen-uine one.

Ricardo de Castro took the next steps. He decided to wait until it was almost closing time at the fuel station, when the employees would presum-ably be in a hurry to close up and go home. He chose one of the larger and busier stations.

While Florence waited nervously at home, Ricardo implemented the plan. One of his close friends had recently joined an underground network.

He borrowed a small truck and became the driver in the test operation. De Castro rode in the passenger seat.

At the fuel station, things couldn't have gone better. A line of trucks was waiting for service as closing time approached. When their turn came, the attendant in the booth reviewed the form, endorsed it, and added it to the stack on his desk. After he waved them forward, the service operator pumped twenty-five gallons into the fuel drum strapped to the truck bed. When he finished, they drove out.

It almost seemed too easy.

De Castro had arranged with his friend to share the proceeds of the initial run equally. Half went to the man's underground network. The remaining gas was bartered by de Castro's friend with black marketers for a list of medicines provided by Florence, including quinine, penicillin, and sulfa drugs.

With great delight, Florence put together the first small shipment of medicines for couriers to smuggle into Cabanatuan. There had even been money left over after the bartering, and she was thrilled to see it was in Philippine pesos. She sent most of them to Carl as well.

It was hopefully the first shipment of many.

THIRTY-SIX

DECEMBER 1942
CABANATUAN PRISON CAMP NO. 1
PHILIPPINES

For Carl Engelhart, the money that arrived through the underground courier service was like receiving another last-minute reprieve from a death sentence, just as he had after the beheadings. It might still mean life imprisonment, but this was another chance to heal, to come back from the brink, to rebuild his reserves. He could only wonder how Florence had done it.

He delivered the medical supplies to the camp hospital. There were more than thirty wards now and doctors were treating hundreds of men, many near death due to the lack of medicines to treat lingering wounds and infections. Her supply would save lives.

Malnutrition was still the principal cause of death among the thousands of men in the Cabanatuan camp. Carl had learned its impact on mental stability with Breitung and Briggs. It also caused a breakdown in mental acuity. One of Carl's hut mates suddenly couldn't remember his wife's name even though they had been high school sweethearts. Another colonel could only remember the names of six of his nine children.

Carl tried to keep his mind focused by recording a summary of important events in his journal.

Mental lethargy began to affect them all to a degree, and the hut mates decided to try to stimulate their minds with some serious discussion. After their evening meal, they would gather together around a table made from scrap lumber and talk until their regular bedtime.

158

The first subject they chose to discuss was "the most important thing in life." It yielded very little discussion because the men were unanimous that food was the most important thing. The follow-up subject was to name the second most important thing. About half the officers responded that it was "a woman to love and to cherish." The rest were convinced it was a pair of comfortable shoes.

One thing they could all agree on was that their chances of surviving the war under the present camp conditions were a definite long shot. Between starvation, disease, and random Japanese cruelty, the consensus was they could last another year at most.

That led to a separate discussion among the married prisoners of what they hoped their wives would do if they died in captivity. To a man, they wanted them to find someone worthy to share their lives, but also hoped they would retain a fond memory of the husband who never came home. They swore to one another that the survivors would visit the dead men's widows after the war.

Carl's outlook about their chances of survival improved with the regular deliveries of pesos and medicine from Florence. The latest amount was enough to buy meat, fish, and a variety of vegetables instead of scraps to supplement the rice ration. If she continued her efforts, he and his hut mates and friends would only get stronger.

As his energy level improved, Carl expanded his efforts to keep sadistic Japanese soldiers from beating the prisoners. One day, Henry Jones, whose farm now showed promise of becoming a substantial food provider in the months ahead, asked him to intervene with another guard.

The guard was responsible for supervising twenty POWs and every day after work he lined them up facing each other in two rows. He then ordered the men in one rank to hit the men opposite in the face. While the guard looked on, giggling, they were forced to take turns hitting each other. If a man did not clout his opposite hard enough, the guard would hit the man in the head with his club.

Carl knew that even if he prevented the violence once, the guard would probably resume his cruelty the following day. He decided that a more permanent solution lay in replacing the American officer supervising the detail with one who had no fear of the Japanese and could possibly make the guard fear him.

Carl knew the right man. He was an army captain named Art Wermuth. Like Bing Smith, he had been awarded the Distinguished Service Cross for his gallantry on Bataan. Wounded three times during the battle, he led a group of Filipino soldiers behind enemy lines to successfully eliminate Japanese infiltrators. Before the surrender, his exploits were chronicled in a *Life* magazine story titled "The One-Man Army of Bataan."

Carl told Wermuth about what was being done to the men in the farm detail and Wermuth volunteered to take over. A day later, Carl approached him in camp and asked what had happened. Wermuth told him everything was fine. His solution had been simple. When the guard lined up the men and ordered them to begin hitting one another, Wermuth spoke loudly enough to attract the attention of the other guards. He proposed that in the spirit of the Bushido Code honoring courage above all else, he and the guard should demonstrate proper punching protocol so his men could learn the correct standard. Instead, the guard ordered the men to go back to the camp.

———

Though for now the abuse subsided, a deadly serious issue arose soon after that threatened the lives of many more prisoners.

Carl was summoned to the Japanese camp headquarters to meet with Lieutenant Colonel Mori. The lieutenant colonel angrily told Carl that one of the POWs had stolen the Japanese guard orders book. He demanded its immediate return along with the guilty prisoner. If he wasn't surrendered for punishment, the food rations for the entire camp would be cut off.

Carl knew what the thief's punishment would be. He also concluded there were only two reasons why the POWs needed paper: one was to roll the cigarettes they made using dried plant leaves. The other was to wipe their asses at the latrines. Carl was pretty certain it was the second reason that accounted for the theft. He could only hope that the guard orders book wasn't already in smeared shreds at the bottom of one of the latrines.

Carl told Mori that he would attempt to recover the order book, but if he were successful, his own officer's code of honor would prevent him from turning over the culprit. Mori didn't respond.

Going straight to the camp POW headquarters, Carl explained the situation to the senior leaders. They agreed that the blocking of food rations for the whole camp would lead to a greater number of deaths.

Carl suggested that the word should immediately be passed throughout the camp that the guard orders book must be returned at once—and what the consequences would be if it wasn't. He added that the book should be passed from man to man through so many hands that no one would know who had actually stolen it.

An hour later, the book was brought to camp headquarters. When Carl looked it over, it appeared to be fully intact. He took it immediately to Mori's office, where it was inspected and found complete.

Lieutenant Colonel Mori demanded to know the name of the prisoner who stole it. Carl explained that this was impossible because it had been passed through too many hands before reaching him.

"Then I have every right to punish you instead," said Mori.

Mori had acted reasonably when the lives of Carl and his hut mates had been in the balance after the attempted escape by Breitung, Briggs, and Gilbert. This time his life was at stake. He told Mori in Japanese that the prisoners were desperate for toilet paper and that if they received it, there would be little likelihood that Japanese books and documents would be stolen in the future.

Mori dismissed him.

Several days later, two rolls of toilet paper were dispensed to every squad of prisoners in the camp. The individual sheets were carefully counted and an equal share allocated to each man.

THIRTY-SEVEN

Florence's life was now compartmentalized into three areas.

The first was her job as a clerk and bookkeeper in the accounting office of the Philippine Liquid Fuel Distribution Union. Along with Soledad Javier and Imelda de Asis, she continued to process ration coupons and record her entries for each transaction in the PLFDU's business ledgers. Occasionally, she took the time to participate in Kiyoshi Osawa's badminton competitions in the park and attend weekend social functions he organized for the staff.

To her coworkers, she appeared to live a quiet and dull existence as a grieving widow. She made no close friends in the office and refused all invitations from men she met at work.

In her secret life, she went to work every morning in a state of nervous excitement, knowing that if she made a single mistake and was caught, she faced a death sentence. Her anxiety was compounded by the increased presence of new Japanese employees who looked over the shoulders of the Filipina workers in every branch of the operation.

There were ninety-eight Japanese working in the office. Dozens of the officers strutted up and down the hallways all day long in full uniform regalia with sabers. Every time an enlisted man encountered an officer he would stop in his tracks to salute him and let out an accompanying shriek. When it happened within hearing range, it never failed to unnerve Florence.

In the accounting department, Japanese accountants and bookkeepers now occupied desks in the same office as the Filipina clerks, and they often began reviewing the ledgers without advance warning.

She and Ricardo no longer acknowledged one another in the office. After their successful test run with the first coupon, they had begun their fuel diversion operation.

Fortunately, the Japanese adhered to the Filipino custom of a two-hour lunch often followed by a brief siesta. Work would resume from three in the afternoon to six, when most of the employees went home. That allowed her ample opportunity to do what was needed. Her principal fear was that she might be searched while leaving the building and the guards would find the false coupons before she could destroy them at home.

Initially, she set a limit of diverting one hundred gallons of fuel per week, secured via four twenty-five-gallon ration coupons. As the reserve supplies of gasoline in the Philippines declined, Florence switched the coupons from gasoline to alcohol and diesel fuel, which were both still in sufficient supply to not warrant a second look.

Ricardo always varied his choice of the fuel stations and never went to the same one twice in a week.

Most of the supplies she received were sent through the underground courier system to Carl Engelhart and the POWs, but Florence delivered a smaller share of supplies to the internees at Santo Tomas.

In February, she decided to increase the amount of fuel she and Ricardo were diverting from one hundred gallons a week to two hundred. The decision followed an introduction by Lucy Hoffman, her fellow former staffer at the Office of Army Intelligence, to Josefa Escoda. After learning in a letter from Carl that Lucy was sending Ray Bibee similar packages, Florence and Lucy joined forces.

Meeting Josefa was one of the most thrilling moments of Florence's life. Josefa Escoda was an admired activist in the country, and a revered role model for Florence when she was growing up. Josefa's husband, the equally celebrated Tony Escoda, was an influential newspaperman and editor at the *Manila Daily Bulletin* prior to the war.

Charismatic and fearless, Josefa led the effort in 1937 to win the plebiscite that granted Philippine women the right to vote. In 1939, she founded the Girl Scout movement in the Philippines, and was also the head of the National Federation of Women's Clubs, a social work organization committed to empowering women in every strata of society.

Now, Josefa told Florence that with the increased food shortages, she and Tony were committed to helping those most in need. She reached out to the young women in Luzon who had been active in her Girl Scout movement and recruited many to collect food, medicine, clothing, and other supplies for delivery to the Filipino and American prisoners of war, the internees at Santo Tomas, and the Filipino poor.

Josefa learned through Lucy of Florence's contributions to the same cause. Without asking Florence how she was doing it, she said she hoped they could work together to expand the reach of Josefa and Tony's network.

Florence didn't dwell on her decision. If the Escodas were willing to put their lives on the line, she would do her best to help them. She confided what she was doing at the fuel union, and promised to secure additional funds for their work. Tony was very impressed with her ingenuity, but warned her to be especially careful.

Aside from her work at the fuel union and her secret activities, Florence maintained her personal life, which extended only to family and close friends. Although the sisters continued to live together, Norma had moved on from the disappeared Manuel and had met a man named Jose Delmar. They had begun a romantic relationship. Florence still cared for Jerry at night and found pleasure in pampering the sweet and curious little boy.

She also found relaxation with the small network of friends she had made before the war. Margaret Cirstens was still living with the Swiss national Alfred Keller, and they often hosted small gatherings on the weekends. Alfred was able to buy spirits, and liquor flowed at the parties, allowing the guests to temporarily forget the occupation.

Dolores became Florence's closest friend, and they spent many evenings together at her apartment on Herran Street in the Paco district. Florence always brought Jerry, who napped in the guest room while the women discussed their lives and their plans to help Bob Hendry and his friends in Santo Tomas.

Dolores disclosed that her two brothers, Marvin and John, had gone into the hills to join the resistance. Marvin had come to detest the Japanese for only allowing their propaganda films to be produced and shown in the theaters, and he had refused to participate. John had joined with Marvin.

Through Dolores, Florence learned that the brothers' small resistance group was one of hundreds now challenging the Japanese army across Luzon. There was rarely coordination between them, so when the army captured a man in one of the networks, it rarely led to others in another network.

Florence didn't tell Dolores about her diversion operation, but the amount of supplies she was able to buy for Santo Tomas began to raise questions with her friend, who knew that Florence was not making a substantial salary. When she asked Florence where all the money was coming from, Florence lied and said she solicited the gifts from others.

At that point, she decided to recruit someone to help distribute the increased load of supplies for Santo Tomas. The possible answer was provided on her next visit to the prison camp when she encountered Fred Comings, who had been the business secretary at the Manila Army-Navy YMCA when Florence went to work there.

Fred was now interned along with his wife and small baby. During the first weeks of confinement, the child had come close to death from acute dysentery but had rallied and was now doing well.

Florence told Fred what had happened to Bing. Fred had known and liked Florence's husband, and was saddened to learn of his courageous death. He told her he had been designated the roll call chief by the Santo Tomas camp leaders, which meant he had the freedom to leave the camp to visit internees in the Manila hospitals, carry messages for those inside, and deliver ration money.

As she left through the gate, she was sure he was the right man to help distribute the bulk of her supplies and money in Santo Tomas, if he was willing to take the risk. Before parting, she asked if he would meet her outside the walls and he agreed.

February 8 marked the first anniversary of Bing's death. In the five months since beginning the diversion operation, Florence and Ricardo had stolen several thousand gallons of fuel and used it to good purpose for the Philippine resistance, the Americans at Cabanatuan, and those imprisoned at Santo Tomas. She hoped he was proud of her.

THIRTY-EIGHT

On May 9, Carl received a letter from his sister Lottie in New York City. It had been written the previous December, but every piece of mail sent to the thousands of POWs in Cabanatuan had to be read and censored by Lieutenant Colonel Mori's Japanese interpreter, who processed about ten letters each day.

In the letter, Carl's sister wrote that his parents were doing well and that his wife Margo, their son Anders, and daughter Karen in San Diego were bearing up under the ordeal of their separation with great fortitude. They all missed him terribly.

Carl had mixed feelings after reading the letter. In the time he had spent at Cabanatuan, he had tried to avoid thinking about everything he was missing with his wife and children. It was the only way to suppress the agony. He hadn't seen Margo or Anders for two years. He doubted he would even recognize Karen. The thought that the war could drag on filled him with renewed torment. It was better to be in limbo except in his dreams. He couldn't help going home in his dreams.

Another officer in Carl's hut was thrilled to receive a letter from his wife. Like Carl, he had sent her back to the States with their two children in 1941. In the note, she expressed how much she missed him and at one point wrote that their new baby was now three months old. Like Carl's letter, the postmark was the previous December. In doing the math, the officer

167

realized that the baby could not be his. He no longer wanted to receive any more mail.

When it came to their basic survival, Carl knew they had turned a corner. The regular arrival of Florence's Philippine pesos made the difference, not only to his hut mates but to the many others he was helping, including Ray Bibee and the other survivors of his intelligence staff from Fort Santiago, and the friends he had made since his arrival at Cabanatuan.

He knew which guards could be bribed to acquire meat, fish, and other foods that allowed them to stabilize their weight. It was no longer painful for Carl to sit on a hard chair and he had even regained some muscle mass. He wasn't ready to fight Joe Louis, but they were all back from the brink.

In addition to the food Carl managed to procure, Henry Jones's vegetable garden began to prove its worth. Now a working farm, the acreage yielded okra, eggplant, squash, and *camotes*—the Philippine sweet potato. The farm's cucumbers were a yard long and its cornstalks were eight feet high.

Finally seeing the results of what they had labored for many months to achieve, the prisoners were excited to harvest the first round of vegetables and have them added to their daily diet. The Japanese had other plans.

When an acre's worth of cucumbers were brought in carts to the warehouse near the camp, a small fleet of trucks was waiting. The outraged prisoners were ordered to load the cucumbers on the trucks, and the American officers on hand were told that the cucumbers would be sold to purchase additional rice for them.

It was clear to the POW camp leaders that some of the senior guards were looking to make a profit from their labor. After bitter complaints to Lieutenant Colonel Mori, the colonel ordered that half the produce should go to the camp kitchens. It quickly made a difference in the health of the general prison population. In addition, men all over the camp were now receiving small amounts of money, soap, and personal items. The underground courier service remained undetected by the guards.

The improved situation led to a growing belief that they might actually survive until the Japanese could be defeated. No one knew when that would be, but Carl now believed it was inevitable. He was receiving regular up-dates on the war from the officer who built the shortwave receiver. In Europe, the Soviets annihilated the German army at Stalingrad and Rommel's Afrika Korps surrendered to the allies in Tunisia. In the Pacific, the Japanese retreated from Guadalcanal after thirty thousand men were killed.

He was sure it was only a matter of time before the American army and navy reached the Philippines as they moved west across the Pacific. With continued luck and Florence's gifts, he might still be alive to welcome them.

Carl and Ray Bibee speculated how it was possible for Florence to do so much, and the first clue arrived in a letter sent to Ray from Lucy Hoffman. Referring to Florence as "the widow," she said they were working together to supply not only Cabanatuan but the internees at Santo Tomas. Even Lucy's six-year-old daughter Lily was part of the delivery network.

A fuller answer was supplied one day in April when a truck arrived at the camp driven by Tony Escoda, whom Carl knew had once been a prominent newspaperman before the war. Escoda and a German priest named Father Theodore Buttenbruch had filled the truck with packages of food and medicine.

After they left, Carl was approached by a friend named Bob Fields, who had survived the Bataan death march and was one of the dozens of recipients of Florence's gifts. Pulling Carl aside, he told him that Tony Escoda had asked that a confidential message be passed to him.

"Tell Colonel Engelhart that his stenographer is stealing the Japanese blind of diesel oil and alcohol at the Philippine fuel union," Escoda said to Bob Fields.

Carl now knew how Florence was managing to do so much for them. He could only smile at the news and hope that she continued to be careful.

As prison life became more bearable, small creature comforts and simple pleasures relieved the tedium. A small cake of soap and a rainstorm meant a satisfying shower. The Japanese allowed several crates of athletic equipment to come through and sports leagues were set up for softball and basketball. A shipment of books arrived through the Red Cross and the camp now boasted a small library.

One morning, the Japanese dumped a huge pile of used clothing inside the gates, and the prisoners formed a line to receive an allotment. When it was Carl's turn, he was given a khaki shirt several sizes too large for him.

Ray Bibee was right behind him in the line and received a pair of black pants. When he started to examine them, Ray laughed out loud. Then he showed Carl the inner band of the waistline. The name "BIBEE" was scored into the cloth. They were the tuxedo trousers he had left behind at the quarters he shared with Carl on General Luna Street the day they evacuated Manila. Carl tried to estimate the odds that the pants could have found their way to their former owner after eighteen months of war. It was inconceivable.

One thing that didn't change was the continued beatings of prisoners by some of the guards. Carl's reputation for stopping the random cruelty had spread throughout the camp. He saved scores of men from serious injury, but with thousands of prisoners it was impossible to be in every part of the camp.

A prisoner named Connell disappeared one afternoon when Carl was out with one of the farm details. According to his friends, he had become ill and was running a high fever when he went missing. However, when he failed to appear for the evening roll call, the guards didn't appear concerned.

The next morning, Connell's body was carried into the camp. The camp leaders were told he had been found dead on the ground, but his face was almost unrecognizable and a doctor said that most of his ribs were broken. His body went out on the burial cart.

On the fifth Sunday of May 1943, the prisoners were given permission by Lieutenant Colonel Mori to conduct a Memorial Day service at the nearby graveyard. Carl had explained in his request to Mori that it was an annual custom in America to honor its dead from all wars. Mori approved the request.

That morning, several thousand prisoners marched in formation to the graveyard as Japanese guards lined the route. When the procession arrived at the field, Carl was stunned to see that the large burial mounds extended far into the distance. About forty men were buried under every one. There

Charles Ebersole Sr., circa 1899, after he
lied about his age to enlist in the US Army
as a medic in the Spanish-American War.
Courtesy of the Finch family

The three youngest Ebersole children born
to Maria Hermoso and Charles Ebersole
Sr. in Isabela Province, Philippines,
circa 1921. From left to right, Norma
(8), Florence (6), and Edward (10).
Courtesy of the Finch family

Studio portrait of Florence in 1934, shortly after
graduating with honors from Manila Central
High School. *Courtesy of the US Military Academy*

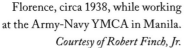

Florence, circa 1938, while working
at the Army-Navy YMCA in Manila.
Courtesy of Robert Finch, Jr.

Edward Carl Engelhart's graduation photo from the US Military Academy in 1920, reprinted from *The Howitzer* yearbook. Engelhart's photograph was accompanied by the words *Veteran Boy Scout*. *Courtesy of the Finch family*

Formal military portrait of Colonel Edward Carl Engelhart, US Army, circa 1945. *Courtesy of Robert Finch, Jr.*

Studio portrait of Norma Ebersole, circa 1938. *Courtesy of the Finch family*

Charles Edward "Bing" Smith relaxing at the Army-Navy YMCA in Manila, 1941 (photographed by Florence). *Courtesy of the Finch family*

Bing and Florence on a stroll at Clark Field in 1941, shortly before the Japanese invasion. (Woman on left unidentified.) *Courtesy of the Finch family*

Bing Smith and his teammates on the Pacific All Fleet baseball team, 1941. (Bing is second from left, holding trophy.) *Courtesy of Robert Finch, Jr.*

Bing and Florence Smith pictured on their honeymoon at the Baguio mountain resort in August 1941. *Courtesy of the Finch family*

Bing holding the puppy he gave to Florence "to begin their family" after their marriage in August 1941. *Courtesy of the Finch family*

The infamous Airport Studio in Manila, the Kempeitai headquarters where Florence was taken on October 16, 1944, and tortured along with many other members of the Philippine resistance. *Courtesy of Colonel Gustavo Ingles, author,* Memoirs of Pain

General Douglas MacArthur wades ashore with his staff during the amphibious landings at Leyte, Philippines, on October 20, 1944. *Courtesy of the National Archives and Records Administration*

US Army photograph of Colonel Charles Willoughby in Australia, circa 1942, shortly after General Douglas MacArthur and his staff escaped from Corregidor. *Courtesy of The MacArthur Memorial, Norfolk, Virginia*

Kiyoshi Osawa upon receiving the Medal of Merit from the Philippines-Japan Society in 1994 for his work building bridges between the two countries. *Courtesy of the Philippines-Japan Society*

Carl Engelhart secretly photographed in a compound inside Cabanatuan prison camp in 1943 by a fellow prisoner with a handmade camera. *Courtesy of Robert Finch, Jr.*

Carl Engelhart's handwritten list of American POWs who had died in Japanese prison camps. The page was soaked in seawater when Carl swam ashore after the sinking of the *Oryoku Maru* in December 1944. *Courtesy of the Finch family*

DEAD	A	N	US MC	CIV	
CAB.	2574	75	55	18	2722
O'Donnell	1532		7	15	1554
Tuay Detail	325	7	7	1	340
Bilibid	111	8	8	4	131
Enroute Japan	9	5	4		18
Enroute Davao	3				3
Steam Hospital	83			4	87
K.I.A.	679	139	80		898
Formally Executed	38	3			41
Informally Killed	38	1	1		48
Died on Marches	98	1	2	5	106
Missing	426	22	7	1	456
					6404

$$
\begin{array}{r}
898 \\
456 \\
\hline
1354
\end{array}
$$

$$
\begin{array}{r}
6404 \\
1354 \\
\hline
5050
\end{array}
$$

Florence in her Coast Guard dress uniform after graduation from basic training, Manhattan Beach, July 1945. *Courtesy of the Finch family*

Florence receiving Bing's Distinguished Service Cross and other medals along with her own Asiatic-Pacific ribbon, the first and only SPAR to ever receive it for her courageous actions in the Philippines. *Courtesy of the Finch family*

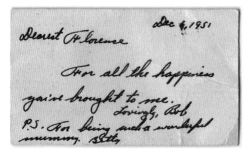

An example of the endearing notes that Bob Finch wrote to Florence on every possible occasion during their marriage, usually accompanied by flowers. *Courtesy of the Finch family*

Betty Finch Murphy and Bob Finch Jr., pictured on Florence and Bob Finch's Christmas card in 1959. *Courtesy of the Finch family*

Florence in Hawaii in 1995 to attend the ceremony in which the US Coast Guard dedicated its new Pacific headquarters building in honor of Florence Ebersole Smith. *Courtesy of the Finch family*

were no written markers, only the mushroom-like humps of soil covering each mass grave. Carl counted the humps as he marched along the edge of the field and finally lost track after sixty.

The Americans called the place Bone Hill. The layer of bulldozed earth over many of the mounds was too thin to prevent the dead men's bones from protruding and gases from escaping, and it stank of death and corruption.

Chaplain Fred Oliver, the senior cleric in the camp and one of Carl's favorite chess opponents, conducted the Memorial Day service. A few of the prisoners fashioned a large wreath from wildflowers and laid it down near the first row of burial mounds.

As a choral group of prisoners sang "Rock of Ages," Carl gazed through silent tears at the sea of faces around him, soldiers from storied army regiments now scarecrows wearing castoff clothing, reduced to servility.

Many were stone-faced, beyond grief as they stared forward at the burial mounds or into the sky. When the choral group finished singing the hymn, the silence was broken by the melancholy sound of men sobbing.

THIRTY-NINE

The days that Florence came to dread most were Mondays. On Monday mornings, all the ration coupons from the fuel stations were collected and collated at the accounting office.

She had fulfilled her pledge to Josefa and Tony Escoda, and she and Ricardo were now stealing 250 gallons of fuel a week. As a result, it took her more time to comb through the stacks of coupons to locate and conceal the false ones and then make the adjustments to the tallies in the ledgers.

With gasoline and diesel oil in increasingly short supply, the alternative fuels of butanol and coconut oil were now her principal targets. The factory that Mr. Osawa built to manufacture the substitute for lubricating oil was yielding record amounts, and they were in the process of refining it further to run internal combustion engines. Osawa's efforts to produce butanol biologically through the fermentation of raw sugar and cow manure were also keeping fuel stocks from dropping rapidly.

It was hard to believe that no one at the fuel union had noticed the loss of thousands of gallons of fuel over the previous nine months, but she concluded that the amounts were a small fraction of the total available supplies. The only serious impact of their diversions was that it left fewer stocks for the private sector.

Florence saw delegations of businessmen from across the country arriving regularly to meet with Osawa, all of them warning that a lack of fuel was causing them to slow down and even stop production of needed goods and materials. Osawa could only ask them to be patient.

In addition to supplying the Escodas, Florence successfully recruited Fred Comings, her former colleague at the Army-Navy YMCA, to distribute the additional money and supplies to the internees at Santo Tomas, while continuing to make her regular deliveries to Carl Engelhart through the underground courier service.

At the offices of the fuel union, it didn't take a mind reader to figure out that the Japanese military knew they were losing the war. Florence could see it in the daily behavior of the officers. Some of them came back drunk after their long lunches, and they were increasingly belligerent, often screaming obscenities at their Filipino coworkers for the slightest hint of a defeatist attitude. One wrong look could unleash a tirade.

The rising tensions led to a growing fear among the civilian staff, particularly the women. In spite of supportive words from Mr. Osawa, many of the clerks began to go through the motions, sluggishly performing their jobs until the closing hour allowed them to go home to their families.

This lethargy allowed Florence to breathe a little easier, even on Mondays.

As the rainy season began, Norma confided to Florence that she was pregnant again. The father of the baby was Jose Delmar. Florence and Norma agreed to not make any change in their living situation as Norma prepared for the baby's arrival in October or November.

At work one day, Ricardo sought her out to say that he had been approached by a close friend to try to arrange a meeting between Florence and Francisco Reyes, a young leader in one of the most effective guerrilla organizations in the country.

She reluctantly agreed, knowing that he would ask her for help. She planned to tell him that she was already operating at the full extent of her capabilities. If she attempted too much, it could wreck everything.

Very lean with intense black eyes, the young Reyes began the meeting by telling her he was fully aware of what she was already accomplishing on behalf of the resistance and that he was deeply grateful.

"I would like you to know how I became involved in the cause," he told her. "When the war began, my younger brother Jose and I were cadets at the Philippine Military Academy in Baguio. Those of us in the junior and senior classes were commissioned as lieutenants in the Philippine Army and went to fight alongside the Americans on Bataan. After the final defeat, we refused to surrender."

Florence could only admire their resolve.

"Along with our other two brothers, Jose and I went up into the mountains to join many of our fellow cadets from the military academy and former ROTC cadets from other colleges and universities," he said. "We called ourselves the Hunters ROTC guerrillas."

Florence had heard of them. The Japanese had vowed to exterminate the group.

"There are thousands of us now," Reyes told her, "all of us committed to liberating our country."

Reyes told her that they were led by another former cadet from the military academy named Terry Adevoso. They began their campaign in 1942 by brazenly attacking an armory in downtown Manila and carrying away hundreds of rifles.

In August, they ambushed a large Japanese military convoy, securing more weapons, ammunition, and equipment. The Hunters soon dispersed across Luzon, with small units raiding Japanese installations and wreaking havoc on their communications. They had taken severe losses but that only strengthened their will to fight harder. The morale of the Japanese troops suffered because they knew there were no safe havens anywhere.

The Hunters had recently complied with an order issued by General MacArthur from Australia to all the recognized resistance networks in the Philippines to "lie low" and wait for his instructions before resuming new attacks. This gave Terry Adevoso and the other leaders time to train and arm their growing number of recruits.

"We need fuel to operate our trucks, machines, and other equipment," he said, "so we can organize in every province and be ready to strike when the time comes for the battle of liberation."

He concluded by telling her that since the American Congress had voted to grant the Philippines its full independence, they could only achieve it by defeating the Japanese.

As with Angelita Alvarez Sobral and the Escodas, Florence was inspired by Reyes's courage and commitment to the cause of freedom, but she was forced to tell him she couldn't take the risk of diverting more fuel. It wasn't so much what would happen to her, but what her arrest would mean to the people she was already helping if she was caught.

Reyes said he understood the risks too. He was assigned by Terry Adevoso to gather intelligence in Manila, and his family's home on Arlegui Street now served as a safe house for the Hunters' leaders when they came to the capital for an intelligence briefing. One false move or a betrayal would mean the crippling of their movement as well.

Florence ended the meeting by saying she would give thought to ways she might be able to help in the future. Reyes thanked her again, saying that the loyalty went both ways and if there came a time when she needed his help, he would be there, or others in his place if he fell.

FORTY

"Even the comfort women are doing their part," announced a laughing Ray Bibee.

When Carl asked what he was talking about, Ray shared the story told by one of the enlisted POWs in his work detail. Three of the POW's hut mates worked for a Japanese sergeant in the freight shed. They had solved a difficult freight-handling problem for him that earned the sergeant a commendation from his superior. As a reward, the sergeant offered to treat all three to a visit to one of the brothels near the camp. The men hadn't been with a woman for years and readily accepted. When the men arrived, they were allowed to pick one of the Filipina women and go upstairs to her room.

All three men then shared the same experience. Once inside the rooms, the women told them they had the "clap" and would only sleep with the Japanese so they could infect them with the same venereal disease. Instead of sex, they gave the three Americans cake and wine and after sufficient time had passed sent them off with all the pesos they had.

———

One day Carl was conversing in Japanese with two guards on the farm detail when an officer from the guard company came up. Carl saluted him respectfully and the officer signaled with his finger to follow him.

176

Intrigued, Carl followed him behind a tall stand of cornstalks where the officer stopped and turned around. He glanced furtively in both directions once more to make sure they couldn't be seen.

The officer began by saying they were both soldiers and he wanted to ask Carl a question as one professional to another rather than as guard officer to prisoner. Carl agreed to talk on those terms.

"Who will win the war?" asked the officer.

Carl had been receiving regular updates from the young officer with the homemade radio, and he knew that the American army and navy under MacArthur and Admiral Nimitz, the commander in chief of the Pacific Fleet, were getting closer to the Philippines every month. It was only a matter of time before the Japanese were defeated.

"What is the greatest blunder a military commander can commit?" Carl asked him.

"To be taken by surprise," the officer responded.

"That is what happened to us at Pearl Harbor," Carl said. "But the second-greatest blunder is the failure to exploit that success. Your aircraft carriers didn't finish the job and you'll never get another chance. Japan has already lost the war."

Hearing the decisive verdict in his own language clearly stunned the Japanese officer. Without saying another word he slowly walked away, his head down and shoulders slumped.

Carl knew his reasoning was hollow. In truth, he believed Japan's defeat was inevitable once America reached its full industrial might, but his argument obviously sounded plausible to the guard officer, and it wouldn't hurt to have him spread a dose of defeatism to his friends.

Pete Pyzick, the Marine Corps major who had successfully pleaded for the lives of Carl and his hut mates after the attempted escape, had been appointed months earlier by the Japanese to create an index card file of all the American prisoners in Cabanatuan, as well as all the other camps in the Philippines. Pyzick and a team of POWs had been working ever since to build a comprehensive list, mostly from the Japanese documents and the rest from their own sources. It grew rapidly and they did as thorough a job as possible to account for every man, particularly those who had died in captivity.

The Japanese regularly gave Pyzick's team updates about the men who had died in other camps. The cause of death was invariably listed on the cards as malaria, dysentery, or "from a fall."

Pyzick observed written notations on the backs of the cards in a Japanese script that he couldn't read. He asked Carl to look at them, and Carl saw that they were scrawled in *gyosho* or *sosho*, two forms of writing the Japanese were sure no American could interpret.

The notations contained the truth. The cause of death would say malaria on the front side of the card but the notation on the back would read, "Executed for defiance of orders" or other behavior leading to death by beheading, gunshot wounds, or beatings.

Carl went through the notations on the back of every card and recorded the actual cause of death in each case on a separate secret list kept by Pyzick. When Carl saw the total number of deaths while in Japanese captivity, he was stunned and horrified.

The population of all the living American prisoners in the camps was barely fifteen thousand. In the months since the fall of Corregidor in May 1942, the number of men who had died in captivity was nearly six thousand.

The sobering news foreshadowed a new and more immediate danger when three hundred enlisted men were rounded up without warning and trucked out of the camp along with a small number of American officers. The Japanese refused to tell the POW leaders where they were being taken or what their ultimate fate was to be. Apprehension settled over the camp as no word was heard of the missing men, and rumors spread they had been executed.

The mystery was solved a few weeks later when a Japanese guard that Carl hadn't seen for some time appeared again at his regular station on the farm and Carl noticed he was wearing a West Point class ring.

Striking up a conversation, he learned where the guard had been. He was part of the escort that accompanied the three hundred prisoners to

Manila, where they were put aboard a freighter and taken to Japan to become slave laborers.

The guard confided that food and water had been severely limited during the voyage and the American officers attempted to supplement the rations of the men by bartering their last possessions of watches, fountain pens, and rings.

It turned out to be just the beginning of what would become a tragic exodus.

FORTY-ONE

NOVEMBER 1943
MANILA

In October, Norma's new son was born. She named him Bobby, and Florence brought them home from the hospital two days later. Like Jerry, he was a sweet-natured baby. Norma decided to give notice at the restaurant to stay home and nurse him.

They were still celebrating his arrival a month later when Manila was struck by the most devastating typhoon to hit the Philippines in half a century. Japanese meteorologists had accurately tracked the typhoon's path, but the army viewed it as confidential military information that could possibly aid the enemy. With no public warning, the Philippine people had no chance to prepare for its catastrophic consequences.

The storm began with torrential rain and punishing winds, wreaking havoc across Luzon. Communications were soon cut off with the coastal provinces where early reports indicated that hundreds of Filipinos had drowned.

When the Manila power grid collapsed, electricity was knocked out across the entire city. Buses and streetcars were immobilized. There was no telephone service and no potable drinking water.

Hour by hour, the level of the Pasig River surged upward until its banks overflowed and tons of water invaded every part of the city, rising in some lower-lying districts to more than eight feet above street level.

Florence and Norma were cut off at home. Together they watched the coursing river of black water overflow the street and engulf Mariano's vegetable garden. Contaminated by sewage, the water surged into the house and continued to rise until it was a foot above the ground floor.

As soon as they realized the dimensions of the storm, Florence and Norma moved everything they could carry to the second floor. The rattan furniture in the living room was too heavy, but they carried up the cushions, lighter furniture, and rugs along with two cribs, the items hidden under the closet floor, their clothing and personal belongings, and food from the kitchen pantry.

When the city water system collapsed, they set bowls out on the second-floor balcony to collect rainwater, periodically emptying them in the bathtub. There was no means to cook anything and they ate what they had carried upstairs.

Eventually, the flood level inside the house stopped rising but they were trapped on the second floor. Between bouts of fitful sleep, their principal activity was feeding and changing Bobby. The easygoing Jerry played with his toys, oblivious to the shrieking wind and rain.

Four days after the typhoon began, the rain finally stopped and the winds ebbed. Looking out from the bedroom balcony, Florence saw that the river of water still inundated Pennsylvania Avenue, fouled with the carcasses of dead animals.

Rescue crews began paddling up and down Pennsylvania Avenue in rowboats and dugout canoes. One came to the front door to make sure they were all right. From the bedroom balcony, Florence told them they were safe, but she and Norma stayed upstairs with Jerry and Bobby until the water receded from the house, leaving behind a thick coating of sludge. One morning, Florence's dog, which had been miserable during the storm, left the house and never returned.

Several days later the power and water were finally restored, and Florence and Norma could begin to clean up the mess. In the end, it was impossible to fully eliminate the odor of mold and mildew.

Newspapers began publishing again and Florence learned that all the major businesses and government offices in the city remained closed until further notice. They also read about the full extent of the disaster in the rest of the country.

Rice plants ready for harvesting had been destroyed across Luzon, and the prices of rice, eggs, corn, sugar, meat, and other staples skyrocketed. Philippine pesos were now worth four times the Japanese military peso and the disparity grew larger every day.

Looting broke out again, and squads of Japanese soldiers took to the streets to try to maintain order. Suspected looters were summarily executed, and their bodies were left hanging from street poles.

When businesses and government offices finally reopened, Florence returned to the fuel union office to a scene of chaotic disorder. Many of their files had been ruined due to prolonged immersion. A number of the Japanese officers who worked for the fuel union were temporarily reassigned to other duties outside the office.

Kiyoshi Osawa brought his diminished staff together to give them encouragement and to say that they would soon be distributing fuel at pre-storm levels. It just meant working harder to process the emergency orders they were receiving from public agencies across the country that were working to restore services to the people.

As she sat listening, the path to helping Francisco Reyes and his Hunters ROTC guerrillas suddenly came to her. The public agencies, including the utility companies, the regional telephone companies, the railroads, and the public transit companies, all received fuel allotments differently than private companies.

The private sector acquired its fuel using ration coupons redeemed at the fuel stations. The public entities needed fuel in far greater quantities and so were given warehouse release orders. These were redeemed where the liquid fuels were stored, from the local refineries or oil tankers from Japan and the Dutch East Indies.

For the public entities, a thousand or even two thousand gallons of gasoline, diesel oil, alcohol, or coconut oil wasn't unusual, and with the national emergency in the wake of the typhoon, orders were coming in from all over to address the required repairs.

The timing couldn't be better to help Francisco Reyes through falsified warehouse release orders. She told Ricardo what she planned to do and he agreed to contact Reyes to say they were ready.

On December 8, Florence marked the second anniversary of the Japanese war. She took heart from the fact that there were so many people fighting back. She was not alone. Everywhere, the people were rising up and risking their lives for freedom. She was proud to be one of them.

FORTY-TWO

One of the medications delivered in quantity to the camp by the Red Cross was an innovative new drug called sulfathiazole. The American doctors were amazed at its effectiveness in curing a wide range of bacterial infections. Carl was prescribed a course of the pills for a prolonged lung infection, and it cleared up the problem in days.

Through the grapevine, the Japanese guards learned that the pills could also cure gonorrhea and other venereal infections. Afraid to confide their embarrassing problem to their own doctors, they offered to buy the pills from the prisoners for enough pesos to purchase a carton of cigarettes.

A few of the POWs immediately recognized the profit that could be made while at the same time adding to the guards' misery. The genuine pill was pure white and imprinted with the letter W, which stood for Winthrop, the company that had pioneered the drug.

The entrepreneurs crafted wooden molds using the genuine pills and began manufacturing imitations made from rice paste and tooth powder. They were excellent replicas, right down to the engraved W. The pills sold briskly to the guards.

The enterprise led to a protest from one of the Protestant chaplains, who went to complain to Lieutenant Colonel Fred Oliver, the senior chaplain in the camp. Oliver was playing chess with Carl but listened as the chaplain declared that selling the imitation pills was immoral since the guards would never receive a cure. Chaplain Oliver reminded him that one of the other Protestant chaplains had been caught stealing food from an American patient in the hospital.

"War is immoral," he told him.

Apprehension swept through the camp again when without notice another five hundred prisoners were rounded up and sent by train to Bilibid prison in Manila to await a transport ship leaving for Japan.

Carl bribed one of the guard officers to find out if the exodus would continue and was told that orders had been received from the Japanese high command in Tokyo to prepare to send all the able-bodied prisoners to Japan, Korea, and Manchuria. Of the approximately seven thousand prisoners currently in the camp, only the sick would remain behind.

Carl easily deduced the reasons. The radio news from KGEI in San Francisco provided one answer. American military forces under MacArthur and Nimitz were driving closer to the Philippines all the time. Guadalcanal had fallen to the Americans in early 1943. The navy then moved west across the Central Pacific and invaded the Gilbert Islands, taking Tarawa and Makin Atoll from the Japanese in November. That was followed by the invasion of the Marshall Islands in January, another two hundred miles closer to the Philippines.

The latest news was that American carrier planes had virtually wiped out the Japanese naval air presence at Truk, in the Caroline Islands, which were only sixteen hundred miles away. At the same time, MacArthur's troops were mopping up the last remnants of the Japanese army deployed in New Guinea to the south of the Philippines.

It was equally clear why they only wanted able-bodied men. Japanese civilian workers were being pressed into the army and navy to replace the hundreds of thousands already killed or wounded. They were desperate for workers in their heavy industries and mines at home and in their conquered territories in Korea and Manchuria.

Aside from the possibility of being worked to death, the prisoners faced another imminent danger before even reaching the home islands. American submarines were now patrolling the sea-lanes into Japan, and according to the radio news, they were sinking dozens of Japanese merchant ships every month.

Carl no longer liked the odds of their survival.

FORTY-THREE

What Florence had been dreading for almost two years finally occurred.

Ken Osawa called an emergency meeting in the PLFDU's amphitheater on the first floor and every employee was ordered to attend. When Florence arrived with the rest of the accounting and clerical staff, Ken Osawa was standing at the podium next to the Japanese general who oversaw the union. The women began whispering to one another about what it all might mean. They went silent when everyone was seated.

"Thousands of gallons of alcohol and coconut oil have gone missing from two of our warehouses, and we believe the fuel was stolen by the Philippine underground," a clearly agitated Osawa declared. He told them the theft was confirmed when the invoices showing the amounts of fuel delivered to the warehouses failed to match the levels remaining in the storage tanks at the end of the reporting period.

"These crimes are now being investigated by the Kempeitai and every employee can expect to be interrogated in the coming days and weeks," he said. "I urge all of you to cooperate fully and to answer every question posed to you to help find the criminals responsible."

Florence glanced across the amphitheater and caught Ricardo looking back at her. She wondered if he had the same sick feeling that knotted her stomach as she thought about the Kempeitai interrogations.

"A team of Japanese accountants will be carefully reviewing all our files and documentation to see if any of the warehouse release orders were stamped with a counterfeit seal."

Florence felt a measure of relief, since they appeared to only be looking for counterfeit orders, rather than genuine ones.

"The army is putting in place soldiers to monitor every new fuel transaction. We are also deploying additional guards at all the union's fuel stations and the warehouses. The criminals who committed the crimes will be found and punished," he concluded.

When Florence returned to the accounting office, she watched as the financial records, ledgers, and fuel orders were removed from the filing cabinets by the Japanese accountants and taken to a secure office for careful examination.

She was able to get a message to Ricardo to meet her after work. There, she told him he must get word to the underground that there would be no more diversions until she could try to figure out a safe plan.

A few days later, she underwent her first interrogation by an officer of the Kempeitai. Alone in a small office, he made her describe in detail her daily responsibilities, often interrupting her answers by insinuating that she had to know more about the thefts and who was responsible.

She denied knowing anything. When he asked about her coworkers, she told him they all seemed loyal and trustworthy. When it was over, she felt relieved that none of his questions related to what she had actually done.

Florence quickly learned from her coworkers that all of them had been treated as if they were guilty of something, and that one of them had actually been accused of abetting the thefts. The woman complained to Ken Osawa and he brought the clerks to his office to reassure them that the investigation was taking several paths, but that the Kempeitai was sure one or more people currently working in the fuel union were members of the resistance and helping to steal the fuel. Until the person was found and punished, all of them would unfortunately be suspect.

Osawa gave them a warning and some advice.

"I know you are in deep distress. Stay calm and steer clear of trouble. I hope you understand what I mean. The time will come when you will be glad you followed my advice."

In the weeks that followed, Florence didn't alter her daily routine. She went to work, carried out her regular tasks, returned home, and spent the evening with Norma and the children. There were no more diversions.

A short note arrived one day in the mail from Josefa Escoda. It was an invitation to a small party being hosted by one of her friends. Thrilled, Florence wrote back that she looked forward to meeting her there.

At the party, Josefa and Tony took her aside. Tony said they couldn't call her because their phones were tapped and they were both under surveillance by the Kempeitai. Josefa explained the reason they wanted to see her. Ever since the November typhoon had destroyed the rice harvests, the food shortages in Manila had grown steadily worse. For the poor, it was especially difficult because they had no money to pay the inflated prices.

Josefa had used her network of young women to set up neighborhood food kitchens in the poorest districts of Manila. There, they served rice and vegetables to the hungry, most of whom were living in the streets and parks.

Unfortunately, their supply of milled rice had been cut off because the mill owners were on strict fuel rationing and only operated for a limited number of hours each day. Some of the operators had agreed to secretly mill rice at night if they could be provided with enough diesel to do it. They estimated several hundred gallons were needed in order to supply the food kitchens.

Florence told them about the new security procedures the army had put in place, and expressed her fear that the resistance men sent to pick up the fuel would be captured and executed.

Tony said he and the others were willing to undertake the risks of obtaining and transporting it if she could provide the required release order. Florence promised to try to find a way to help.

FORTY-FOUR

MAY 1944
CABANATUAN PRISON CAMP NO. 1
PHILIPPINES

Early on the morning of May 11, Carl Engelhart awoke to the sounds of shouting outside his shack. Rushing into the sunlight, he saw a small group of prisoners yelling at a Japanese soldier, who was prodding Chaplain Fred Oliver across the camp compound with the stock of his rifle.

Carl was immediately alarmed when he saw the soldier's uniform and the prominent arm band on his sleeve. He was a Kempeitai military policeman, and there hadn't been one in the camp in the eighteen months Carl had been there.

He watched as Fred staggered and was clubbed in the back to hurry him along. Catching up, he saw that blood was dripping down the chaplain's face from a wound on his scalp. Carl asked the military policeman in Japanese what was happening, but he was ignored.

As they approached the main guardhouse, Carl saw a group of about twenty American prisoners squatting on the ground, surrounded by a squad of Kempeitai. Fred Oliver was shoved inside the cordon.

After the first American was taken inside the guardhouse for questioning, less than a minute went by before he screamed in pain. There had been no time to ask a question and it was obvious to Carl they were softening the prisoners up before asking for whatever information they wanted. Japanese interrogation techniques weren't subtle. A heavy length of wood, an iron bar, brass knuckles, metal-toed boots, a water hose, studded belts—they employed them all.

As the beatings continued, more prisoners were brought from the barracks compound and pushed inside the cordon, including two other chaplains and Lieutenant Colonel Jack Schwartz, the senior doctor in charge of the camp hospital.

Desperate to help, Carl went straight to the new senior guard officer and offered to serve as an interpreter during the men's questioning. The guard officer was clearly nervous and Carl knew why: a Kempeitai officer had the power to arrest, torture, or execute anyone. The guard officer ordered Carl to stay away from the prisoners or he would be punished along with them.

The beatings went on into the night before the prisoners were taken away in a truck. In the morning, Carl set out to discover what had caused the violent roundup. It was impossible for him to believe that Fred Oliver had committed any overt acts against the Japanese.

After a bribe, one of the guards disclosed that the men had been identified as recipients of messages or contraband carried by an underground agent who was intercepted and arrested near the camp. Under torture, the courier disclosed that contraband goods were hidden in the freight wagons that brought food supplies into the camp. This led to the arrest of the six Americans who were the carabao oxen drivers. A careful search of their wagons yielded more hidden messages from friends of the prisoners.

The twenty men were moved to the Kempeitai headquarters in Cabanatuan. The following day an American doctor in the camp hospital was taken to the jail to treat an injured prisoner. He returned to say that it was Fred Oliver and that his neck had been broken during one of his beatings. The doctor had fashioned a crude cast to stabilize him.

When Carl realized that Florence's regular gift of pesos hadn't been delivered, he could only hope she or Lucy Hoffman hadn't been among the people whose messages were intercepted.

He was glad they had taken precautions over the two years in case a courier was caught. The letters and packages for Carl and Ray were always addressed to Margo, Carl's wife, and Florence never signed the notes. The men who collected the packages at the freight shed knew that a package for Margo was one for him or Ray. Time would tell if she had been compromised.

FORTY-FIVE

At her desk, Florence silently fought against sheer terror. The fear wasn't personal. It was for the men who were going after the diesel fuel to allow the rice mill operators to supply Josefa's food kitchens. Pretending to focus on the work in front of her, she tried to control her racing emotions and get through the rest of the day.

Florence had considered every option for how to divert another three hundred gallons of diesel without being caught. She had ruled out the warehouses. They were being monitored too closely.

She recalled that in her recent interrogation by the Kempeitai there wasn't a single question related to her earlier diversions using ration coupons. And she still had a small reserve of them at home.

Three hundred gallons of diesel fuel could be broken up into thirty-gallon increments using ten of the coupons. If the agents were successful in acquiring the fuel, she would still need to recover the falsified coupons and adjust the tallies in the ledgers. She thought the best chance of success lay in redeeming the coupons at just two fuel stations over the course of two or three days. Early the following Monday morning, she would be waiting in the office to retrieve the false coupons and post the altered tallies in the ledger.

She met secretly with Ricardo de Castro to discuss the plan and he agreed to contact Francisco Reyes to make the arrangements and provide enough men with different trucks to hopefully avoid suspicion.

The three days chosen to conduct the operation were pure torture for her. One slipup, one wrong word, a suspicious fuel station attendant . . . there were so many possibilities for discovery and disaster.

Florence was at home on the third evening when she received the coded telephone call confirming the mission was successful.

Her relief was almost tangible. The following Monday, she was the first clerk at the office. She located the ten coupons from the targeted stations and concealed them in her newspaper as the other staff members arrived and began work.

By the time she was able to gain access to the needed ledger, she saw that one of the other clerks had already entered the original tallies from the stations. Attempting to change them at that point would only draw attention to her. She could only hope that the discrepancy wouldn't be noticed.

She had already decided that if the latest diversion succeeded, it would be her last one. The constant threat of exposure had finally begun to affect her mental health and vitality. She was listless and detached both at work and home. Norma was the first to notice it, asking her if she was ill. Florence assured her that she was fine, simply tired.

One evening she tuned the shortwave radio to a station in Australia and heard the news that the Americans and British had invaded Europe at a place called Normandy. She listened to General Eisenhower's stirring words as he talked about the great crusade taking place to free the European people.

The news left her with mixed feelings. If successful, the invasion would lead to Germany's defeat, which she truly hoped would come soon. But it was Japan that had attacked the United States, first in Hawaii and the Philippines.

How long would the Philippines have to wait for its deliverance?

In early June she learned from Lucy Hoffman that several leaders of the Manila underground networks had been arrested by the Kempeitai. Each one had been a supplier to the American prisoners at Cabanatuan. Angelita Alvarez Sobral was suspending her deliveries until she thought it was safe to operate again.

Essential services in Manila began breaking down. There were frequent blackouts, both day and night. Florence's phone line was often dead. Many of the city's schools shut down because they had no paper, pencils, or even books.

She noticed that new Japanese troops were arriving in the city almost every day. When she asked Ken Osawa about it, he said that they were coming by ship from across the Japanese Empire and it meant that the army planned to defend the Philippines with all the resources they had. It was their final stand.

Florence saw that the new arrivals were no longer cocky and screaming "Banzai" like the ones who marched in the victory parade after they took Manila in January 1941. These men looked apathetic as they trudged along on their way to whatever military destination had been assigned to them.

Francisco Reyes brought her some heartbreaking news at the end of June. Tony Escoda had been arrested by the Kempeitai and was now a prisoner in Fort Santiago. Reyes told her that in addition to all his other resistance work with Josefa, he had secretly been helping General Vicente Lim gather military intelligence in preparation for the invasion of the Philippines, which would be led by General MacArthur.

Vicente Lim was the most famous soldier in the Philippines. The first Filipino to graduate from West Point, he had commanded the famed 41st Division in the fighting on Bataan. After the surrender, the Japanese puppet government tried to trade on his immense personal popularity by attempting to recruit him to head their pro-Japanese constabulary.

Pleading illness, Lim admitted himself to a Manila cancer hospital and had his doctors tell the government officials that he was too ill to accept any appointment. Secretly, he began working to gather intelligence on Japanese military dispositions across the country.

In early June, Lim received a summons from General MacArthur to join him in Australia to help plan the invasion. General Lim, Tony Escoda, and other resistance leaders were to travel by schooner to the island of Negros. There, an American submarine would be waiting to take them to MacArthur's headquarters in Brisbane.

A paid Filipino spy learned that Lim was leaving the country and informed the Kempeitai. Fast Japanese patrol craft were dispatched to find and search every small vessel crossing the narrow stretch of sea between Luzon and the island of Mindoro.

Off the Batangas coast, Lim's schooner was intercepted and the passengers and crew brought on deck. The masked informer identified General Lim and Tony Escoda. They were brought back to Manila and imprisoned in Fort Santiago.

Reyes said there was no doubt they were now being tortured to reveal the names of the people they worked with in the underground. He suggested that Florence leave Manila to join the Hunters organization in the hills.

As she considered her decision, Florence could only imagine the emotional torment being borne by Josefa. Florence yearned to be free from the constant fear, and knew that the Hunters had learned how to avoid capture after two years in the hills. But if she escaped from Manila, it might be viewed as an admission that she was a member of the resistance and place her family and friends in jeopardy.

She told Reyes she would stay.

FORTY-SIX

The flattering whispers from MacArthur's admirers in Washington, DC, reached his ear all the way across the Pacific, and they unleashed within the general the grandest ambition of them all. The dream of becoming president of the United States had always lurked in the recesses of his mind, but as he waited in Australia for the continued buildup of the forces he needed to return to the Philippines, the allure became something he couldn't control.

To MacArthur's thinking, a man of his lifelong attainments shouldn't have to run for the office. He believed the presidency was his ultimate destiny. It would be bestowed upon him like the laurel wreath crowning the head of the victor in the Olympics of Ancient Greece.

He had grown to detest Roosevelt and his New Deal. In 1939, while serving as the field marshal of the newly created Philippine Army, MacArthur felt free to confide to his closest aides his opinion: "The greatest disaster that could possibly visit the world today is the continuation of Roosevelt as president of the United States."

In the spring of 1944, MacArthur was riding high in national polls that asked Americans who they thought would be the strongest Republican candidate against Roosevelt. Politically, he hadn't been hurt by escaping from the Philippines two years earlier. It had been portrayed by the national press as a heroic act for which he earned the Congressional Medal of Honor.

MacArthur's own public relations staff in Australia worked overtime to send glowing reports of his popularity with the troops under his command.

After being asked repeatedly by the press if he planned to seek the nation's highest office, he finally released a public statement that seemed to close the door on a run.

"The only hope and ambition I have in the world," he stated, "is for victory for our cause in the war."

Privately, he continued to stir the fires that he hoped would generate a groundswell of support across the country and lead to a coronation at the Republican convention.

MacArthur dispatched his intelligence chief, Charles Willoughby, to reach out privately to influential Republicans like Congresswoman Clare Boothe Luce, the wife of the publisher of *Life* magazine. Willoughby made it clear to her that the general was available for anointment and described him as a combination of Napoleon, the Duke of Wellington, and Robert E. Lee.

Senator Arthur Vandenberg, the powerful Republican from Michigan who was leading the effort in Washington to propel a MacArthur candidacy, wrote a piece for *Collier's* magazine titled "Why I Am for MacArthur" that resonated with many Republicans and elevated the general to the ranks of the greatest war leaders in history.

The undoing of MacArthur's ambitions began when an obscure Republican congressman from Nebraska named Arthur Miller publicly released the private correspondence he had exchanged with the general over the previous year. The congressman apparently thought it would help speed up the MacArthur bandwagon.

Miller first wrote to MacArthur in the fall of 1943, strongly urging him to run for president and writing, "Unless this New Deal can be stopped this time, our American way of life is doomed."

MacArthur replied with a respectful note confirming, "I unreservedly agree with the complete wisdom and statesmanship of your comments."

In his next letter, Miller urged MacArthur to lead the charge to "destroy this monstrosity . . . which is engulfing the nation and destroying free enterprise and every right of the individual." MacArthur thanked him for his "scholarly letter" and wrote that the congressman's views were "calculated to arouse the thoughtful consideration of every true patriot."

When the hopelessly naïve congressman decided to publicly release the letters, he did not consult MacArthur. Their publication created a public furor. MacArthur was forced to release a statement in which he wrote, "I entirely repudiate the sinister interpretation" that his words in the letters were intended as criticism of Roosevelt.

MacArthur's superior, General of the Army George Marshall, was astounded that the man commanding army forces in the Pacific could allow such efforts to have continued for so long without disavowing them.

For his part, President Roosevelt was neither surprised nor angry. He had known MacArthur intimately for ten years, ever since the general had been the chief of staff of the army. He was well aware of MacArthur's presidential ambitions and his monumental vanity as he angled closer to becoming a candidate. But just as Roosevelt had outmaneuvered his rivals in the Democratic Party to win an unprecedented nomination for a fourth term, he saw a new way to manipulate MacArthur to his own advantage by maintaining an excruciating silence.

When the uproar showed no sign of dying down, MacArthur beat a final retreat, releasing a statement that as far as the Republican presidential nomination was concerned, "I do not covet it nor would I accept it."

It was a personal humiliation that stung deeply, but he soon discovered that he hadn't been the only one dealing in machinations. While he was pursuing his political ambitions, the most senior admirals in the American navy were maneuvering to bypass the invasion of the Philippines.

For months, Admiral Ernest King, the commander in chief of the US Fleet and Nimitz's superior, had been quietly making the case to the Joint Chiefs of Staff that instead of invading the Philippines at great cost in men and materiel, the next move in the Pacific should be an invasion of the Chinese island of Formosa, which was more lightly defended and closer to Japan.

King's plan was based on the presumption that the Japanese home islands would have to be conquered in order to defeat them. Formosa was not only hundreds of miles closer to the home islands, but a better staging area for American bombers to begin the destruction of Tokyo and other strategic targets prior to the final invasion.

MacArthur was outraged at the navy's end run and considered it a personal betrayal. He had promised the Philippine people he would return to liberate them with all the might of the American armed forces behind him.

Now it would be up to President Franklin Roosevelt to make the final decision on the question: the commander in chief who General MacArthur had sworn to loyally obey and had so recently betrayed.

On July 6, MacArthur received orders from George Marshall to come to Hawaii to attend a strategic military conference set for July 26. Marshall refused to tell him the purpose of the conference, but MacArthur could only assume it was the pending decision on the Philippines or Formosa.

Roosevelt was about to have his political revenge. Instead of attending the Democratic National Convention to accept his fourth nomination for president, he secretly left for Hawaii, arriving at Pearl Harbor aboard the heavy cruiser USS *Baltimore*.

There, he waited with Admiral Nimitz aboard the ship for the arrival of General MacArthur. Loud police sirens began wailing in the distance, and a few minutes later MacArthur pulled up at the dock in a chauffeured red convertible with a full motorcycle escort.

As they shook hands, MacArthur was privately shocked at the president's physical condition, noticing the dramatic loss of weight, the pallor of his skin, and the tremors in his hands. He concluded Roosevelt would be dead before the ultimate victory.

The president's first order of business was to sit for a series of ceremonial photographs. For Roosevelt, it was the political gold standard to be pictured as commander in chief in the midst of a world war while flanked by two of the most popular military heroes in the country.

MacArthur knew he was being used for political purposes but was powerless to do anything about it. More importantly, he needed to convince the president to choose the Philippines for the next major invasion. He decided to handle it all good-naturedly.

At one point, he asked Roosevelt what he thought of Republican governor Thomas Dewey's chances in the upcoming presidential election. Roosevelt responded by saying he was too busy to think about politics. At that, MacArthur leaned back and roared with laughter. After a few seconds, the president joined him.

The three war leaders spent the rest of the day touring Oahu's military facilities, conducting inspections, and finally having dinner with senior army and navy staff officers at the home of a wealthy American businessman. Late that evening, Roosevelt, MacArthur, and Nimitz adjourned to the living room to discuss the next move in the Pacific war.

Nimitz went first, articulating the navy's view that Japan was the ultimate prize and that taking Formosa brought them much closer to the home islands than a costly invasion of the Philippines, which could bog them down for months.

MacArthur spoke next, forcefully arguing that the United States had a moral obligation to liberate the country they had abandoned at the start of the war. Further, he told the president that he already had all the resources in manpower, ships, and planes to carry out the invasion. The only thing he needed was the order.

When Roosevelt expressed his concern about massive casualties in a Philippine invasion, MacArthur declared that his losses would be very light as a result of the superiority of American soldiers, weapons, and aircraft. He also outlined the elements of a plan to isolate the Japanese positions on Luzon with superior tactics based on his familiarity with the island's complex terrain.

The meeting broke up at midnight with the president leaving the decision unresolved. Privately, he concluded that there was merit on both sides, but the moral component of freeing the Philippines gave MacArthur the edge.

MacArthur left to return to Australia the next morning. The president remained in Hawaii for an additional day of tours, photo opportunities, and inspections before boarding the USS *Baltimore* to make the run back across the Pacific. At the conclusion of his whirlwind visit, the president faced the press.

"We are going to get the Philippines back," he told them, "and without question, General MacArthur will take part in it."

The invasion of the Philippines was on. The only question was when.

FORTY-SEVEN

When Florence saw Ken Osawa come into the accounting office trailed by several Kempeitai officers, she knew they had discovered the theft of the diesel fuel. She felt a wave of nausea at the thought that this might be her final day of freedom.

Gathering the accounting staff together, Osawa announced that all work in the office would cease until the Filipino accountants and clerks could be questioned individually about another very serious matter.

Osawa was present for each interrogation. Florence drew the same Kempeitai officer who had questioned her previously. This time he didn't start with a question. He began by accusing her of forging ration coupons and being part of a black market gang.

His voice rose to a shrill scream as he charged her with stealing three hundred gallons of fuel vital to the Japanese army. Her offense was punishable by death, but if she confessed and revealed the names of the others, her punishment would be less severe. Although Osawa never said a word, his presence was somehow reassuring to her.

In the face of his repeated threats, Florence denied the charges again and again. At one point, the Kempeitai officer moved threateningly close to her chair and she thought he was going to strike her.

After her repeated denials, he opened a bulging folder on the desk and showed her the files inside. They were the ration coupons processed by the fuel stations the previous week. He then gave her a blank coupon and an office pen and ordered her to copy the information from one of the processed coupons in her own hand.

Florence did so in the same precise lettering she always used. The processed coupon he'd chosen wasn't one of hers and the lettering didn't match. The officer grabbed it from her and said her handwriting would be matched against all the forged coupons they had found in their search of the records.

She had destroyed all ten falsified coupons, so there was no evidence to betray her there. At the end, the officer warned her not to discuss the interrogation and threatened that her next one would be at the Kempeitai headquarters.

After the officers left, the other staff members confirmed that each one had been accused of forging coupons. Later, Osawa brought them together in his office and repeated many of the encouraging words he had used in the past.

Another calamity struck a week later. Florence and Norma were at home with the boys when there was a furious pounding on the front door. Florence opened it to see a Japanese soldier standing on the portico. Speaking in broken English, he said that their house was needed by the Japanese army and that she had twenty-four hours to remove clothing and personal items before the officers assigned to live there arrived. The furniture, bedding, and kitchen equipment would have to remain.

A stunned Florence told the soldier they had nowhere else to go. She pleaded with him to allow them to remain in the house until she could appeal to someone in the occupying authority. His answer was to say that if they weren't out of the house within the required time limit, they would be forcibly removed.

After the soldier moved on to deliver the same message to the next set of occupants on Pennsylvania Avenue, Florence desperately tried to think of a place where they could go. The massive influx of Japanese troops in the previous weeks and months had led to housing shortages everywhere.

Florence and Norma had no family in Manila and their friends were already living in overcrowded conditions. The plantation of her childhood was not even worth considering. There was only one person she felt she could turn to for help. It was the guerrilla Francisco Reyes who had told her at their first meeting that the loyalty would go both ways. He had given her a telephone number where she could leave a message for him, and he returned the call later that same evening. When she told him what had happened, he said he would come by in the morning.

Florence spent her last evening in the house packing up clothes and personal things in boxes and suitcases. She emptied the hiding place under the closet floor and buried Bing's pistols and ammunition in the backyard. She hid her American passport and army identification in one of the boxes filled with clothing.

Early the next morning, Reyes arrived at the house in a horse-drawn dray. He told Florence and Norma that he had found a temporary place for them to live and would take them there in the wagon.

It was agonizing to leave. This was the first and only real home she had ever known. Standing at the open door to the living room, she began to weep as she thought back to all the special moments she had shared here with Bing, of waking up next to him every morning to plan their days and nights during the idyllic months before the war.

As they slowly rode in the dray across the city, Reyes told her about the new place, an apartment used by members of the Hunters guerrillas when they came to the city on intelligence-gathering missions. Unfortunately, it was in the Tondo district, he said, which Florence knew was one of the worst slum neighborhoods in the city. He assured her that he would try to find something better in the days ahead.

It was hard to feel anything but gratitude that they had someplace to go. When they reached the northern section of the city, Reyes pulled up to a three-story frame building in a block of shabby apartment houses. The narrow street wasn't paved and their building was less than a block from the Tondo Canal. Small children played happily on the packed-earth street.

The sluggish canal was the receptor for much of the raw sewage from the neighborhood, and the air had a corrosive smell. Behind their apartment house was a maze of crudely built shacks with tarpaulin roofs and walls.

The apartment was one large room in the basement of the building and only reachable through a door in an alley. It was furnished with two cots, a small dining table, and a few chairs. There was an open kitchen area with a cast iron, wood-burning stove. A single tap provided running water. There was no bathroom and they had to share the outhouse in the backyard with the other tenants.

As they were moving their things inside, it suddenly struck Florence that there was no way she could get to her office every morning from this location. Tondo not only lacked basic services like telephones; there was no regular public transportation.

She felt a wonderful sense of liberation. As long as she had been able to use the diversions to support the prisoners at Cabanatuan and Santo Tomas, she would never have quit. Now, the diversion operation was fatally compromised.

There would be nothing suspicious about her quitting her job, because it was the Japanese who had confiscated her home and ended her ability to reach the fuel union office. The unbearable tension she had endured through her secret life was ending.

Florence decided she would write a letter to Ken Osawa explaining that her house had been taken by the army and she had been forced to move to Tondo. She would give him her new address so that her last paycheck could be sent there. She would also write to Ricardo de Castro to let him know what had happened and that she would no longer be able to join him in their "family activities."

When Francisco Reyes finished helping them get settled, he again apologized for its inadequacies, and asked Florence to join him outside for a moment. He asked if she had any money left and she said very little. She had received no pesos from the last diversion and she had sent most of what remained from the previous operations to Carl Engelhart and to Fred Comings at Santo Tomas.

Reyes promised to return with some money and food to tide them over until he could find them a better place. Just before leaving in the wagon, he gave her the bad news he had been holding back.

"The Kempeitai arrested Josefa Escoda," he said. "They've taken her to Fort Santiago where Tony is being held."

It was one more crushing blow. Josefa had been a beacon of goodness in every way, a role model for every young woman in the Philippines. Reyes told Florence the Kempeitai had come to the Escoda home and taken her out in front of her frantic daughter.

Florence's world was collapsing around her. She could only try to survive.

FORTY-EIGHT

Two months after Chaplain Fred Oliver was taken to the nearby Kempeitai jail, he was returned to the camp hospital after suffering a heart attack while undergoing another round of interrogations.

Carl was shocked at the chaplain's condition when he went to visit him in the ward. Fred still wore the neck cast. On a semi-starvation diet, his cheeks had hollowed out, his nostrils were glazed with a mucus infection, and he was suffering from dysentery. When Carl took his hand, he opened his eyes and smiled.

"I didn't tell them anything," were his first words.

He said the Kempeitai wanted the names of the people in Manila who were supplying the camp with contraband goods. Although he hadn't given names, he believed that one of the other prisoners might have done so under torture.

Carl updated him on what had happened in camp since his arrest and told him about the departures of the Americans to Japan. From a peak of around eight thousand prisoners at the beginning of 1944, now less than half remained in the camp. Of those sent to Japan, he said that many had never arrived.

The last ship to sail from Manila carried nearly a thousand Cabanatuan prisoners. According to a guard, it had been torpedoed by an American submarine and most had drowned. To the American submarine captain, it

208

had simply looked like another enemy transport ship, with no designations or markings to show that it was carrying prisoners.

Fred brightened up when Carl told him that KGEI, the radio station in San Francisco, was proclaiming a succession of American victories over the Japanese and that a big carrier task force was reportedly attacking targets in Philippine waters.

The accuracy of the news report was confirmed on the morning of September 21. Carl was accompanying a work detail out to the farm when he heard the distant drone of airplane engines. The throbbing grew louder as the formation passed overhead.

The pilots flew too high to distinguish their markings, but he could see that there were fighter planes escorting a large cluster of bombers. One of the prisoners began pointing toward another cloud of specks high in the sky that were headed south toward Manila.

The formation above them continued flying west and a short time later they heard the faint detonation of explosions. Carl knew that Nichols Field lay to the west. It was now a Japanese air base.

The prison guards seemed to sense what was happening and nervously ordered the detail back to the camp. They were walking inside the gate when two fighter planes roared over at a height of a couple thousand feet. As the prisoners watched, the lead plane burst into flames and dove down out of control, exploding beyond the boundaries of the camp.

The victorious pilot circled around as black smoke rose from the crash site. To Carl, the markings on the plane's wings were unfamiliar: a white dash, a white star, another white dash. The last time he had seen an American warplane, the insignia was a white star with a red center and blue background.

One of the navy officers called out that it was a new American carrier plane. The exciting news was met with silence. Every face was animated, but the men remained quiet in fear of retribution as the American fighter disappeared in the sky.

Liberation was finally coming. Would it be in time?

FORTY-NINE

SEPTEMBER 1944
PHILIPPINE LIQUID FUEL DISTRIBUTION UNION
METROPOLITAN THEATER BUILDING, MANILA

Kiyoshi Osawa sat in his sun-filled corner office, reviewing the production estimates for the factories producing alcohol and lubricating oil. It was a beautiful morning, unusually cool, with a bluebird sky.

The quiet was suddenly shattered by the staccato bursts of a nearby anti-aircraft battery, quickly followed by the throbbing roar of a large formation of approaching planes. Over the previous few weeks, Osawa had participated in many air-raid drills with his employees, but now that it was the real thing, he chose to remain in the building and watch the battle unfold...

The first formation of American fighter planes flew in low from the sea and began making strafing runs at the docks, piers, and military facilities along the edge of the harbor. Explosions shook the warehouse district as another formation of fighters came from the north and attacked the ships moored in Manila Bay.

The anti-aircraft battery located in the park near his office opened fire as the third wave of planes arrived, which included dozens more attack bombers and torpedo planes. The air was filled with the screams of their bombs falling and the constant blasts of the flak cannons.

Osawa watched as one of the enemy planes running the gauntlet of the anti-aircraft cannons caught fire and fell in flames into the harbor, but the others survived to deliver their payloads on the ships in the bay.

210

There were more than thirty vessels anchored there: warships, freighters, and tankers of all sizes. One by one, they were lit on fire by bombs and torpedoes. The aim of the pilots was deadly accurate and they unleashed their payloads only a few hundred meters over their targets.

Each time a ship was hit, a column of flame and smoke erupted above its decks. So quickly was it all happening that it seemed to Osawa the bay itself was on fire. A few ships had been loaded with ammunition, and when they exploded, the blast felt like an earthquake. It made the floor shudder under his shoes.

After the attack ended and the planes disappeared, Osawa watched, distraught, as the ships of the empire sank in front of him, at least twenty, sending clouds of greasy smoke into the blue sky. At that moment, he realized the war was lost. And Osawa knew it was only the beginning of the bloody harvest that had been sown by the Japanese after attacking the Americans at Pearl Harbor. He could only pray that his wife and two small children in Japan would be spared the same destruction being delivered to his countrymen in the Philippines.

FIFTY

Florence's life was reduced to a constant search for food.

In the wake of the American air attacks, deliveries to the marketplaces in Tondo had been interrupted. Most of the shelves in the stores were bare. If one still had money, it was possible to buy rice and other staples under the counter, but Florence only had the remaining Japanese pesos from her final paycheck.

Francisco Reyes had promised to come back with a small amount of money and food to tide them over, but she had heard nothing from him since the day he first dropped them off in the horse-drawn dray.

During the bombing attacks in late September, Florence watched the formations of American planes with a mixture of excitement and apprehension. It meant the Americans were closer to returning, for which she couldn't be more thrilled. But they had bombed several military targets close by, and she worried that an errant strike could hit their neighborhood.

In the wake of the air attacks, martial law was declared. It didn't prevent a descent into chaos and disorder. For Florence and Norma, it became too dangerous to go out at night, and they locked themselves in the apartment as soon as darkness approached. Marauding gangs of young men roamed the narrow streets looking to steal anything they could sell for food and alcohol.

Prostitutes were living in the shacks behind their apartment, and they entertained men at all hours. Fights would break out between men drunk on home brew and spill into the open yard behind their building.

During the day, Florence searched the open-air markets, hoping to purchase milk for Bobby, fruit and vegetables, or a small portion of fish or meat to make soup. As her money ran out, she was forced to barter for food with her watch and the few pieces of jewelry Bing had given her.

One afternoon Florence found a teenage boy standing next to his bicycle outside the alley door to their apartment. He said he didn't want to leave it because he knew the bike would be stolen as soon as he did. The boy said that he had been sent by Ricardo de Castro and handed her an envelope. She opened it to find a short letter and a small trove of Philippine pesos. To Florence, it was a fortune. By then, the Philippine pesos were worth twenty times more than the Japanese ones.

In his note, Ricardo wrote that Francisco Reyes had told him of their plight and that he wanted to help them. He had sent the boy because there was a good chance the money would have been stolen if he had put it in the mail.

He said that the PLFDU was no longer dispensing fuel to the public. The remaining stocks of gasoline, diesel, alcohol, and coconut oil were restricted for use by the army and the large utilities. Most essential services had broken down or operated sporadically.

At the end of his note, Ricardo answered the riddle of why she had not heard from Francisco Reyes. Before he was able to help her, he had been arrested along with his three brothers.

Aside from Ricardo and Angelita Alvarez Sobral, almost everyone she had worked with in the underground was now in prison. She could only pray that the Americans would invade soon enough to end the nation's nightmare.

On the morning of October 16, five days after celebrating Florence's twenty-ninth birthday, Norma was making breakfast for Jerry and Bobby on the woodstove when there was a loud banging on the basement door.

When Florence went to open the door, two Japanese soldiers were standing on the landing holding rifles with bayonets. One of them removed a folded piece of paper from his breast pocket, handed it to her, and shouted, "Florence Smith?"

"I am Florence Smith," she said, bowing deeply as she always did.

The paper was obviously an official document, but aside from her name, the words were in Japanese and she had no idea what they meant. The one thing she did recognize was the small red sphere at the top of the page. It was the Kempeitai logo.

The first soldier was nervous, as if expecting resistance. He barged past her with his rifle pointed into the room and began shouting in Japanese. Jerry and Bobby began wailing loudly at the frightening intrusion.

When Florence showed her confusion, the soldier motioned with his rifle for her to come along with them. She had on a blouse, skirt, and sandals. They gave her no time to bring anything else. As she was leaving, she turned to look at her sister and saw her stricken expression. Florence gave her a reassuring smile before she was prodded by the first soldier up the stairs and out into the alley.

The local markets had opened for the day and the neighborhood was already teeming with people. The main street bordered the sluggish Tondo Canal, and the air reeked with the odor of human and animal waste. The rainy season was ending but the early morning temperature was chilly and she wished she had had time to take a sweater.

Florence expected the Kempeitai to have a car or truck waiting but the soldiers were on foot and motioned her to walk between them. There were no sidewalks in this part of Tondo, only packed dirt paths under the tin awnings of the shops. The street was choked with bicycles, fruit vendors, and pony carts. The vendors behind the stalls glanced furtively at her as she passed by.

She had tried to be so careful. Florence wondered how they had learned where she was living and concluded it had been a mistake to send her new address to Ken Osawa after writing to give him notice. They walked for nearly an hour through the residential neighborhoods that led into the commercial heart of the city. Arriving at Azcarraga Street, Florence looked up to see a huge building with a hexagonal tower rising five stories above the pavement. A vertical sign attached to the tower read AIRPORT STUDIO. Although she had never been inside, she knew that before the war it had been a popular photography studio where cameras and photo supplies were sold.

The soldiers led her past two guards at the entrance and toward a bank of desks on the far side of the lobby. They stopped at one and saluted an officer before handing him the paper with her name and information on it.

After the officer took a moment to scan the page, he grunted something in Japanese and the two soldiers left. The officer set the paper down on his desk and told her in English to follow him.

At the rear of the lobby was a broad staircase leading down to the next level. It was the lowest floor and consisted of one large, well-lit room with no windows. In the center of the space was a rectangular in-ground pool with three-foot-high cement walls around it.

The now empty pool was about twelve feet long and six feet wide and surrounded by planked wooden benches that had once provided customers with a place to relax and observe exotic fish while waiting for a photo shoot or considering a camera purchase.

As she reached the foot of the staircase, Florence felt a rush of indescribable horror. A man was lying on his back on one of the benches. Naked to the waist, his wrists and ankles were shackled together beneath the edges of the bench. He was unconscious or dead, and his chest and swollen stomach were smeared with blood. There was a horrible smell in the room.

The nightmares she had endured for more than two years of what would happen if she were caught were no longer dreams. She was in a pit of hell. The stench triggered the sudden urge to vomit but she fought it down.

The Japanese officer pointed toward a closed door.

Florence thought of Bing and what he had done, sacrificing his life for his shipmate during the battle for Bataan. When others were in immediate danger, Bing always ran toward it. She hoped she had a fraction of his strength and courage.

FIFTY-ONE

General Douglas MacArthur was about to keep his promise.

Two years and eight months after escaping from Corregidor on *PT-41*, he boarded the light cruiser USS *Nashville* to launch his invasion of the Philippines and free its people from the yoke of the Japanese Empire.

His invasion plan was a classic one-two punch. The Japanese expected the invasion to take place in Lingayen Gulf on the northern coast of Luzon, which was where they had launched their own landings in 1941.

Instead, MacArthur decided that the first landing would be on the island of Leyte, a smaller island southeast of Luzon. There the American forces would enjoy significant advantages in strength and numbers and could construct airfields to begin attacking Luzon.

The Japanese had steadily reinforced the Philippines in the previous months and now had an army of 430,000 soldiers prepared to die for their emperor, but only a small fraction were deployed on Leyte.

Leyte was sparsely inhabited, so civilian casualties would be light. One hundred thirty miles long from north to south, the invasion site chosen by MacArthur was on its eastern coast and sheltered by two nearby islands. The landing beaches were only accessible by sea through two bodies of water: the San Bernardino Strait to the north and the Surigao Strait to the south, making the location more defensible from a counterattack by the Japanese navy.

Once Leyte was secured, MacArthur would launch the invasion of Luzon, defeat the Japanese army, save his beloved Manila, and free the thousands of American soldiers held in Japanese prison camps.

The decision to invade Leyte was predicated on two assumptions made by his intelligence chief, Colonel Charles Willoughby. The first was that the Japanese navy would not risk its home fleet to defend the Philippines, and the fleet would remain in the Sea of Japan to protect the home islands. In this he was supported by the navy.

The second was that General Tomoyuki Yamashita, who commanded the army on Luzon, would retain his forces there in prepared defensive positions rather than reinforce the small force on Leyte.

MacArthur was commanding the largest naval force ever assembled in the Pacific. It included 730 ships, 34 aircraft carriers equipped with 2,000 fighters, dive-bombers, and torpedo planes. The fleet also contained 12 battleships, 24 cruisers, and 166 destroyers to escort the transport ships carrying 200,000 battle-tested soldiers fresh from their defeat of the Japanese army on New Guinea.

On the moonless night of October 20, MacArthur arrived with his armada at the landing beaches. All the ships were blacked out, and the troop transports employed radar to anchor at their preplanned positions off the beaches.

At dawn, MacArthur's twelve battleships and twenty-four cruisers unleashed a massive artillery barrage to destroy military targets that ranged five miles from the beach, then walked back the distance until the enormous shells were pounding the invasion beaches.

When the barrage ended, the first assault wave of thousands of troops left their transports in landing craft. Once ashore, the men stormed inland to attack the remaining military targets, which had been identified by networks of the Philippine resistance in the weeks leading up to the invasion.

By one o'clock in the afternoon, MacArthur decided it was time to join his men. The moment had finally arrived to once again set foot on the soil of the Philippine archipelago and to do so with all the epic drama his public relations staff could devise.

After finishing lunch, he went to his stateroom and dressed in freshly starched khakis. Picking up the loaded derringer that his father, Arthur MacArthur, had carried through the Civil War, he slipped it into his back pocket.

When he emerged on deck, the general was wearing his old Philippine Field Marshal cap with its salt-stained mass of gold braid on the visor. His senior staff was already waiting aboard the *Nashville*'s motor launch when he joined them for the ride to the beach.

They were still a good distance from shore when the launch ran into a sand bar. An aide radioed the beach master controlling traffic flow to send an amphibious craft out to ferry the commanding general and his staff into shore.

The harried beach master famously replied, "Let 'em walk."

News photographers were waiting on the beach and recorded the dramatic moment when a grim-faced MacArthur stepped off into the sea and began wading through the knee-deep water toward the shoreline.

Ashore, he strode up the beach toward the command headquarters. Japanese snipers were still hiding in firing perches just beyond the beach, some strapped to trees, others in deep foxholes covered by coconut palm fronds.

A light Nambu machine gun began firing at the group of officers as they headed across to the headquarters. While members of his staff ducked for cover, the general seemed oblivious to the rounds thudding into the sand nearby.

A few of the Japanese soldiers spoke English and began yelling taunts at the Americans from their hidden positions in the jungle. General George Kenney, MacArthur's air commander, heard one of them scream, "FDR EAT SHIT!" as MacArthur approached the command post. If he heard it, the general didn't react.

His first and only task was to deliver a radio broadcast to the Philippine people telling them that he had returned, as he pledged he would in March 1942. A small communications truck had been brought ashore for this purpose. The radio equipment in the truck would transmit

MacArthur's words to a more powerful transmitter aboard the *Nashville*, and his words would then be broadcast around the world.

A steady rain began to fall as MacArthur took the microphone from an army radio technician standing under a canvas canopy. Rifle and artillery fire could be heard in the background as MacArthur read the remarks, his deep, mellifluous voice shivering with emotion.

People of the Philippines, he began, *I have returned. By the grace of almighty God, our forces stand again on Philippine soil—soil consecrated in the blood of our two peoples... The hour of your redemption is here... Rally to me. Let the indomitable spirit of Bataan and Corregidor lead on. As the lines of battle roll forward to bring you within the zone of operations, rise and strike. Strike at every favorable opportunity. For your homes and hearths, strike! For future generations of your sons and daughters, strike! In the name of your sacred dead, strike! Let no heart be faint. Let every arm be steeled. The guidance of Divine God points the way. Follow in His name to the Holy Grail of righteous victory.*

MacArthur was already back aboard the *Nashville* when reports arrived from the generals commanding his troops ashore that all the objectives targeted for the first day of the invasion had been achieved. He slept soundly.

FIFTY-TWO

There was only blackness. It had no bottom, no hint of light around the edges of the solid door. There were no windows in the little room and no movement of the stale, stifling air.

Florence's cell was three feet by four feet—the size of a broom closet, which it once had been. Apart from the tin chamber pot she had seen when they locked her in, the room was empty. Florence could only sit or squat on the bare concrete floor. As the hours passed, she found it easiest to remain in the lotus position with her legs crossed.

She was terribly thirsty. She hadn't been given water since her arrest. As the hours passed, she lost track of time and no longer knew if it was night or day. She would doze off, only to be ripped back to consciousness by another harrowing scream, prolonged and horrible, from somewhere nearby in the basement area.

They finally came for her.

She heard the lock moving in the door and it opened to reveal a young Japanese guard. He motioned for her to come out and then pointed down the dimly lit corridor. She walked ahead of him past a number of closed doors until they arrived at an open one and he pointed inside.

A Japanese man in a wrinkled white suit was standing in the reception area outside another office with a closed door. He was no more than five

220

feet tall with a plump face and thinning gray hair. In his right hand was a two-foot-long bamboo baton.

"I am interpreter," he said, pointing to a chair. "You sit."

A few minutes later, a voice called out in Japanese from the room beyond the reception area. The little man opened the door and waved her inside, shutting the door behind them.

Her eyes were alert to every detail. It was a large, windowless office with a desk and conference table. A Japanese officer was sitting at the table. Powerfully built, his head was shaved and he had a pencil-thin mustache. He wore an army uniform with high, black leather boots and the insignia badge of a captain. The white armband on his left shoulder bore the Kempeitai logo. His saber lay on the table to his left. At the far end of the table were stacks of file folders.

Florence waited for him to look up from the file he was reading before she made the traditional deep bow. With a curt nod, the officer pointed to one of the two chairs across from him. The interpreter sat in the chair next to her.

"These are charges against you," the interpreter said, handing her a single sheet of paper.

It was typed in English and had many misspellings. She found her name at the top of the sheet along with the date when she began working for the Philippine Liquid Fuel Distribution Union.

The first charge accused her of falsifying fuel ration coupons to aid the enemy forces in the Philippines. The second charge accused her of sabotaging critical fuel supplies. The third charge was that she had supplied money, medicines, and other contraband to American military prisoners in the Cabanatuan prison camp.

The charges were all true, but did they have proof? Had she been betrayed?

The Kempeitai captain began the interrogation with a short question in Japanese that she knew included her name. The little interpreter translated his words.

"You are Florence Smith?" he asked.

"Yes, Captain," she said, looking at the officer.

"You are American?" was the next question.

"No, Captain," she said. "Filipina."

Without warning, the interpreter swung around in his chair and slapped her in the face. It shocked her more than it stung.

"You will tell truth," he said.

The Japanese officer spoke again and the interpreter translated it.

"You are American?"

"My father was American," she answered. "My mother is Filipina."

The next questions quickly went to the heart of the matter.

"Do you admit that your job was to write the names of applicants on the rationing coupons for gasoline, alcohol, and diesel fuel?" he asked.

"Yes," she said.

"Did you use coupons to steal fuel for the enemy underground?" the interpreter asked.

"No," she said.

He turned and slapped her in the face again.

The officer spoke at length, and the interpreter said, "We have a witness who said you gave coupons so he and his friends in the resistance could acquire gasoline and diesel fuel. You still say you did not steal Japanese fuel?"

"No," she said, and this time he punched her on the side of the face with his closed fist, knocking her out of the chair. Momentarily dazed, she glanced up at the officer. He showed no visible reaction and casually waved his finger for her to resume her seat at the table.

Florence could feel the side of her face swelling as she sat down again. She waited for the captain to identify the person who had betrayed her, but he moved on to a different question related to the fuel diversions.

She knew that if she confessed to the charges of stealing fuel for the underground, the punishment would be death. The laws set down by the occupying authority were explicit about aiding the enemy.

And if she did confess, they wouldn't stop there. The next round of interrogations would make her inform on the others. Ricardo de Castro, Francisco Reyes, the Escodas, Lucy Hoffman, Angelita Alvarez Sobral, Fred Comings—they would all face the same consequences.

The questions began coming faster. Who were her couriers into the Cabanatuan camp? Who picked up the fuel with her falsified ration coupons? How and when did she plan the thefts? Who were the others in her underground network?

Each time she denied a charge, the interpreter delivered another blow. After one answer he didn't like, he raised the bamboo baton high in the air and brought it down hard on the backs of her hands. The searing pain caused her to cry out.

The interrogation hadn't gone on for very long before Florence heard the low whine of an air-raid siren. It was soon joined by the wailing of others across the city. The Kempeitai captain stopped in the middle of his question.

Standing up, he strapped the saber to his leather belt and left the office. The interpreter followed him into the corridor. The young guard returned and motioned her into the reception area before locking the door of the inner office.

She sat and waited as her face began to throb with pain. One of the blows had loosened some of her teeth. As the sirens continued to whine, the interpreter returned and wearily sat down, as if tired from the beating he had given her. She could smell whiskey on his breath.

"You will be taken back now," he said. "It will only be harder on you tomorrow. If you tell the truth, I will do what I can to help you."

The same young guard escorted her back to the closet. Before locking her in, he patted her down as if searching for a concealed weapon, while staring at her the whole time.

Alone, she again lost track of time in the darkness until the door opened once more. In the pale light from the corridor she saw a Filipina woman standing by a metal pushcart. After emptying Florence's chamber pot in a metal drum, she handed her a small bowl and a can of water. The bowl contained a clump of rice. The water was warm and brackish.

Her swollen jaw continued to throb as she slowly ate in the darkness. The air-raid sirens had temporarily given her a reprieve and it could only mean the Americans were coming closer. She wondered if they would arrive in time to save her. If they would even know where to look.

FIFTY-THREE

The Leyte invasion was going just as MacArthur planned.

From the beginning, Leyte was intended to be the easy phase of the one-two punch, yielding a quick victory that would soften up the Japanese before MacArthur invaded Luzon. All the early objectives were achieved in the first two days. The date for the Luzon invasion was set for December, little more than a month away.

MacArthur was already thinking ahead. As soon as his army was ashore on Luzon and engaged with General Yamashita's defense forces, MacArthur planned to send a fast flanking force straight through to Manila to free the capital.

All it required was swift success in the battle for Leyte.

That victory still rested on the two critical assumptions made by Willoughby and his intelligence staff during the planning phase of the invasion. He had assured MacArthur that General Yamashita, who commanded more than four hundred thousand soldiers on Luzon, would not reinforce his small force on Leyte.

Yet as soon as Yamashita received word of the invasion, he began dispatching reinforcements to Leyte, making a full commitment to the battle with three well-trained divisions and an eventual force of fifty thousand additional soldiers.

The second assumption made by Willoughby was that the Japanese navy would not permit its home fleet in the Sea of Japan to be sent to contest the Leyte invasion. Once again, he was dead wrong.

On October 23, two American submarines in the South China Sea spotted a large Japanese naval task force heading for the Philippines. It was actually one of four heading toward the Leyte landing beaches to destroy MacArthur's invasion ships.

Alerted to the planned invasion by their own intelligence staff, the Japanese hoped to inflict the kind of decisive defeat of the Americans that would eliminate the possibility of their invading the home islands. It was an incredible gamble, with everything at stake for the Japanese in one throw of the dice. The Battle of Leyte Gulf was about to become the single biggest naval engagement in history.

The Japanese plan was complicated but sound. Since they had lost most of their carrier planes in previous naval battles, they decided to use four of their remaining aircraft carriers as bait to lure away the principal American naval force guarding the San Bernardino and Surigao Straits, the narrow passages of water leading to MacArthur's landing beaches from the north and south.

If the Americans took the bait and chased the decoy carriers, the passages would be left undefended. A second and even bigger Japanese naval task force commanded by Admiral Takeo Kurita would then dash through the strait and wipe out MacArthur's troopships, transports, and supply ships with overwhelming firepower. Kurita's force included the most powerful battleships and heavy cruisers the Japanese still possessed.

The third and fourth Japanese task forces, consisting of more battleships, cruisers, and destroyers, would converge at Surigao Strait, the southern passage to the landing beaches, and attempt to join forces with Kurita to complete the destruction.

Once MacArthur's transports and supply ships were destroyed, General Yamashita's 430,000 soldiers on Luzon would be sent as needed to Leyte to eliminate the 200,000 American soldiers trapped there under MacArthur.

The Japanese plan worked to near perfection. The principal American fleet commanded by Admiral William Halsey pursued the decoy carriers and left the San Bernardino Strait unprotected. Hours later, Kurita swept through with four battleships, eight cruisers, and eleven destroyers.

The only remaining obstacle between Kurita's force and MacArthur's transports and supply ships was a thin screen of small escort carriers and a handful of destroyers. With astonishing bravery, the captains of four American destroyers attacked the battleships and cruisers in an almost suicidal effort to block them from the landing beaches.

Although each of the destroyers was sunk in turn, they managed to draw close enough to launch torpedoes. At least one struck home and knocked a heavy cruiser out of the battle line. The American escort carriers then launched all their aircraft to attack the Japanese task force, damaging two more cruisers.

It was the crucial moment in the battle. Because the Japanese commanders had been ordered to maintain radio silence, Admiral Kurita was unaware that the principal American fleet had taken the bait and was already hundreds of miles away, chasing the carriers.

Now no significant warships stood between Kurita's powerful task force and the defenseless transports and supply ships. The landing beaches were less than thirty miles away, but the heroic sacrifice by the American destroyers and the pilots from the escort carriers led Kurita to believe he was facing the principal American fleet rather than a final screen of defenders. He decided to save his fleet from further damage and retreat from Philippine waters, thus losing the last and greatest opportunity for the Japanese to inflict a decisive and crushing defeat on MacArthur's invasion force.

While narrowly avoiding a disaster by sea, MacArthur faced a mounting challenge from the Japanese on the ground and in the air. Willoughby's intelligence estimates of Japanese air strength on Luzon were as wrong as his other assumptions. Four days after the invasion, the Japanese launched daily attacks on both the American infantry positions and the ships anchored near the landing beaches.

For the first time in the war, the Japanese began kamikaze attacks, the suicidal missions by brave Japanese pilots who dove their planes into American ships. They came every day from airfields on Luzon and there were too many to shoot down. The loss of ships and men began to mount.

The weather was abysmal too. A succession of storms and typhoons dumped thirty-five inches of rain on Leyte, slowing down construction of the new airfields. The storms also prevented the Americans from mounting coordinated attacks against the Japanese infantry positions.

It was clear to MacArthur's battlefield commanders that the invasion of Luzon would have to be postponed. At first, a deeply frustrated MacArthur refused to alter the timetable for it. Finally, he bowed to reality.

His promise to free Manila by Christmas would not be fulfilled.

FIFTY-FOUR

Florence's second interrogation session followed the same pattern as the first.

The Kempeitai captain would ask the questions in Japanese. Each time he didn't like her translated answers, he nodded at the little interpreter in the white suit, who used his fists or the bamboo rod to beat her face and upper body.

Florence continued to deny falsifying the ration coupons and supplying fuel to the enemy. She insisted she was not part of an underground network, and therefore could not identify members of the Philippine resistance.

About two hours into the second session, a hard blow to the back of her head with the bamboo rod knocked her unconscious. By the time she recovered her senses, the captain was gone. The young guard was summoned and she was taken back to her cell.

The time alone in the blackness between interrogations seemed endless, but the thought of the next torture session was far worse. Each time she heard the sound of boots clicking down the corridor, she prayed the guard wasn't coming for her again.

Her only other visitor was the Filipina woman who came to the cells once a night to empty the prisoners' chamber pots and give them each a small portion of rice and a can of water. Mentally exhausted, Florence's few hours of troubled sleep provided a release from her dread of what they would do to her next.

The third interrogation proved to be different than the first two. In addition to the bullet-headed captain and the interpreter, a third Japanese man was sitting at the conference table when she arrived. In front of him on the table was what looked like an electronic transformer for a toy train set. The machine was already plugged into a wall socket.

The interpreter ordered Florence to hold out her hands and the third man unwound two long wires from the machine. He wrapped the ends of them around her index fingers and secured them with tape.

"We begin again," said the interpreter.

Did she falsify coupons to supply fuel to Japan's enemies in the underground? he asked.

When Florence answered no, the Kempeitai captain motioned to the man with the machine and he turned a knob on the transformer. The shock was instantaneous, sending hot shooting pains through her whole body. Leaping from her chair, she screamed.

The interpreter got up and pushed her back into her seat, standing behind her and pressing her shoulders down so she couldn't move. He repeated the first question: Did she falsify coupons to supply fuel to the enemy underground?

When she again said no, the man with the machine delivered an even stronger jolt of electricity. It coursed through her nerves like a river of pain. After ten seconds, he dialed the knob back to where there was only a deep burning sensation in her fingers and she could breathe normally again.

The interpreter repeated the same question a third time: Did she falsify coupons to supply fuel to the enemy underground?

Before she said no, the man delivered an even more powerful burst of electricity. This time it was unbearable. Sobbing with agony, Florence lost control of her bladder and urinated in her underwear.

The torturer seemed to know just how far he could amplify the surge without causing her to lose consciousness. He would smile as he ran the current through her and she cried out each time. In the sea of agony, she could only pray for the ordeal to end.

She saw that the Kempeitai captain wasn't paying attention anymore to what they were doing to her. He left the questions to the interpreter while doing other paperwork and smoking cigarettes.

As it went on and on, Florence became disoriented, trying to hedge some of her answers rather than saying no and being punished for it. After what seemed like an eternity, the captain finally ended the session and the man removed the terminal wires from her fingers.

"We start again tomorrow," said the interpreter.

Following the third inquisition, she was taken to a washroom where a Filipina attendant helped her remove her soiled clothing. For the first time since her arrest, she was allowed to clean herself with soap and water.

In the washroom mirror, two black eyes stared back at her from her bruised and swollen face. There were welts and contusions covering her shoulders and stomach. The skin on her index fingers had turned pasty white.

When she had finished washing herself, the attendant gave her a pair of clean cotton pajamas. Still trembling and physically unstable from the effects of the shocks, she needed the assistance of the Japanese guard to help her down the long corridor to her cell. After he locked her in the darkness, she collapsed on the floor.

Untold hours later, Florence heard the sound of boots clicking down the hallway again. They stopped outside the door. Not again, she thought. It was too soon. The key turned in the lock and there was a momentary gleam of pale light as the young guard stepped inside, shutting the door behind him. He was no longer wearing his pistol belt.

She knew what he was planning to do as soon as he began pulling at her pajama top in the darkness. The rankness of his body revolted her as she felt him drag down her pajama bottoms.

She went limp as he forced himself inside her and could only endure the nightmare in silence. Who would notice or care if she screamed out in torment? The howling shrieks of the prisoners were a constant in the basement of the Airport Studio.

For a time, the only sound in the room was his harsh grunts. When it was over, he stepped back into the corridor and locked the door again. She knelt on the concrete floor and vomited in the chamber pot.

Incapable of sleep, she forced herself to think about what to do next. Her fingers still ached from the agony of the last interrogation. How long could she endure without confessing? If she told them everything she had actually done, they would execute her, but as much as she wanted to survive, she realized there was no way she could undergo repeated torture without them eventually breaking her will.

She felt something else well up inside her. A silent rage over what the Japanese were doing to her, to Josefa and Tony Escoda, Francisco Reyes, and to so many others. Like them, she had to fight back as long as she could.

She decided that at the next interrogation she would deny the more serious charges and confess to sending money, food, and medicine into Cabanatuan. It would implicate no one new. They had already caught the courier who had brought her last package to Carl Engelhart.

They couldn't execute everyone who had given the American prisoners help.

FIFTY-FIVE

As Carl wandered through the vast deserted compound for the last time, the place reminded him of a dusty ghost town in the old west. Under the brutal sun, the hundreds of barracks that had once housed eight thousand prisoners lay silent and empty.

The prisoners who could walk were moving out. The only men who would remain behind were the five hundred or so serious hospital cases and the handful of doctors attending them.

Carl had spent two and a half years of his life in this wretched place, alternately starving, watching his friends die, living under the threat of execution, and sweating under the tropical sun every day as he and the others strove to survive.

The only visual reminders of what they had endured were heaped piles of tattered clothing, battered tin cups and plates, and discarded bedding. And, of course, the earth mounds at Bone Hill to the south of the camp, where thousands of Americans lay buried.

One thousand prisoners were leaving the camp that day. A week earlier, another 1,750 officers and enlisted men had been marched to the nearby railroad siding to be put aboard a train that carried them south to Manila to await the next available ship leaving for Japan.

Previously, the Japanese had done a physical examination of each prisoner to make sure they weren't carrying diseases back to the

233

Japanese homeland. Now, the only requirement was that they could walk.

In the last days before leaving, Carl had eaten as much of Henry Jones's farm produce as his stomach could hold. He knew there would be very little food aboard the ship and it would be good to have a few extra pounds to shed.

When he boarded the train at the railroad siding, it looked like the same cattle car he had ridden in to the camp two and a half years earlier. Once again there was no water to drink and they were packed in so tightly there was no room to sit down.

Arriving in Manila, they were marched to Bilibid prison in time to see the previous group of 1,750 prisoners leaving to board an old Japanese freighter, the *Arisan Maru*. Carl was able to wish good luck and godspeed to a number of close West Point friends. All of them attempted to put on a cheerful air at the parting.

"See you soon at the Jap coal mines," one of them joked.

The Bilibid cell blocks were just as Carl remembered, with bare concrete walls. There was nothing to do but sit on the floor in the muggy heat and wait for their ship to come. Once a day, each man received a cup of boiled rice.

Early one morning he awoke on the concrete floor to the growing whine of an air-raid siren. Japanese guards quickly swarmed into the cell blocks and ordered the men to fasten down the solid wood shutters that covered the open, barred windows.

Through the cracks in the shutters, the prisoners watched a host of carrier planes attacking the ports, docks, and the warehouse district. More followed the next day. It could only mean that an invasion of Luzon was coming soon.

Carl was certain of only one thing: if the American army reached Manila before the prisoners were put on a ship to Japan, the Japanese would herd them all out into the prison yard and machine gun them from the catwalks.

The alternative of being aboard a Japanese ship, trying to run the gauntlet of American carrier planes and submarines to get back to Japan, was no better risk. This was confirmed two weeks later.

An American doctor who was treating a Japanese officer learned something so catastrophic that after confiding it to the senior POW leaders, the news was restricted to avoid setting off a wave of panic.

The *Arisan Maru*, the freighter carrying the 1,750 men from Cabanatuan, had been sunk in the China Sea by an American submarine. None of the prisoners had been wounded by the torpedo explosions and the Japanese crew allowed them to climb down the cargo nets into the sea before the freighter sank. One of the other ships in the convoy rescued the Japanese crewmen who had escaped in a lifeboat.

They left the Americans floating in the empty sea. In the end, only nine of them survived.

FIFTY-SIX

It no longer seemed as if the Kempeitai were interested in the truth, only in inflicting pain. The grinning man controlling the transformer no longer restrained the power surge to his previous limits. At times, he would dial it to the maximum setting, driving Florence into insensibility. She would regain consciousness, and the questions would go on.

In agony, she was assisted back to the room after each session and left in the darkness. The young guard did not attack her again, possibly because she was no longer allowed to clean herself. The process of degrading her in every way was designed to break her spirit and make her confess.

In between interrogations, they forced her to witness what might lie ahead for her if she didn't cooperate. On one occasion, she was brought back to the expansive room in the basement with the cement-walled pool and the wooden benches. Three men were being tortured there. One Filipino had been beaten so severely that his arms and legs were almost completely blue. His voice was gone, and the man was reduced to making tiny yelps with each new blow from a metal rod.

A second man was lying on his back on the concrete floor. One end of a garden hose had been shoved into his mouth and an interrogator was holding it inside his throat. Flowing water was running through the hose from an open spigot and the man's stomach was hideously distended. As she watched, a second interrogator stepped onto his abdomen, and water gushed out of his mouth. Mercifully, the man appeared to be unconscious and uttered no sound.

The third prisoner was leaving the room after whatever had been done to him. Too weak to walk, he could only crawl forward on his hands and knees as a guard prodded him to keep moving.

By then, Florence had confessed to sending small amounts of money and medicine to the American prisoners at Cabanatuan. As she had feared, he immediately demanded to know the names of her couriers, how she had acquired the money and contraband drugs, and who she had sent them to in the camp.

She told them that she did not know any couriers and that someone unknown to her would pick up the packages at her home. The money and medicine were donated by friends she had asked for help, she said, and the supplies were meant for all the prisoners, not a specific one.

It only meant more hours of beatings from the little interpreter and repeated shocks from the transformer as Florence continued to deny stealing fuel and diverting it to the friends in the underground.

In between sessions, she lost track of time again, but at some point realized that something strange had taken place. With the repeated infliction of the electric shocks, her sensitivity to them seemed to have dulled or possibly her nervous system had shut down in a way. And knowing what to expect somehow made it easier to endure it. Part of her terror had been the unknown. Now it was all too well known.

For the first time, she thought there might be a chance she wasn't going to break.

About a week after her arrest, Florence was alone in the blackness when she heard the familiar clicking of boots coming down the corridor and the key turning in the lock. The sound no longer reduced her to frantic terror.

When pale light filtered into the room, she saw a different guard. He motioned her to come out and pointed down the hallway. Assuming this would be her next interrogation session, she steeled herself for another round of questioning.

Instead, the guard took her back to the washroom. There, she was allowed to bathe for the first time since her arrest. Glancing into the mirror, she was horrified. Florence had no idea how much weight she had lost but her bruised body was now angular and gaunt.

The attendant gave her another pair of clean cotton pajamas and the guard took her to a different wing of the basement. It was an actual cell block and the cell doors were iron bars. Unlocking the door to one of the cells, he waved her inside.

There were already six women there, sitting on the floor. The cell wasn't big enough for any of them to lie down. After being told that speaking was forbidden, she assumed the lotus position. A single bare bulb in the ceiling provided illumination. It was never turned off. The cell block was silent except for the random screams of men and women being tortured in other parts of the basement.

A few days later, a guard unlocked the cell door and motioned for Florence and two of the other women to come out of the cell. They were taken to the rear entrance of the building. Outside, a truck was parked on the street. Its engine was running, and the guard helped them onto the covered freight bed. The women were blindfolded, and the truck moved out.

FIFTY-SEVEN

NOVEMBER 1944
UNITED STATES ARMY COMMAND HEADQUARTERS
TACLOBAN, LEYTE

Douglas MacArthur stood on the open veranda, calmly smoking his corncob pipe as he watched the Japanese fighters come in for another strafing run. His new headquarters was a mansion in Tacloban, the port city closest to the landing beaches. It was the largest and most impressive building in the town. After the Japanese overran Leyte in 1942, they had chosen it for their own headquarters. Rightly assuming that MacArthur would adopt it as his, they now made every effort to destroy it and him.

War correspondent Turner Catledge of the *New York Times* stayed at the mansion while covering the battle and reported that it "had been strafed repeatedly and was pockmarked inside and out with machine gun bullet holes. My room had a gaping hole through the wall."

The Japanese came very close to killing the general. During one air attack, a .50-caliber bullet plowed through the wall of the office where MacArthur was working and buried itself a foot behind his head. As aides watched, he dug it out of the wall and said, "Not yet."

The Japanese destroyed many of the facilities around the mansion, including a direct hit on the officers' mess. Two American newsmen were killed, along with a dozen Filipino soldiers. MacArthur's staff was amazed by his seeming willingness to court possible death rather than seek shelter in the bunkers of the main complex.

The general claimed there was a purpose to his behavior, telling his personal physician Dr. Roger Egeberg, "If I do it, the colonels will do it. If the colonels do it, the captains will do it, and so on."

His mordant sense of humor often emerged during the periods of greatest personal peril. During one attack, an American anti-aircraft battery began firing at its lowest depression above the ground to knock down a Japanese Zero coming in at treetop level. One of the rounds blasted a hole through the wall of MacArthur's bedroom. Miraculously, it was a dud and didn't explode. The next morning at breakfast, MacArthur dropped the round on the table in front of the officer in command of the batteries.

"Bill," said MacArthur, "ask your gunners to raise their sights just a little bit higher."

Five weeks into the battle, MacArthur's ground forces finally made progress against the reinforced Japanese troops dug in on Leyte. In spite of the torrential rain and typhoons, the American Sixth Army slowly began reducing the Japanese positions one by one.

In mid-November, General Yamashita became despondent over the final outcome after American carrier planes intercepted a Japanese troop convoy sent to reinforce the Leyte garrison. Ten thousand Japanese troops drowned when their ships were sunk.

Yamashita had dispatched sixty-five thousand elite troops to Leyte, but they were now on the defensive and being divided into ever-smaller pockets of resistance. The final result was foreordained when Yamashita informed his commander on Leyte that no further reinforcements would be sent.

The Japanese had gambled everything at Leyte and lost. Dozens of their major warships lay at the bottom of the sea, their air force assets were decimated, and Yamashita's sixty-five thousand troops on Leyte would eventually be annihilated.

MacArthur could now focus on freeing his beloved Manila.

FIFTY-EIGHT

When the guard removed her blindfold, it took only a moment for Florence to know where she was. The Bilibid Prison for Men was a dominant landmark in Manila with its twelve-foot-high stone walls, barbed wire, and electrified fencing. The complex took up a dozen square city blocks.

At the intake office, Florence was registered as a prisoner facing trial before she and her two fellow prisoners from the Airport Studio were taken to one of the cell blocks. In the lavatory, a male guard ordered them to take off all their clothes, spread their legs, and bend over. Another half dozen guards stood and watched as the humiliation of an intimate search was followed by an order to shower. Afterward, the women were issued pajamas stamped *U.S. Army Medical Corps.*

The men's clothing was far too big for the emaciated Florence and hung on her like a tent. Still barefoot, the women were separated and led to different cells. When the door to Florence's cell was unlocked and she stepped inside, the first thing she noticed was a terrible stench.

There were seven women in the room and they were all either kneeling or sitting on the concrete floor. One of the women raised her finger to her closed lips, signaling that talking was forbidden.

The cell was about six feet square. The door consisted of iron bars. A thick mesh screen covered the single window on the outer wall. The dreadful smell appeared to come from the far corner, where there was a circular

241

hole in the floor. It was where the women relieved themselves. In the other corner, there was an iron pipe and a water spigot. A few tin cups sat underneath it on a bare shelf.

Florence joined the others on the floor and assumed the lotus position.

The hours passed slowly as a guard marched up and down the corridor beyond the bars of the door. Sometime in the afternoon, the door opened again and a Filipina attendant handed out food to each prisoner. The meal was a small helping of rice gruel served in a coconut shell.

After eating, the women resumed their sitting or kneeling positions. Except for sporadic visits to the fetid hole or to take a drink of water, they remained in their positions until nine thirty that night, when the light in the ceiling was turned off and they were allowed to sleep. Throughout the night, clouds of mosquitoes buzzed through the iron bars of the door to further torment them.

Florence could only look at her new quarters as a reprieve from the inquisition at the Airport Studio. Her index fingers were still acutely painful. The prolonged burning from the wires had penetrated through the epidermis into the deeper tissues of her skin, turning them both a charred black. She hoped they would now have time to heal.

She quickly learned the daily prison routine. Before dawn every morning, someone emptied the metal bin holding their waste from under and outside the cell. They were awakened at six thirty and ordered to assume the rigid sitting positions on the floor. At nine thirty in the morning and three thirty in the afternoon, the women received their rice ration, sometimes supplemented with a topping of seaweed or greens. Florence was always hungry.

Occasionally they were served a weak, unsweetened tea with the afternoon meal. Depending on the mood of the guards, the women were allowed to go to the washroom to shower once every two weeks. It was a luxury Florence came to treasure.

On most days, they were permitted to go outside into a small, high-walled courtyard to walk for fifteen minutes before being returned to their cell. It was during one of these initial outings that she made her first friend in prison.

The woman introduced herself as Dorothy Fuentes and told Florence that she was an American who had posed as Italian to deceive the occupying authority and spy on the Japanese. She described some colorful adventures before she was caught by the Kempeitai along with another female prisoner named Maria, who was also in their cell. Maria was from a very wealthy Spanish family in Manila.

Dorothy had been imprisoned at Fort Santiago for four months and tortured to reveal the names of the people in her network and the prisoners she had supplied at Cabanatuan. She had refused to incriminate her friends and, like Florence, was now waiting to be tried by a Japanese military court for her crimes. In her late thirties, she was spirited, funny, and upbeat.

As they bonded, the two women quietly joined forces to do their best to survive while waiting to learn their individual fates. One way they relieved the tedium was to share favorite recipes using ingredients they could only dream about.

Sitting close together near the iron bars at the front of the cell, they would wait for the guard to head down to the end of the corridor before whispering to each other. One of Dorothy's concoctions was "Waffles a la Bilibid," made with flour, eggs, cream, butter, cheese, and bacon. When their rice gruel was served, Florence pretended it was the waffle.

One morning, another guard approached unexpectedly from the opposite direction and caught Florence whispering to Dorothy. Thrusting his saber between the bars while she was looking away, he slammed her in the head with the flat edge, knocking her out. When she finally regained consciousness, she was only grateful the penalty hadn't been more severe.

Then she discovered the other reason for the terrible stench.

A number of the cells in their block contained male prisoners, and many were being subjected to regular beatings and torture for whatever crimes the Japanese believed they had committed. Florence and her cell mates were often awakened by their howling screams in the middle of the night. As these men approached the end of their suffering, they were carried to the cell adjoining the women's.

At least one died every day, often as many as four or five. The corpses would sometimes lie for days unattended, decomposing in the tropical heat. A few of the more sadistic guards would stroll by the cell and laughingly call out, "No *patay*?" No dead?

During one of her fifteen-minute exercise periods, Florence was walking in the courtyard near the high wall that separated their cell block from the next one when she heard a chorus of American voices coming from the other side. From the bits of their conversation, she realized they were American prisoners of war and wondered what they were doing in Manila instead of Cabanatuan. Was it possible Carl was there too?

Their daily routine was permanently changed a few weeks after her arrival. Early that morning, air-raid sirens began going off all over the city, and Florence heard the approaching roar of many planes. For the next few hours, Manila received the heaviest bombardment she had ever personally experienced.

The warplanes returned every day and the women were no longer allowed to walk outside. Sitting or lying in their cell, the women could feel the concussions through the floor and hear the spent shells of the Japanese anti-aircraft guns falling like hard rain on the roof of the prison. Each night, Florence prayed that Norma, Jerry, and Bobby were safe at the apartment in Tondo or wherever they had gone.

Dorothy learned through the prison grapevine that the Americans had landed on Leyte. It was only a matter of time until they invaded Luzon. Florence took heart from the thought they might all soon be free.

When Dorothy was taken away for her trial by the Japanese military court, she returned less than an hour later with a bruised face. One of the judges hadn't liked her attitude or answers and had told the interpreter to punch her. Florence was quite familiar with that courtesy.

Dorothy said she had pleaded guilty to the charge of sending supplies to the men at Cabanatuan but was surprised when the judges did not sentence her after the so-called trial. Before dawn the next morning, Florence was awakened by the voice of a guard inside the cell. In the shadowy light, Dorothy and Maria stood up. After being roped together, they were taken away.

A few days later, Florence was notified that her own trial date had been set. The night before it was to take place, Florence was on her way back to her cell from the lavatory when she encountered a male prisoner being driven toward her along the corridor by a guard. He could barely remain on his feet and bore the familiar marks of a man already half beaten to death.

The prisoner somehow looked familiar and Florence was stunned when she realized who it might be. But that was impossible. Francisco Reyes had told her that Tony Escoda had been imprisoned in Fort Santiago.

When the man looked back at her, she saw recognition in the battered eyes of his ruined face. Then he was past her, struggling down the corridor at the prodding of the guard walking behind him.

It was only when she was back in her cell that Florence remembered Dorothy telling her that she too had been imprisoned in Fort Santiago, and that the Kempeitai had transferred her to Bilibid after they had finished questioning her.

FIFTY-NINE

Carl Engelhart and the rest of the prisoners from Cabanatuan had now spent six weeks in the Bilibid cell blocks, and the rice ration had been cut twice since their arrival. When the American air attacks on Manila had resumed in mid-November, it gave them hope that the invasion by MacArthur was imminent, but the attacks ceased near the end of the month.

Carl was sure that the Japanese would take advantage of the lull to organize a new convoy to Japan and his assessment proved accurate. A Japanese liaison officer announced they would be boarding a ship for Japan the following day so they could "enjoy the better living conditions" in Japan.

On December 13, the Americans were organized into four columns at the prison entrance gate. Weakened by hunger, they made a ragged march to the boarding terminal near Pier Seven in the Manila dock area. The roof of the terminal building had been shattered by bombs and they were ordered to sit on the debris-strewn floor for most of the day as nearly two thousand Japanese civilians, mostly women and children, boarded the ship from the pier. Most of them were the wives and children of Japanese officers and businessmen. As they went up the boarding stairs, they tearfully waved goodbye to their husbands and friends. The civilians occupied the staterooms above decks. The Americans would occupy the cargo holds.

It was late in the afternoon by the time the prisoners were herded to the boarding gates. Approaching the ship, Carl saw that its name was *Oryoku Maru*. When he reached the deck, Carl's group was directed to the bow of the ship and into the forward cargo hold. Another line of prisoners went to the stern hold.

As he descended the ladder into the darkness, Carl saw that a wooden platform had been constructed four feet above the bottom of the compartment. After reaching the deck, each of the prisoners was ordered to take a sitting position on either the shelf or the deck and to draw their knees up to their chests.

Six hundred prisoners were crammed into the hold before the Japanese decided it was full. The heat in the confined space soon became appalling. Although the hatch cover remained open, there was no air flow and some of the men jammed under the platform began to suffocate.

That evening, the ship slowly steamed away from the dock to an anchorage in the bay. The 1,600 Americans in the holds had been given no food or water since they had marched from Bilibid, and a few began to shriek hysterically in the darkness. Their cries died down as they were comforted by friends.

At dawn, Carl heard the low rumble of the ship's engines as it began to move. Once underway, a hint of hot air began to circulate downward through the open hatch. By then, a number of Americans had died from heat stroke.

They had been steaming for two hours when Carl heard the distant drone of approaching aircraft. A few minutes later, the scream of fighters could be heard as they began diving toward the convoy. Men in the hold started cheering even though they were on the receiving end of the attack. In the distance, Carl could hear deep "whumps" as bombs were dropped on other ships in the convoy.

A piercing torrent of .50-caliber machine gun bullets began tearing into the decks of the *Oryoku Maru* and Carl couldn't remain still any longer. He climbed to the top of the compartment ladder and poked his head above the edge of the hatch. A Japanese lieutenant came charging toward him with his pistol drawn and shouted that if he came farther up the ladder he would be shot.

Before descending again, he saw that the bridge superstructure and the tiers of cabins along the deck were riddled with bullet holes. Two of the other ships in the convoy were on fire and dead in the water.

Back in the hold, Carl heard a crewman above them scream "Banzai!" and he knew that one of the American planes had been shot down. Another rain of machine gun bullets from one of the planes slashed through the deck plates above them, spraying the cargo hold.

Carl felt a sudden stab of pain in his left elbow. With his right hand, he tore a strip of cloth from his shirt and bandaged his flesh wound. Others were more seriously wounded or dead, including Major T. K. MacNair, a West Point friend.

The ship's captain attempted to speed up and elude his attackers, to no avail. When darkness fell, the captain dropped anchor and the crew secured the hatch cover over the cargo hold.

Another night passed in the stifling compartment with no water or food, and many more prisoners died from lack of oxygen or wounds. Soon after the hatch cover was removed again in the morning, Carl heard the sound of returning aircraft followed by the shriek of falling bombs. He felt the ship shudder and shake like it was coming apart when the *Oryoku Maru* absorbed a direct hit.

As the ship began to settle downward, a Japanese officer suddenly appeared at the open cargo hatch. Shouting in English, he called out to abandon ship and ordered the prisoners to leave their gear in the hold. By the time Carl stepped onto the deck, there was blood and chaos everywhere.

The bomb had hit the stern section of the ship, where nearly a thousand Americans were jammed into the rear cargo hold. The survivors were pouring out of the smoking hatch and launching themselves off the side of the ship into the water.

Close to their own hold, Carl saw the bodies of dozens of Japanese women and children lying in neat rows along the deck after being removed from the machine-gunned cabins during the night.

Looking toward shore, he saw that the ship was in Subic Bay near the former American naval base, now on fire from the bomb strikes. The closest shoreline was at least six hundred yards away.

The Japanese had placed a cargo net on the hull of the ship and Carl was able to clamber down it before pushing off into the warm sea in a slow side stroke, using his unbound arm to gain passage. He was about twenty yards from the ship when a flight of five American fighters came in low for another attack. By then, hundreds of prisoners were in the water and desperately trying to make it to shore.

The lead pilot in the formation banked his wings to get a better look as the men frantically waved up at him. The pilot must have recognized who they were because the fighters flew on without attacking the ship again.

Carl was still narrowing the distance to shore when he found himself alongside a Japanese guard paddling in the same direction. Together, they came up on an American lieutenant who was towing one of the chaplains in his arms.

When the lieutenant saw the Japanese guard, he let go of the chaplain and swam smoothly over to him. Grabbing his head, he forced it underwater and held it there until the guard ceased to struggle. When it was over, he swam calmly back to the chaplain to continue their journey. The chaplain made no comment.

A weary Carl finally reached the beach and crept ashore on his hands and knees. Japanese soldiers with machine guns pointed in the direction the men were supposed to go. A half mile inland, he arrived at their new home. It was a single clay tennis court surrounded by a high chain-link fence. The hundreds of survivors were herded into the enclosure.

There was a water spigot in one corner of the court, and he stood in line for another hour to get his first sips of water since leaving Bilibid two days earlier. While he was waiting, he felt a tap on his shoulder and Carl turned to see Ray Bibee, equally haggard but safe and unwounded. He had been in the stern hold when the bomb hit and somehow made it out.

The two friends hugged one another and thanked their maker.

SIXTY

The day after Florence saw Tony Escoda staggering down the cell block corridor, she was summoned before a Japanese military tribunal to stand trial for providing illegal contraband to the American prisoners at Cabanatuan.

Since she had already confessed to the same charge under torture at the Airport Studio, her conviction was a foregone conclusion. The only question was what her sentence would be for the crime.

An hour before the trial, a guard escorted her to a windowless chamber in another prison building. When she arrived, several clerks were sorting paperwork. There was a broad dais at the far end of the chamber with five chairs behind it. The guard motioned her to take a seat at a table in front of the dais.

A few minutes later, a Japanese man in a tropical suit walked into the room. Joining her at the table, he introduced himself as her defense attorney. In his thirties, with an easygoing self-assurance, he spoke fluent English and told her he was a graduate of the Harvard Law School.

She was still considering the absurdity of this notion when a door opened behind the dais and five Japanese officers filed into the room and took their seats. The officer in the middle chair pounded a gavel and said something in Japanese.

Florence stood up and bowed low to the court. One of the clerks began reading from a paper in Japanese and Florence's lawyer whispered that it

250

was a summary of the charges against her. When the clerk finished reading, the judge spoke for less than a minute in Japanese.

"You are found guilty," said her lawyer, getting up from the table.

"What is my sentence?" asked Florence.

"Only three years of hard labor," said the lawyer, smiling.

He shook her hand and wished her luck as the guard came up to take her away. As she was going out the door of the chamber, a male prisoner in shackles was being led inside. The entire trial had taken all of two minutes. Her supposedly Harvard-trained attorney never said a word.

Back in her cell, she resumed the monotonous routine of sitting in either the lotus position or with her knees drawn up to her chest from six thirty in the morning until nine thirty at night. She felt a sense of relief at being given a prison sentence instead of a death sentence, but that vanished when she learned the fate of two other women in her cell.

The two young Filipina girls were sisters and no more than twenty years old. They had already had their trial and been sentenced to two years hard labor. Florence didn't know what they had done but they were accused of aiding a resistance group.

A week after her own trial, they were taken out one morning and didn't return. She was horrified when one of her other cell mates learned through the prison grapevine that they had been beheaded.

On December 18, she was taken to a prison discharge area and placed aboard a truck with several other female prisoners. Over the previous two months, her senses had been dulled by the emotional and physical ordeal, but she still very much wanted to live and could only pray that the truck wasn't taking them to an execution site.

She knew the war was almost over. She only needed to survive a bit longer.

The truck took them east out of the city into the rural countryside. They traveled for miles over bumpy roads before finally arriving at another high-walled complex of buildings. A sign at the gate to the complex read WOMEN'S CORRECTIONAL INSTITUTION: MANDALUYONG.

Inside the prison office, she was issued a burlap dress made from a rice sack and a pair of used sandals. A female official informed her that she was now a military prisoner rather than a provincial prisoner and was there to work at hard labor for the duration of her sentence. Her job would be to grow vegetables in the prison garden. If she attempted to escape, the penalty was death. She was to have no contact with the outside world.

At the end of the interview, Florence was issued a blanket, a soup spoon, and a shovel. The segregated wing for military prisoners turned out to be a circular one-story wooden building with a large open courtyard in the center of it. She was assigned to a cell that had four long benches topped with grass-filled pads. After sleeping on the floor for two months, it looked like heaven.

On her first night, Florence discovered that her heavenly sleeping pad was infested with bed bugs. Finally giving up the battle to sleep, she spent the rest of the night on the floor.

The sentence of hard labor meant working seven days a week, outside under the harsh sun. The work stopped for thirty minutes at midday for lunch in the communal mess hall.

Lunch turned out to be a misleading word. The rice ration was even smaller than the ones they had received at Bilibid, less than half a cup of rice gruel mixed with boiled weeds from the garden.

At her first meal, she saw that there were about forty prisoners in her wing and was happy to discover that Dorothy Fuentes was one of them, along with Maria, the young woman from the wealthy Spanish family.

Dorothy, who had clearly lost weight since leaving Bilibid, confided to Florence that they would starve to death unless they were rescued by the Americans or could bribe a guard for additional food. She added that she had nothing left with which to bribe them.

The vegetable garden consisted of a large plot of dry, stony earth. Florence's job was to turn over the soil with her shovel and prepare the ground for the planting of new seeds. The seedlings had to be watered by hand every day, and the soil was not fertile.

The spinach, *camotes*, and cassava sprouts that had been growing for weeks were stunted and fragile. According to Dorothy, few of the plants survived for harvesting because desperate prisoners risked execution to plunder the garden at night and eat the raw plants and roots.

Lack of food became their greatest threat to survival. Florence was startled at how quickly her energy drained away each day. Since her arrest, she knew she had lost body mass. Still, she was shocked after stepping onto the scale in the prison kitchen one day to find that she now weighed eighty-five pounds.

The minimal rice ration the prisoners received could not compensate for digging most of every day under the sun. At night, her stomach groaned with hunger, but there was nothing she could do about it.

With no ability to contact anyone beyond the prison walls for help, she was on her own. She could only hope that she didn't end up like the skeletons they carried to the outbuilding, called the dead house, near the front gate of the prison.

SIXTY-ONE

All but one of Carl Engelhart's personal possessions now lay at the bottom of Subic Bay in the hull of the sunken *Oryoku Maru*. The most important object he possessed was still with him, even if soaking wet. It was the personal journal he had maintained at Cabanatuan in the steno pad he had carried since Corregidor, including the detailed list of numbers compiled by Pete Pyzick of all the prisoners who had died in the Philippines while in Japanese captivity.

In a corner of the tennis court, he laid out the sodden pages of the journal and waited for them to dry in the sun. He now had many more names of dead friends to add to the list. The POW leaders had taken a new roll call of the survivors from the ship. The total of missing and presumed dead stood at 278, most killed by the bomb that hit the stern cargo hold. Three of them had been Carl's hut mates during his two and a half years at Cabanatuan.

For the next three days, the prisoners stood or sat in the open enclosure under the broiling sun. At night there was only room for each man to sit between the legs of the man behind him. A few dozen men were wounded and given space to lie down. Lieutenant Colonel Jack Schwartz, the senior medical officer from Cabanatuan, attempted to treat them but he had no instruments or medical supplies, and they soon began to die.

The Japanese had given them no food since the sinking, but they had plenty of entertainment. Large formations of American carrier planes returned each day to hammer the Japanese military installations around Subic Bay, sending flames and smoke from the ammunition and fuel dumps high into the sky.

At the end of each attack, a few fighters would veer away to fly over the tennis court, and the pilots would waggle their wings to give the prisoners a small measure of hope that help was on the way.

Their situation became increasingly dire. Carl noted it in his journal.

16 Dec. No food, no clothing. Many men nude, having removed clothing to swim ashore. Suffering from sun in daytime, cold at night.

17 Dec. Received one spoonful of rice grains per man. Ate it raw. Wounded dying.

18 Dec. One spoonful raw rice, ½ spoonful salt. Old Jap underwear issued to naked men.

19 Dec. 1 spoonful raw rice grains. Groups taken out of tennis court for 1 hour under nearby trees.

On December 20, a convoy of trucks arrived to take half the prisoners to the provincial jail in a nearby town. Carl was put in command of this contingent by the senior American officer and he immediately began to organize plans to save his starving men.

First, he found space for the wounded and their doctors. He ordered junior officers to dig latrines in the prison yard and he assigned another group to set up a rude kitchen. Going to the officer in command of the jail, Carl requested in Japanese sufficient cooking pots, fuel, and enough rice and vegetables to feed his men. The young officer was intrigued by this half-naked scarecrow talking his own language and complied with the requests.

Carl appointed one of his captains, Will Bianchi, to run the kitchen. Bianchi had been remarkably resourceful in helping his fellow prisoners at Cabanatuan, and had become known as the Great Samaritan. During the Battle of Bataan, Bianchi had earned the Congressional Medal of Honor for personally destroying two enemy machine gun positions while sustaining three serious wounds.

On the morning of December 21, Bianchi and his kitchen team produced the first cooked meal of rice and vegetables the prisoners had enjoyed since boarding the *Oryoku Maru* more than a week earlier. He repeated the feat that same evening.

The good times didn't last.

At three in the morning on Christmas Eve, Carl was awakened by a Japanese officer and was told that his men would be leaving on a freight train for the coastal town of San Fernando. There, they would board another ship headed to Japan.

The 679 men were divided into three boxcars, with the wounded prisoners riding on the roofs. A Japanese officer sarcastically told Carl that the men on the roofs were welcome to wave at any attacking American fighters.

Arriving at San Fernando, the men disembarked from the boxcars and were marched to the port area. There, they were reunited with the men from the tennis court who had been convoyed to a separate jail to avoid overcrowding. Another roll call yielded the fact that there were now 1,071 men remaining from the original 1,620 that had sailed on the *Oryoku Maru*.

Before dawn on December 27, the men boarded a ship named *Enoura Maru*, which was bound for the Chinese island of Formosa, the next stage of the voyage to Japan. Once again they were jammed into the ship's three cargo holds.

Carl descended the ladder into the middle hold to discover that its previous occupants had been a troop of horses. A thick layer of excrement-covered straw coated the deck and the reek was overpowering. Wooden buckets were passed down to the men to use for their own waste and the hatch cover was sealed tight.

The temperature in the compartment rose alarmingly quickly until a doctor with a thermometer called out that it had reached 135 degrees. With the hatch cover closed, there was no light for the doctors to treat the wounded.

Risking the wrath of the Japanese officer in command, Carl climbed the ladder and pounded on the underside of the hatch cover, demanding in Japanese that they remove it before the men suffocated. Japanese crewmen finally detached the wooden covers, but not before several more men had died.

As daylight paled the sky each morning, the newly dead were carried to the foot of the compartment ladder and hoisted in a cargo net to the deck of the ship, where the Japanese dumped them overboard. At the end of each day, the men received their food ration; a few tablespoons of rice along with four ounces of foul drinking water for each man.

The wooden buckets overflowed with human waste and more than half the men came down with dysentery. Others were so dehydrated they fell unconscious.

The nights were beyond imagination; scenes of living hell. Some of the starving men became hysterical, screaming out incoherent diatribes and attacking fellow prisoners with mess kit knives, attempting to drink their blood. Other prisoners were forced to physically immobilize them.

The *Enoura Maru* finally reached Takao Harbor on the southern coast of Formosa. Once anchored, the men waited to be brought up from the holds, but the Japanese officer in command did not appear. They stayed in the compartment for a full week, subsisting on the spoonfuls of rice and brackish water while more of them died.

The prisoners had no way of knowing that January 9 was the date MacArthur had chosen to invade Luzon. To prevent reinforcement from Formosa, every port and every ship on the southern coast was targeted by American carrier planes.

The distant buzz of engines grew steadily louder as American fighters and bombers approached Takao Harbor to deliver a mortal blow. The men trapped in the three cargo holds could only pray for deliverance from the falling bombs.

In the next ten minutes, the *Enoura Maru* absorbed three direct hits.

As one bomb exploded amidships, Carl looked up to see the heavy steel cross beams that supported the hatch cover blasted down into the compartment, killing and wounding dozens of men. Metal splinters from the bomb sprayed death in every direction.

The air in the hold was suddenly filled with a cloud of straw-packed horse manure. When it finally settled down, Carl took in the full extent of the disaster. A marine master sergeant sitting near him looked uninjured except that his left eyeball hung halfway down his cheek. Another officer groaned as he stared down at his missing leg.

Luck had finally run out for Captain Will Bianchi, the Congressional Medal of Honor recipient who had survived the Bataan death march and the sinking of the *Oryoku Maru*. He was killed instantly, like so many others.

Carl sustained a superficial chest wound. Trying to help the more seriously wounded in the semidarkness, he could see that the steel bulkhead separating the forward and middle cargo holds had been ripped open like tin foil.

An officer went to look through the torn bulkhead into the forward hold. A bomb had penetrated the upper deck and exploded inside the compartment. Hundreds of men lay mangled and dead.

Moments later, the wounded survivors began screaming in agony.

SIXTY-TWO

To confront General MacArthur's invasion, General Tomoyuki Yamashita had initially deployed thirty-six thousand troops to meet the American invaders on the beaches. He was forced to reconsider the decision after learning that the Japanese air force was too depleted to attack the battleships and heavy cruisers in the invasion force. Yamashita knew how devastating the American artillery fire would be to his men on the beaches and he withdrew them.

As the American fleet drew closer, waves of kamikaze planes attacked the armada; the suicide pilots sank or damaged forty warships. It was a punishing blow but only a small fraction of MacArthur's firepower, and by the time his forces arrived at Lingayen Gulf, the kamikazes were temporarily spent.

Yamashita decided to concentrate his army in three provinces of Luzon. The first and largest disposition of 160,000 troops was made in the mountain ranges east of the landing beaches. Concentrated above Luzon's central plain, he hoped to attack MacArthur's land forces as they moved south.

A second army group was deployed to defend Clark Field. Yamashita knew that if MacArthur could capture it, the American air force would soon dominate the skies everywhere in Luzon. He deployed his third army group to the south near Manila. Although he recognized that the capital

259

was strategically worthless, he hoped to engage the American army from both north and south before it reached the city.

At dawn on January 9, American carrier planes attacked a wide range of military targets in Luzon, including Manila and Clark Field, as well as the key target of Takao Harbor in Formosa. The navy pilots sank or damaged every ship in the anchorage, including the *Enoura Maru*.

Prior to his troops landing, MacArthur's battleships and heavy cruisers blasted every potential target within two miles of the beaches. After the barrage ended, the first sixty thousand men stormed ashore. Four hours later, MacArthur followed them.

As he rode toward the beach in his motor launch, he remembered his earlier landing during the Leyte invasion and the dramatic photograph of him wading ashore that had appeared in almost every newspaper in the States. This time his staff arranged for navy Seabees using bulldozers to construct a small jetty extending out from the beach that would allow him to land without wetting his pants.

MacArthur would have none of it. Telling the boat captain to stop, he stepped off the launch into the calm surf and waded up to the beach in front of the phalanx of news photographers.

Safely ashore, his first communiqué from Luzon was broadcast to the world.

```
The decisive battle for the liberation of the
Philippines . . . is at hand. General MacArthur
is in personal command at the front and landed
with his assault troops.
```

MacArthur's hunger for self-glorification could not erase the fact that he had crafted a superb plan for defeating Yamashita's defense forces. It was as if he had divined Yamashita's intentions and dispositions before the Japanese general even made them.

Unlike Leyte, the battle for Luzon went incredibly quickly as MacArthur drove his commanders relentlessly toward his ultimate goal of freeing

Manila. He moved so swiftly that a flank attack from Yamashita's main forces in the mountains never took place.

Early on, he felt his battle commanders were still advancing too slowly. At considerable personal risk, MacArthur moved his headquarters thirty miles forward of the main battle line, goading his commanders not to linger.

In every town, he was greeted by crowds of loyal Filipinos as a conquering hero. Young girls draped his jeep with flowers and hung even more garlands around his neck. MacArthur later wrote, "It embarrassed me [to] no end."

Saving Manila was uppermost in his mind, and he issued orders to launch a daring drive for the capital with a small mobile force, comparing it to the end runs that Confederate General Jeb Stuart was famous for pulling off in the American Civil War. Manila was now only a hundred miles away.

His exact words to the commander of the 1st Cavalry Division were, "Go to Manila. Go around the Nips, bounce off the Nips, but go to Manila. Free the internees at Santo Tomás. Take Malacañang Palace and the Legislative Building."

Even more dazzling thrusts quickly followed.

Clark Field fell to the Americans on January 23. They now controlled the air.

With his forces moving steadily south down the Luzon plain, he undertook another amphibious landing on January 29, just three weeks into the invasion. A full army corps went ashore near Subic Bay on the western coast of Luzon, just sixty miles north of Manila. They captured the port without a single casualty and headed south.

MacArthur also ordered a rescue team of army rangers and Filipino guerrillas to attempt to save the remaining American prisoners at Cabanatuan Camp No. 1. The Japanese commander there had received orders to execute all five hundred remaining prisoners if the Americans drew near.

The rescue team penetrated the Japanese lines and traveled thirty miles to the camp without being discovered. On the night of January 30, they launched the raid and freed the prisoners still held at Cabanatuan because they were too ill to work as slave laborers. The rescue team was able to lead or carry all the prisoners back thirty miles through the Japanese lines to safety.

MacArthur landed another mobile force at Mariveles on the southern tip of the Bataan Peninsula, cutting off the Japanese troops on Corregidor and defeating the remaining Japanese on Bataan in just seven days.

On January 31, MacArthur ordered a third amphibious landing forty miles south of Manila. Ten thousand paratroopers landed ashore to join the attack on the capital from three different directions.

On the night of February 3, forward elements of the 1st Cavalry Division broke through the Japanese defense lines north of Manila and streaked toward the Santo Tomas internment camp.

Dolores Gardner was with Bob Hendry in his canvas hut on the grounds of the university when they heard the rapid bark of automatic rifle fire followed by exploding hand grenades as a vicious battle erupted outside the prison walls.

The firefight continued in the darkness. Suddenly, five American tanks burst through the stone perimeter walls and drove the remaining Japanese defenders inside one of the university buildings. The four thousand American and British civilians who had survived since January 1942 were finally free.

On February 4, forward units of the 37th Division fought their way against ferocious resistance to the walls of Bilibid prison. After two days of hand-to-hand combat, resistance finally collapsed and 1,300 American and Filipino prisoners were freed from its cells and torture chambers.

MacArthur had triumphed. Only one step remained and that was his victory parade through the streets of Manila at the head of his forces. He had gambled that Yamashita would declare Manila an open city, just as he had done in 1941, to avoid civilian casualties and because it had no strategic importance.

He waited for the news that the American flag was again flying over Malacañang Palace.

SIXTY-THREE

Florence knew she was finally dying. With the passage of each day, she could feel the life draining out of her. She collapsed one afternoon while trying to wield her shovel in the rocky soil of the garden. Seeing her condition, a prison trusty relieved her of regular work duties. But lying in her bedbug-infested cot, she steadily lost strength and was only able to summon the energy to get to the chamber pot.

During her waking hours, Florence listened to the roar of the warplanes flying overhead, the dull pounding thuds of the anti-aircraft batteries trying to shoot them down, and the piercing shrieks of falling bombs exploding in the distance.

Dorothy Fuentes came by one afternoon to cheer her up. She was in the midst of assuring Florence they would soon be rescued when rifle shots rang out from the grounds of the adjacent hospital. They heard the crack of several more volleys before it was quiet again.

Later that day, a Filipino guard confided to Dorothy that Japanese soldiers had marched into the hospital and ordered the American and British patients outside into the courtyard. There, they were all shot.

Florence still believed rescue would come, but could only wonder if she would be alive to see it. She hadn't weighed herself on the scale in the kitchen for many days, but it no longer mattered. The results spoke for themselves. A familiar expression kept repeating in her mind. *Skin and bones. Skin and bones.*

Florence had also done something terrible, and she felt deeply ashamed.

None of the prisoners were supposed to have contact with the outside world, but it soon became clear that the regulation was not enforced with every prisoner. Maria, the young Spanish woman from a wealthy Manila family, had bribed a senior guard to contact her mother. When her mother came to the prison, she was allowed to give her daughter a large basket of provisions. Maria stored them under her cot in the cell she shared with Dorothy.

Maria used a small portion of the food to hire a fellow prisoner to do her work in the garden while she "supervised" her. It caused serious resentment, but there was nothing the other prisoners could do. Maria had the complicit support of the prison authorities, who were receiving substantial bribes.

Maria's personality seemed to change overnight. It was as if she were no longer a prisoner, but the child of privilege she had been before the war. She made it clear to her cell mates that she had no intention of sharing her newfound bounty with them or anyone else.

A few days later, Florence surrendered to overwhelming temptation. Once she made her decision, she went forward, waiting until Maria was outside in the garden supervising the other prisoner.

Slipping inside her empty cell, Florence pulled Maria's hoard out from under her cot. Most of the provisions were in their original packages. Maria would certainly notice if she stole one of them. There was also a wooden bowl under the cot that contained newly cut chunks of fresh meat from a coconut. Grabbing one of the pieces, she shoved the rest of the food back under the cot.

Back in her cell, she wolfed down the coconut meat. Within moments of finishing it, she felt deeply ashamed. The sliver of coconut would not make a serious difference to her survival, but it violated the values that guided her life. Regardless of what happened from then on, she vowed she wouldn't steal food again.

On February 8, Florence awoke to the third anniversary of Bing's death. Since her arrest and torture at the Airport Studio, she found it harder to remember his face. So much had happened since he had left her.

His spirit and courage had been an ongoing source of emotional strength, but it was now ebbing away. Food became her sole obsession, born from the desperate hunger that gnawed away inside like it was consuming her.

Their rice ration had already been cut twice since she arrived. They were now receiving two spoonfuls of thin rice gruel in the morning, a spoonful of rice with a small topping of boiled greens or weeds at noon, and a half cup of watered-down rice at five.

One afternoon Dorothy came to her cell and brought a miracle. With a grin, she handed Florence a small, paper-wrapped parcel. When Florence opened it, she almost swooned. It was half an egg sandwich. She had no idea where it came from, but didn't take the time to ask. She finished it in less than a minute. For the first time in weeks, her stomach stopped groaning but the abrupt jolt to her digestive tract led to a round of diarrhea.

The aerial bombing continued every day and the smell of the smoke from the fires over Manila became an irritant to breathing. On February 10, Florence was lying in her cell when someone in the courtyard screamed, "Soldiers . . . Soldiers!"

She could only assume it meant the end and that Japanese soldiers were coming to execute them, as they had done to the American and British patients at the nearby hospital. Weeks earlier, Dorothy had showed her a storage closet off the kitchen where they could hide if the Japanese came, but Florence was too weak to try to reach it.

There were more shouts, and then she heard the single word of deliverance.

"Americans," someone cried out.

Slowly getting up from her cot, she made her way out into the courtyard. The sight of soldiers in American army uniforms reduced her to uncontrollable tears. Smiling and confident, the Americans strolled across the compound with their rifles held across their chests. Most of them were as tall and rugged as Bing.

Florence watched as Dorothy kissed one soldier and then cried her own tears of joy. Another American came toward Florence. Seeing her condition, he pulled a chocolate bar out of his pocket and gave it to her, warning her not to eat it all at once.

The Americans were from the 1st Cavalry Division and led by Lieutenant Colonel Charles Young of El Paso, Texas. Gathering the remaining female prisoners together, he told them that the Japanese had mined the approaches to the prison but they had staked out a safe path to the truck waiting on the nearby highway. Florence told him she wasn't sure she could walk that far, but the soldier who had given her the chocolate said he would carry her.

When they reached the truck, Colonel Young told the women he was planning to take them to Santo Tomas. Florence was momentarily confused. She couldn't understand why they had to go to another prison camp until he explained that Santo Tomas had been freed a week earlier and was now in American hands.

In a state of quiet euphoria, Florence and Dorothy rode south toward Manila in the open truck, following the colonel's jeep. It was slow going because the roadways were choked with convoys of tanks and trucks filled with soldiers.

Once inside the city, she was horrified to see the extent of the destruction that had taken place during the fighting. Whole city blocks were no more than bombed-out cavities in the earth. The stately trees that had lined the boulevards were burned trunks without fronds or branches. Fires still raged throughout the heart of Manila and she could hear the sounds of machine guns near the Intramuros.

Corpses littered the sidewalks, a few Japanese soldiers but mostly Filipino civilians. Many of the bodies were hideously bloated from having lain there for days. The smell of death hung in the air.

When they finally reached the Santo Tomas campus, more American soldiers were guarding the perimeter and the British and American internees were roaming free inside. It was one of the few safe zones in the city and a crowd of civilians had gathered near the gates, seeking protection.

After their truck came to a stop in the compound, an exhausted Florence was carried in the arms of the soldier to the medical clinic. The first examination by a doctor revealed her weight to be seventy-eight pounds, forty-seven less than she had weighed before entering the Airport Studio. She told the doctor she hadn't menstruated for almost six months.

Florence asked one of the nurses if an American prisoner named Bob Hendry was still alive and the nurse promised to check. An hour later, Florence was savoring a second glass of chocolate milk when Dolores and Bob appeared in the doorway of the clinic. Bursting into tears, Dolores rushed to enfold Florence in her arms. When they both stopped crying, Dolores could only repeat that it was a miracle. After Florence disappeared, she had reluctantly assumed her friend had been executed.

Bob told Florence that food and medical supplies were pouring in every day since their liberation and life would soon return to normal. Dolores invited Florence to live with them in Bob's canvas-walled shack on the grounds of the campus until the Battle of Manila was over.

It sounded like paradise.

SIXTY-FOUR

Kiyoshi Osawa barely clung to life.

In his rare moments of consciousness, he wondered if he would live. If he did live, would he ever be able to walk again?

The nightmare began on the morning he had called his senior staff into his office to tell them that MacArthur's forces would soon reach the outskirts of Manila and would eventually capture the city.

"Round up as much food and personal belongings as you can carry. Don't forget rubber bands to stop the bleeding of a wound . . . you may have to live for some time in the mountains."

The American air attacks were now coming every day and night and he no longer traveled to his home nestled above the Wack Wack Club. He ate all his meals at the Manila Hotel, where General MacArthur had lived in the penthouse before the war, and slept each night on his office conference table with a large mosquito net spread above him.

As the Americans drew closer, he ordered the fuel union office files burned in the incinerator behind the building and prepared to join the exodus of Japanese military to their mountain stronghold at Baguio.

His final responsibility as head of the fuel union was to organize a sixteen-vehicle convoy of oil tankers and delivery trucks to transport the remaining stocks of liquid fuel to the Japanese army garrison 150 miles to the north. Due to the speed of the American advance, he knew it would

268

be a dangerous undertaking. Aside from the American army, guerrilla resistance groups might ambush him along the way.

It was slow going from the moment they set out. Every time Osawa heard the roar of American aircraft, he ordered the caravan of vehicles to find temporary refuge under the canopy of the trees lining the road.

They had gone only forty miles when Osawa learned that a vital bridge they needed to cross had been destroyed and would require several days to repair. If the lightly armed convoy was discovered in the meantime, the fuel would probably be captured by the Americans or the guerrillas. He reluctantly decided to turn the convoy around and head south to find protection among Japanese military units. By then, night had fallen and the unlit highway was shrouded in darkness. Osawa's sedan car brought up the rear.

The convoy was further slowed by thousands of Filipino civilians who had fled Manila with their families to escape the fighting and now clogged the highway. In the chaotic melee, Osawa's tanker convoy soon became separated.

Around midnight, the veiled headlights of Osawa's car came upon a truck that had driven off the road into a ditch. It was one of his, and heavily loaded with fifty-gallon oil drums vital to the Japanese army.

Osawa collected a group of Japanese soldiers from the other military transport vehicles to pull the truck from the ditch. With the truck driver accelerating in reverse gear, the soldiers pushed from the front and sides.

Osawa was standing by the rear as the truck suddenly freed itself from the ditch and roared backward. Losing his balance in the darkness, Osawa fell under one of its massive rear tires. After it rolled over his thighs, the wheel dragged him along the rocky ground for another fifteen feet.

The soldiers pulled him from under the truck and laid him on his back. Although the lower half of his body was completely numb, Osawa could feel the warmth of his blood coursing down onto his hands from his mutilated thighs.

Looking up at the dark sky, he saw a red star in the heavens. With the fatalism that had always defined his life, he resolved that if he was dying, it would be with a clear conscience. His only regret was that he would never again see his wife Katsuko, his daughter, and the son he had yet to meet.

"Bind my thighs," he called out to one of the soldiers.

Rubber bands wouldn't help here. The soldier found two leather belts and buckled them tightly above the wounds.

Another man in Osawa's convoy had been the branch manager of one of his fuel stations and was a superb driver. Osawa asked him to drive straight to the Philippine General Hospital in Manila where Osawa's personal physician, Dr. Antonio Sison, maintained his practice.

While a soldier kept Osawa's legs suspended in the air in the back seat, they set out on the traffic-choked road for the hospital. As the shock of his injuries wore off, the pain became unbearable. The shooting jolts of raw agony caused him to scream aloud.

In moments of lucidity, he called out, "Where are we now?"

Mercifully, he fell unconscious for most of the journey. When the vehicle reached the hospital, Osawa was carried to an operating room. His personal physician couldn't be found, but a young Filipino surgeon named Ambrosio Tanco examined the extent of his injuries under the bright overhead lights in the surgical theater.

Osawa's khaki trousers had been ground into his flesh along with small rocks and dirt from being dragged under the wheel of the truck. Dr. Tanco put him under general anesthesia and his surgical team worked for four and a half hours to cut away the trousers from inside his legs, to clean the deep wounds, and to reconnect the strands of his nerve fibers.

After completing the operation, Tanco thought Osawa's prospects for survival were dim. Apart from the loss of blood and the risk of infection in the surgical field, the man's thighs had been literally crushed to the bone.

While Osawa slept fitfully under the potency of a morphine drip, the American army captured his truck convoy, which carried the last of the Japanese army's fuel reserves.

SIXTY-FIVE

The American prisoners who survived the final leg of the journey from Formosa to Japan called it the final voyage to hell. Carl Engelhart recorded the day-by-day conditions aboard the ship in his personal journal.

13 Jan. Joined convoy. Began twisting course to Japan through the Okinawas and Ryukyu Islands. Weather very cold. Men dying. Average meal ⅓ cup of rice, less than 3 oz. of water. Usually one issue of water, frequently none, frequently salt sea water.

Of the 1,620 Cabanatuan prisoners who had boarded the *Oryoku Maru* on December 13, nearly three hundred had died by the time it was bombed and sunk in Subic Bay. Another four hundred men died in the forward hold of the *Enoura Maru.*

The survivors were forced to lie with their dead companions for three days before the Japanese removed the decomposing corpses in cargo nets and dumped them over the side. Carl watched as the first net swung up from the cargo deck. In the entangled pile of bodies, he recognized the faces of several of his friends and broke down in tears.

On the third day, the prisoners were finally allowed to climb out of the blood-soaked holds. They were immediately transferred in a motor launch to another freighter named the *Brazil Maru*. The following evening it embarked for Japan.

The weather turned very cold. The nearly naked men in the damp and freezing holds had no blankets and they huddled together to conserve body warmth. At dawn each morning, those who had died during the night were carried to the center of the cargo deck for removal in the cargo net. The heap of bodies was never less than six men and often more than twenty-five. They died from lack of food and water, exposure, wounds, and chronic dysentery.

One of the camp chaplains at Cabanatuan was a charismatic and caring Roman Catholic priest named William Cummings. In the camp, he never stopped ministering to those in need. Each day during the voyage of the *Brazil Maru* he performed a service for the dead. In the evening, he delivered a closing prayer to the men in the darkness.

Carl found himself deeply affected by his eloquent words and sought out Father Cummings to tell him that his prayers had given him more spiritual comfort than any he had ever received in his life. The worn-out Cummings thanked him as he lay down to sleep. He passed away that same night and in the morning was hauled up with the other dead in the cargo net to be slung overboard.

The men shared their stories about Father Cumming's bravery at Cabanatuan and a number credited him with saving their lives. No one else took up the job of leading the evening prayer, but it didn't stop the men from praying for their own deliverance.

On January 29, the *Brazil Maru* arrived at the port of Moji on the island of Kyushu, Japan. During the two-week voyage, five hundred more men perished in the icy and filthy holds.

When the men from the two cargo holds assembled together on the dock, Carl was happy to see that his closest friend Ray Bibee had made it through. Now gaunt skeletons, he and Ray vowed to try to help one another make it to the end of the war, whatever came next.

At the pier in Moji, the enlisted men were separated from the officers and told they were being sent to a labor camp to serve the emperor. The prisoners who couldn't walk due to injuries and wounds were taken away in trucks, although no one knew where.

The last two hundred officers from Cabanatuan were issued overcoats and after a night on a blacked-out railroad train arrived at Fukuoka Camp No. 1. It was bitterly cold as the prisoners marched to the camp and were assigned to different barracks buildings.

A group of British prisoners, most of them veterans of the Burma defeat in 1941, welcomed them to their new home and gave them some hard-learned lessons about surviving in the cold.

There was a small iron stove in each barracks, but it barely heated the frigid air. The British showed the Americans how to fold their blankets so there was a thick layer underneath and another layer covering their bodies like a cocoon, leaving only a small hole for breathing.

The day after their arrival, the Americans were deloused with a fumigating spray and then assembled to compile an official roster. Each man was weighed, and Carl was appalled to see that he was now just eighty-five pounds, a bit more than half his regular weight of one hundred and sixty.

In his first days at the new camp, he became progressively weaker. He found he could no longer lift his feet when he walked, dragging them along as if crippled. Late one night he was outside on his way to the latrine when he tripped over a tree root and fell facedown on the frozen ground. As hard as he tried, he could not raise himself up. He was still lying there when another prisoner found him. The man was too weak to lift him, but he went for help, and four men got him back to the barracks.

The saving grace at this camp turned out to be the food supply. Each morning the men were given a cup of *lugao*, a soft rice mush flavored with greens or small fish heads. It was far more substantial than what they had survived on in the hell ships, and the prisoners received a second offering of *lugao* in the evening. Drinking water was also plentiful.

If the double food ration continued, Carl thought he could regain some of his strength. The greatest threat was the bitter cold. The weakened men couldn't be outside more than ten minutes without feeling the effects of hypothermia. Many of the officers remained under their blankets day and night.

With time on his hands, Carl recorded the names of the dozens of friends he had lost since Cabanatuan in his journal and the torments they had endured. As a lark, he wrote down the dates and descriptions of his six wounds. It struck him that the score was now five to one: five on the left side and one on the right.

Ray Bibee had been assigned to a different barracks, but Carl saw him every day after breakfast. On one frigid morning, Carl went to have their regular tête-à-tête and found him dead under his blanket. Carl knew Ray had been steadily weakening, but thought the additional food ration would bring him back. He had paid the ultimate price when the stove in his barracks went out during the night.

For Carl, Ray's death was the closing chapter of all that had happened since the Japanese had invaded the Philippines. Ray had survived the battle of Bataan, the infamous seventy-mile death march without food or water, nearly three years in Cabanatuan, and the voyages of the three hell ships, only to die from the cold of a Japanese winter.

Carl removed the ring from Ray's finger that had been fashioned by a camp artisan at Bilibid from a silver peso. His gold wedding ring had been traded years earlier to a Japanese guard for food he needed to survive.

The camp artisan at Bilibid had fashioned the ring by tapping the edge of the coin with a stone until it was flattened out equally all the way around. He had then drilled the center of it to fit Ray's finger.

Carl pledged that if he made it back home, he would personally deliver the ring to Ray's young widow.

SIXTY-SIX

The rattle of gunfire and the crump of explosions greeted Florence's every return to wakefulness, but she reveled in the fact that she was finally safe and with friends. For the first time in three years, she slept without fear in Bob Hendry's canvas-walled shanty on the campus. She remained awake long enough to enjoy the simple meals prepared by Dolores and then went back to sleep.

While she slowly recovered, the savage fight for Manila raged outside the walls.

General Douglas MacArthur had assumed that General Yamashita would not fight for Manila since it had no strategic importance to either side. He was correct in that assumption, but there was another factor he didn't anticipate.

Before withdrawing his troops from the city, Yamashita gave explicit orders to Admiral Sanji Iwabuchi, who commanded a rear guard of sixteen thousand Japanese marines and other naval personnel, to blow up the port facilities and then publicly declare Manila an undefended and open city to minimize civilian casualties before following the army north.

The fanatical Iwabuchi disobeyed Yamashita's orders and resolved to defend the city to the last man. He ordered his marines to erect barricades in every neighborhood using barbed wire, land mines, furniture, oil drums,

275

trucks, and streetcars. Each defensive position was manned with automatic weapons, hand grenades, flame throwers, and mortars.

Manila's major public buildings became ramparts for sand-bagged machine gun nests, and Iwabuchi ordered that the windows and entrances be honeycombed with snipers, every man ready to fight to the death.

Knowing that the Intramuros was the best natural defensive position in the city, Iwabuchi ordered thousands of his marines to dig in behind the twenty-five-foot-thick walls that encircled its ancient stone buildings and churches. The ten thousand civilians living in the Intramuros were to be used as hostages.

In the bastion of Fort Santiago, hundreds of Filipino prisoners suspected of guerrilla activity were still confined in the dungeon cells desperately hoping for release by the Americans as the battle raged beyond the walls. One day, they were brought up and taken outside into a courtyard. Their prayers for deliverance were met by armed and merciless Japanese marines standing near metal fuel drums. Helpless and horrified, they could only scream as they were drenched with gasoline and set afire.

For the Japanese marines, death was their only future, and the contagion of inflicting pain before they died spread through their ranks as the American troops advanced into the capital. Building by building, floor by floor, room by room, street by street, the battle for Manila was fought out.

One million Filipino civilians were trapped in the city and the Japanese would not permit them to leave. Direct orders were issued from Iwabuchi's staff for how they were to be dealt with.

```
All people on the battlefield with the
exception of Japanese military personnel,
Japanese civilians, and special construction
units will be put to death. . . . When Filipinos
are to be killed, they must be gathered into
one place and disposed of with the
consideration that ammunition and manpower must
```

```
not be used to excess. Because the disposal of
dead bodies is a troublesome task, they should
be gathered into houses which are scheduled to
be burned or demolished.
```

His marines responded with fanatical determination.

Four hundred civilians who lived near St. Paul's College were rounded up under the guise of protecting them from danger. The Japanese herded them into a dining hall, which was already rigged with dynamite, and detonated the explosives. Those few who survived the slaughter were murdered by bayonet.

Another marine unit attacked the International Red Cross building and bayoneted or beheaded everyone there, most of them women and children. At the Manila German Club, five hundred civilians had gathered inside to escape the fighting. The Japanese poured gasoline on the furniture and rugs and set the building on fire. No one survived.

The Bayview Hotel was designated by the Japanese marines as their rape center. Hundreds of women were brought there after a roundup in the city's wealthiest neighborhoods. There they were repeatedly raped. Some of the women were sexually mutilated before they were killed.

Thousands of other atrocities went unrecorded because they involved victims in individual homes and small churches where people had come together for mutual protection. The rampaging marines broke down the doors and butchered everyone they found.

The American army was powerless to stop the indiscriminate slaughter. They could only move to eliminate the Japanese defensive positions street by street, often in brutal hand-to-hand fighting.

———

Santo Tomas was an oasis in the sea of carnage.

On the campus grounds, combat engineers constructed a vast white screen to display projected information about what was happening in the war along with other public announcements. At night, they began showing Hollywood movies.

Accompanied by the crump of artillery explosions, Florence watched her first performance of "Rhapsody in Blue" by George Gershwin. The music was a blessing. Its haunting melodies became her favorite piece for the rest of her life.

In late February, Bob Hendry received a letter from his wife in the States saying that they were no longer married. She had divorced him in the middle of the war, but there had been no way to let him know. Now free to marry Dolores, Bob formally proposed to her on one knee and they celebrated their engagement with Florence over a dinner of roast Spam.

As Florence regained her strength, she began walking three times a day around the grounds of the sprawling campus. Crowds of women and children stood several feet deep outside the walls, each of them shoving empty containers between the iron bars and begging for food or clean water. The American troops did their best to supply them, but the numbers were too great. Her heart went out to them, but Florence knew that only the end of the fighting would allow relief convoys to enter the city.

The smell of war was even more horrible than the sound of it. Tens of thousands of decomposing corpses now lay everywhere in the city under the pitiless sun, and the odor of death wrapped around them in the air like a physical thing. She could only wonder what had happened to Norma, Jerry, and Bobby Delmar, and prayed that they had survived the holocaust.

The section of Manila north of the Pasig River was secured first. South of the river, the battle went on for weeks. By the end of February, resistance was limited to the Intramuros with its thousands of hostages.

Loudspeakers were employed outside the walls to assure the Japanese marines in their own language that if they surrendered, they would be honorably treated as prisoners of war. Few of them came out.

When it was finally over, there was no victory parade for General MacArthur, no waving to cheering crowds from a convertible. There was no city left to hold the parade. The ancient buildings in the Intramuros had been destroyed along with the Manila business district and three-quarters of the residential neighborhoods south of the river.

The sixteen thousand Japanese defenders had been wiped out along with the one hundred thousand civilians they had murdered, most of them women and children. Thousands more had perished in the cross fire between the Japanese and the Americans.

The journalists who wrote about the slaughter called it the Manila Massacre.

SIXTY-SEVEN

FEBRUARY 21, 1945
CITY ICE AND FUEL COMPANY
MECHANIC STREET, BUFFALO, NEW YORK

Mabelle Ebersole Lewis was at her desk in the office when the telegram arrived. It was addressed to her in care of the City Ice and Fuel Company and it was from the Provost Marshal General's office of the US Army in Washington, DC. She slit open the envelope and pulled out the telegram.

AM PLEASED TO INFORM YOU THAT INFORMATION RECEIVED INDICATES THE RESCUE BY OUR FORCES OF FLORENCE EBERSOLE SMITH STOP. YOU MAY SEND FREE THROUGH AMERICAN PRISONER OF WAR INFORMATION BUREAU THIS OFFICE ONE ONLY TWENTY FIVE WORD MESSAGE STOP.
    LERCH PROVOST MARSHAL GENERAL

"My God," said Mabelle to her coworkers, "she's alive."

The last news from Florence had been a letter received more than three years earlier in November 1941. Florence had written that she was newly married and the letter included a wedding picture of her with Bing.

The day after the attack on Pearl Harbor, Mabelle had written Florence to say she had heard on the radio that Manila was also being bombed and to please write to let her know that she and her husband were safe. When

280

the envelope came back marked "undeliverable" and there was no further word as the years passed, she had feared the worst.

Life had gone on during the war as it did in every family with relatives overseas in harm's way. Cut off by war, Mabelle could only wait to find out what had happened to them and pray for their deliverance.

In the meantime, she tracked the movement across the Pacific by MacArthur and Nimitz and the vast forces they led with colored pins on a map of the Pacific she kept current on the kitchen wall.

Mabelle raised her daughter Norma and doted on her two grandchildren, Paul and Carol Ann, along with Leah, the daughter of her older sister May, and Leah's sons with her husband, Charles Tillotson. As the war dragged on, their oldest boy Rodger decided to serve and by 1945 was a lieutenant in the army. Charles Jr. was still at home and in high school.

When the news came that Florence was alive and freed from captivity, Mabelle was in the process of separating from her husband. Her immediate thought was that Florence should come to Buffalo and move in with her.

SIXTY-EIGHT

Florence felt stronger with the arrival of each new day. The battle for Manila was over, but she and the Hendrys remained on the grounds of the university because they had no other place to go. That was when Florence received some stunning news.

It arrived in the form of a handwritten message brought to Bob Hendry's shanty. The message was from Norma and it said she was outside the gates of Santo Tomas, but the American guards wouldn't let her inside.

An overjoyed Florence ran through the compound and out into the throng beyond the front gate. Scanning the faces in every direction, she finally saw Norma coming toward her and moments later they were in each other's arms.

The reunion was what Florence had been praying for every day since she had recovered from her own ordeal. They found a quiet place to talk and Norma told her of the terrible days and nights she had borne with Jerry and Bobby as Japanese marines roamed through the Tondo neighborhood, murdering everyone they encountered.

Norma had tried to barricade the alley door to their basement apartment by wedging it closed with a piece of furniture. She knew the Japanese had arrived when she heard a door being smashed open upstairs. It was followed by the sound of boots pounding across the floor and then continuous screaming that suddenly stopped. More screams erupted as they broke into the other apartments in the building.

Norma waited in terror for the alley door to be smashed in, but nothing happened. She heard more shouting and screaming from the house next door and then it was quiet again. Apparently, they had missed seeing the entrance.

An hour later, she thought it might be safe to go outside. Leaving Jerry and Bobby in their bed, she climbed the stairs and removed the furniture blocking the door. Outside was a scene of horror.

The young mother who had lived upstairs was lying on the ground with her toddler. They lay entwined in a pool of blood, both of them knifed or bayoneted to death. Looking up the street, she saw a dozen more corpses of men, women, and children lying where they fell.

A disoriented woman came toward her from one of the buildings across the street. She had been at her window when the Japanese swept through the neighborhood armed with swords and rifles, and had watched as they broke down the doors of each house and went inside. In a minute or two they would come out again and move on to the next building. The woman's husband had hidden her in a crawl space just before the Japanese arrived at their apartment. When she heard them leave, she thought he might have been spared. She had come out to find her husband lying beheaded on the floor.

A few hours later, a small American truck convoy brought relief supplies to the Tondo district and Norma was able to feed Jerry and Bobby for the first time in days. One of the soldiers told her that the Japanese troops had moved south of the Pasig River and she decided to try to reach the apartment of Jose Delmar's sister, Salud, which was close to the University of Santo Tomas. When she found the row house, it was still undamaged and Salud happily took them in. Of Jose, there had been no word. Like so many thousands of others, he had gone missing during the battle.

Florence joined her at Salud's apartment after gathering a basket of food at Santo Tomas. She was thrilled to see that Jerry and Bobby did not seem traumatized by the horrific events that had occurred around them. For the next few weeks, she spent her nights with Dolores in the shanty and her days with Norma and the children.

One morning, an announcement was projected onto the large camp screen that all American citizens would be given the opportunity to return to the United States. Although Florence's American passport had expired, Norma had kept it safe along with Florence's wedding certificate and the identity card from her work with Army Intelligence.

For Florence, the idea of traveling thousands of miles to a strange place was intimidating. If she stayed, she was sure that her work experience would earn her a good position. At the same time, the business district of Manila was now little more than piles of rubble. It might be many months before there was any return to normalcy.

On February 27, a radiogram arrived from her Aunt Mabelle in Buffalo.

CONGRATULATIONS: WILL SEND MONEY IF ADVISED
WHERE STOP. CAN HAVE HOME WITH US IF POSSIBLE
GET HERE STOP. HAVE YOU INFORMATION ABOUT
OTHERS OR SMITH STOP. LOVE WRITE

Florence wasn't aware that the army had contacted Mabelle Lewis as her next of kin, but the radiogram tipped the balance in favor of going to the United States. Before making any final plans, Florence assured Norma that she would find a way to help her and the boys reach America as well.

The officials processing the departure applications informed Florence that as the American widow of a decorated naval chief petty officer who had also worked for US Army Intelligence, she was high on their priority list and would be placed on one of the first ships.

Her journey began on April 9, 1945, when she went aboard a US Coast Guard transport ship named the USS *Admiral E. W. Eberle*. Belowdecks, she found herself billeted in a sizable compartment filled with long ranks of four-tiered bunk beds. There were 2,899 other American passengers.

Before leaving Philippine waters, the ship briefly anchored off the island of Leyte to pick up additional military personnel. Standing at the rail of the passenger deck, Florence understood for the first time the vast military force required to challenge the Japanese. As far as she could see, the anchorage was filled with warships, hundreds of them, including carriers, battleships, cruisers, and destroyers preparing for the next invasion.

Aside from the sleeping arrangements, the voyage became another helpful step in the recovery of her strength. The sea air, plentiful food, and the much-needed exercise of walking the decks all combined to give her a healthy new glow. Her fingers slowly healed but they remained stiff and prone to numbness. She was leaving behind one life and about to embrace a new one.

Nothing could dampen her spirits as she put the past chaos and death behind her. Even when they sailed into a typhoon that caused the ship to roll so frighteningly that her baggage sailed back and forth across the compartment, she was undaunted. While most of the passengers became seasick, she remained focused on the next stage of her life and what the future might hold.

She spent much of her time reading the latest books in the ship's library, just as her father Charlie had done on his first voyage at seventeen from New York to the Philippines, in 1899. There were other pleasures too. Although the ship was blacked out at night in case of a roving Japanese submarine, a full orchestra played a concert every afternoon on the passenger deck.

Florence wrote to her Aunt Mabelle from aboard ship after the passengers were informed by loudspeaker that President Franklin Roosevelt had died on April 12 in Warm Springs, Georgia. Although she had only seen him in movie newsreels, she was deeply saddened that he hadn't lived to see the end of the war.

At Sea . . . We're on the way at last . . . When we get to the States people will never believe we ever went through starvation and worse. Gosh, the food is swell and so much of it—pork and beans, Spam, eggs, bread, butter, ice cream (four scoops), that is just what we had yesterday. And it's like that every day.

Yesterday we had Protestant services on deck—a memorial for President Roosevelt—and more tears shed by me. Will wire you as soon as it is possible to let you know of our arrival date. With loving regards to all, your niece, Florence

In late April, the *Eberle* docked at Terminal Island in San Pedro, California. At the pier, the new arrivals were met by officials from the army, navy, Coast Guard, and the American Red Cross.

After brief interviews, the passengers were driven in buses to the Elks Building in Los Angeles, which had been leased by the Red Cross. Florence was assigned a hotel until her transportation could be arranged. Like the others, she was advanced a gift of $130 in cash to purchase clothing and luggage at a local department store.

The train trip across the United States took four days and three nights aboard a succession of rail lines. Florence spent most of the daylight hours in a coach window seat, taking in the glorious panorama of the snow-capped Rocky Mountains, the Great Plains, and finally the Alleghenies before arriving at Central Station in Buffalo on the snowy morning of May 3, 1945.

After stepping down from the passenger car, she first noticed how much colder Buffalo was compared to Los Angeles. As the snow continued to fall, she looked up to see four people rushing toward her on the platform.

Florence recognized two of them right away from their photographs: her aunts Mabelle and May. The third woman turned out to be May's daughter Leah, Florence's first cousin. The young man with them was introduced as Charles Tillotson, Leah's husband.

The three women began crying as Florence hugged each of them in turn. Charles took the baggage claim check from her and suggested they go on to the waiting room where it was warm.

There, Mabelle told Florence how thrilled they were to have her join the family. They had all read the citation of Bing's Distinguished Service Cross and told her they were deeply moved by his sacrifice. They had no idea of what Florence had endured and she didn't tell them what she had accomplished at the fuel union or what the Kempeitai had done to her at the Airport Studio. As always, she didn't want to burden anyone with her personal suffering.

May reminded Florence that she was the first member of the Ebersole family to return to America after her father Charlie had left to fight in the Spanish-American War. He had never returned, but all these years later, one of his daughters was finally home.

"You must be very tired," said Mabelle as Charles returned, carrying Florence's small army trunk. "Let's go home."

And she did.

SIXTY-NINE

Florence's first month in Buffalo sped past in a blur. The sights and sounds of upstate New York were as profoundly strange to her as Manila had been at the age of seven, after she left her father's plantation for the first and last time. Spring had officially arrived upstate, but snow kept falling. For someone who had lived all her life in the tropics, it was a striking change.

For the first few weeks, Florence stayed with her cousin Leah's family, at their home on North Street.

Aunt Mabelle and Aunt May welcomed Florence like a new and treasured daughter. In an effort to help her adapt quickly, they immersed her in regular family gatherings, neighborhood fish fries, the latest movies, church activities, local sports events, and a visit to the Peace Bridge over Niagara Falls.

At the end of May, Aunt Mabelle was ready for Florence to move into her small home on Arlington Street. She and her husband had recently separated, and Mabelle was looking forward to her company.

Florence's life fell into a comfortable and easy routine built around church and family. Physically, she was completely recovered, but as the days and weeks passed, she felt increasingly like the proverbial fish out of water and somehow unfulfilled.

Each day she read the *Buffalo News*. Although the war in Europe was over, she saw that the Pacific war showed no sign of ending anytime soon. Fierce combat raged on an island near Japan called Okinawa, and it had

288

become the bloodiest battle in the Pacific theater. More than twelve thousand American marines and soldiers had already been killed, along with three times that number of Japanese.

In Washington, military leaders were preparing for the invasion of the Japanese home islands and cautioned the American people that with every Japanese man, woman, and child seemingly ready to fight to the death for their emperor, a million Americans might be killed or wounded in the final campaign.

Some of the people Florence had met since her arrival seemed ignorant of the human cost of the war or didn't want to be reminded of it. She was invited to celebratory lunches and dinners where enough food scraps were thrown out to have fed her and her Bilibid cell mates like royalty for a month.

At one party, she listened to a neighbor complain about the food rationing system, and how he hadn't had enough coupons to buy a decent steak. Most people were tired of the war, and the things they were excited about did not excite Florence. The men looked forward to the new automobile models the Detroit auto manufacturers were presenting for the first time in four years. She didn't know how to drive and couldn't have cared less.

With each passing day, Florence realized that her pledge to Bing to do everything in her power to help defeat the Japanese was unmet. It was still an unclosed chapter. The Pacific war might go on for years and now she was out of it.

She decided to volunteer for military service and rejoin the fight. When she told Mabelle and May, they were dumbfounded, scolding that she had just miraculously escaped death and should now enjoy her new life away from the war.

But when her mind was made up, she was immovable.

In considering which service branch to join, she remembered the superb quality of the Coast Guard men and women she had encountered aboard the *Admiral E. W. Eberle* on her voyage across the Pacific. The Coast Guard had installations in all the naval war zones and a recruiting office in Buffalo.

Taking the bus downtown, Florence met the recruiting officer, Lieutenant Pearl Kheel. After filling out the application forms, Lieutenant Kheel reviewed them for several minutes and then asked her to describe in detail her work for Carl Engelhart as well as the circumstances leading up to her arrest by the Kempeitai.

It was the first time Florence related in detail what she had done during the war. As she described the fuel diversions and the assistance to the American prisoners at Cabanatuan, Lieutenant Kheel seemed incredulous and at a loss for words. Florence made it clear she wanted to rejoin the fight against the Japanese and was hoping for an overseas posting. Lieutenant Kheel promised to forward the request with her paperwork.

SEVENTY

MAY 1945
INCHON PRISON CAMP
INCHON, KOREA

Spring had finally arrived when Carl and the remaining survivors from Cabanatuan were put aboard another ship at Fukuoka, and once again jammed into a cargo hold. The ship left the port under cover of darkness. None of the prisoners had any idea where the Japanese were sending them. Inside the hold, they could only wait again in fear for the familiar roar of American attack planes.

Two days later the ship arrived at its destination and the prisoners were assembled on the dock. Carl learned from a guard that they were now in Korea and that the new camp was located in the port city of Inchon. Close to the camp was a factory that made Japanese uniforms. The prisoners would be required to sew the buttons on the uniform shirts.

In spite of the Geneva Convention declaration that no officers were required to perform menial labor, no one protested. The food at the camp was adequate and the warmer weather was a welcome relief from the months of bitter cold. The end of the war could not be far off.

Carl's chances of personally seeing the end nearly foundered after one unfortunate incident. A prisoner stole a recent Japanese newspaper from the camp commander's quarters and secretly brought it to Carl to see if it contained valuable war news. A Japanese guard caught him reading the newspaper and took him to headquarters, where he was savagely beaten.

An officer told him the penalty for what he had done was death, pending approval by the camp commandant of the execution date.

When the camp commander called him into his office before pronouncing sentence, he asked Carl why he had disobeyed one of the most serious camp rules. The war would soon be over, Carl told him, and any American who understood the Japanese as a people and could speak their language would be able to help to cauterize the wounds of war between the two nations. He had simply been trying to expand his understanding, he lied.

The commander told him that a decision to reprieve him from a death sentence had to come from a higher authority. He called the general in command of the Korean prison camps and delivered Carl's explanation. Perhaps it was because the general also knew the end was so near, but he commuted his sentence.

On August 7, 1945, rumors circulated that a single bomb dropped by an American plane had completely destroyed the city of Hiroshima. A second bomb supposedly obliterated the city of Nagasaki on the ninth.

A few days later, all the prisoners in the camp were ordered to assemble in the main compound. Of the 1,620 men from Cabanatuan who had left the Philippines aboard the *Oryoku Maru*, 113 were left.

The camp commandant formally marched out of the headquarters with all his officers and addressed the prisoners. "The war is over," he announced to them. "You are no longer prisoners of war."

Although Carl and the other prisoners knew the end of the war was approaching, the words of the commandant still came as a stunning shock. As the news sank in, the prisoners were excited to discover that they were no longer under guard and could roam the camp at their will. Food was still scarce, but they were told by the commandant that a relief column of Americans was on its way.

On September 8, 1945, a platoon of American soldiers arrived to escort them out of the camp. They were taken in a truck to the harbor where motor launches ferried the prisoners out to a hospital ship to begin the long journey home.

Carl had been in Japanese hands for three and a half years.

When the ship briefly stopped over in Manila, he attempted to find out what had happened to Florence and the other civilian staff members of his former G-2 Office of Army Intelligence.

Near the Red Cross office, he was stopped in the street by an American soldier. Shaking his hand, the man told him that he owed Carl his life. He was being beaten to death by one of the guards at Cabanatuan and Carl had somehow stopped it. Carl didn't remember the soldier. There had been so many similar incidents. But the encounter filled him with pleasure.

Through the Red Cross, he was able to track down Angelita Alvarez Sobral, who had barely survived the Battle of Manila. Her younger brother had died in her arms after the church in which they were hiding took intense machine gun fire from both sides. Angelita had no idea what happened to Florence, but told him that Lucy Hoffman and her eight-year-old daughter Lily were murdered by the Japanese.

SEVENTY-ONE

AUGUST 1945
US COAST GUARD HEADQUARTERS
MANHATTAN BEACH, NEW YORK

In June, Florence was officially sworn into the Coast Guard and reported to its training facility at Manhattan Beach in Brooklyn, New York. She was now a SPAR, a seaman apprentice in the women's branch.

Boot camp lasted six weeks, during which she and the hundreds of other new recruits drilled every day, learned to march, and took courses in history, communications, and office administration. She was delighted to discover that the physical instructor for the training base was the world-famous heavyweight boxer Jack Dempsey. Once again, she felt the camaraderie of working together with all kinds of people dedicated to the same cause.

With her customary determination, Florence excelled among her peers. For her extraordinary performance during training, she was named "SPAR of the Week," chosen to represent the achievements of all the women in the Coast Guard. The award was presented to her in Washington, DC, by Captain Dorothy Stratton, the commander in chief of the SPARs.

As part of the honor, she was asked to appear on a nationwide radio news program, *Report to the Nation*. She was uncomfortable with the idea, but Captain Stratton told her it would help recruiting efforts with young women who would be inspired by her bravery. The script was written by a Coast Guard public information officer and the program aired on Sunday, August 5, at 6:30 p.m.

HOST: The war has brought to light many heroic stories, the accounts of dangerous assignments carried out with quiet courage. But courage is not a badge worn by men alone. Our guest of honor is a woman whose story is a banner of bravery.

The thirty-minute program briefly recounted Florence's father's journey to the Philippines, her marriage to Bing, his gallant death off Bataan, and her underground work supplying food, money, and medicine to Colonel Carl Engelhart and the prisoners of Cabanatuan. It concluded with the account of her arrest and torture by the Japanese and her rescue by soldiers of the 1st Cavalry Division.

Listening to the program at her home in Richmond Hill, Queens, that night was Lottie Engelhart Friz, Carl's sister. She had heard no news about her brother for two years and feared he was dead. From Florence she learned he had still been alive in the fall of 1944, and it gave her and Carl's mother renewed hope.

Following the radio appearance, Florence put in another request to be assigned to one of the Pacific war zones. She was still awaiting a reply on Tuesday, August 14, when a voice came over the public address system at her training base in Brooklyn, announcing that the Japanese had surrendered unconditionally and the war was over. She wrote to Mabelle the following day.

After the announcement, the national anthem was played. I went into an awful fit of crying hysteria, then out like a light and at midnight I came to in the hospital. Guess it was just too much for me. Really my first emotional breakdown since hearing of Bing's death in May 1942.

In September, an awards ceremony was held at the Coast Guard headquarters in Sheepshead Bay. On that day Florence became the first and only woman in Coast Guard history to be awarded the Asiatic-Pacific campaign ribbon authorized by President Truman. At the same ceremony she received the posthumous medals awarded to Bing Smith, including the

Distinguished Service Cross, his Presidential Unit Citation, the Purple Heart, and the Asiatic-Pacific ribbon he had also earned.

Following the ceremony, she was invited as an honored guest to the New York homecoming of General Jonathan Wainwright, who had just received the Medal of Honor from President Truman. When Florence was introduced to him, she was struck by how gaunt and physically spent he was after his years in a Japanese prison camp. It made her wonder if Carl had survived.

General Wainwright had been informed of her own confinement and torture as well as the circumstances surrounding Bing's gallant death off Bataan, and he told her how honored he was to meet her. Although it was a day for celebration, it all left her saddened and thoughtful.

Returning to her quarters, she found a handwritten letter sent to her from Manila. It was on American Red Cross stationery, from Carl Engelhart.

My Dear Florence,

I just received a telegram from my sister that you are alive and serving as a SPAR. You don't know what the news meant to me. I have been frantically trying to trace you in Manila. Lucy Hoffman's dead and little Lily too. That made me fear the worst about you. It has been so long since I heard from you. I'm still trying to find Bob Field's wife. He's dead too. Ray Bibee died in my camp in Japan. Raymond and Keeler are dead too. So is Sauer I think—Scotty too. In fact Florence, I am afraid I am the sole survivor. See you before Christmas. My Love, Carl

The news in the letter hit her hard, particularly the murder of Lucy Hoffman and her precocious little daughter. The loss of almost all her friends in the Office of Army Intelligence was another striking blow. Somehow she had hoped that most of them had made it and could only remember them as they had been before the war, young and ardent and hopeful.

Florence's first official assignment as a SPAR was at Coast Guard headquarters in Washington, DC. With the war over, it was necessary to provide liaison to all the Coast Guardsmen and SPARs who would soon be demobilized and returning to civilian life.

In October, Florence and Carl reunited in Washington, DC, for the first time since they said goodbye to one another in Fort Santiago on Christmas Eve 1941. It was very emotional for both of them, punctuated with long, repeated hugs, and tears flowed freely as they sat together and talked about all the friends they had lost in the war.

Carl was still visibly weak from his three and a half years as a prisoner, but had sprouted a small potbelly from overeating rich foods since his release. He was clearly embarrassed about it, and later she could only smile as she thought about everything he had gone through at the point of starvation.

Carl was anxious to learn exactly how she had accomplished her life-saving feats, and Florence explained the steps she had taken until her arrest in September 1944. He was astounded at the combined results of her resistance work and told her she deserved to be officially recognized for it. True to character, Florence said her contributions were trivial compared to all their friends who had given their lives.

One of Carl's stops while in Washington, DC, was at the War Department to find copies of the intelligence reports he had submitted from Manila about the imminence of a Japanese invasion in December 1941, and which were ignored by his old nemesis Charles Willoughby. He was outraged after discovering they had all been destroyed and suspected it was on orders from now General Willoughby.

Carl invited Florence to join his family for the Thanksgiving holiday at his mother's home in Richmond Hill, Queens, and she accepted. Carl's mother was a widow and supplemented her small social security income by renting out rooms in her house.

The day after the holiday feast, the front doorbell rang, and Florence opened it to find an army sergeant inquiring if a room was available to rent. Ruggedly good-looking with a cheerful smile and a head of unruly brown hair, he said that his best friend had recommended Mrs. Engelhart, and introduced himself as Bob Finch.

Although he wasn't officially discharged yet from the army, he told Mrs. Engelhart that he was undergoing outpatient treatment at the Fort Dix army hospital after suffering serious ear damage from combat shelling during the Battle of the Bulge. He said he would soon receive a medical discharge and in the meantime hoped to start college.

Mrs. Engelhart offered him one of her rooms.

Before Florence returned to Washington, DC, she and Bob breakfasted together and found it surprisingly easy to open up to one another. Florence explained her relationship to Carl Engelhart and her life in Manila during the occupation, without revealing the details of her torture and rape by the Japanese.

They found they had a good deal in common. Neither was a wide-eyed young person any longer. Bob was thirty-one and Florence had just turned thirty. They had both seen the horrors of war firsthand and lost their spouses. Bob's wife had sent him a Dear John letter, after falling in love with someone else, while his unit was fighting in Germany.

Bob's parents died during the war. Florence hadn't been in contact with her mother Maria for many years. They both loved books and were broadly read. Bob had aspirations for bettering himself through higher education and a successful career. It was clear he was attracted to her, and promised to come down to visit her in Washington, DC.

For Florence, it was the start of her second serious relationship, and one she soon became confident would lead to marriage and hopefully children. After his first visit to Washington ended, Bob wrote to say he was in love with her.

Medically discharged from the army in April 1946, Bob enrolled at Long Island University to study chemistry. Florence received her own discharge from the Coast Guard a month later and was accepted at the Packard Business School in Manhattan.

Bob proposed in July and they were married in October 1946 at the home of Florence's cousin Leah Tillotson in Buffalo. Aunt Mabelle was Florence's maid of honor and one of Bob's friends from the army, Gerry Nielson, was the best man. Carl had been transferred to a base in California and couldn't attend.

After a brief honeymoon in Boston, they returned to Richmond Hill. With millions of veterans returning to the States at the same time, and many starting new families, there was an acute housing shortage in parts of the country, and they moved in at Mrs. Engelhart's.

To give them additional privacy, Carl's mother converted a small bedroom next to their living room into a primitive kitchen and dining area. Water for cooking on a hot plate was brought from the bathroom. Dishes were washed and rinsed in roasting pans.

Worried that he would be too old to find a good job in his field, Bob accelerated his effort to secure his degree by going to summer school while working part-time jobs. Florence found work as a bookkeeper for a dentistry practice.

In the fall of 1947, Florence was shocked to receive a letter from the War Department in Washington, DC. It was only a few sentences long and got straight to the point. *I have the honor to inform you that the Medal of Freedom has been awarded to you by the Commander-in-Chief...*

On November 7, Florence received the highest recognition an American citizen could attain for her heroism during the war. With Bob by her side, the medal was presented by Colonel Lathrop Bullene on behalf of President Truman before five hundred guests at the twenty-fourth annual Women's International Exposition.

MRS. FLORENCE E. FINCH,
CITIZEN OF THE UNITED STATES.

FOR MERITORIOUS SERVICE WHICH AIDED THE UNITED STATES IN THE PROSECUTION OF THE WAR AGAINST THE ENEMY IN THE PHILIPPINE ISLANDS FROM JUNE 1942 TO FEBRUARY 1945. UPON THE OCCUPATION OF THE PHILIPPINE ISLANDS, MRS. FINCH (THEN MRS. FLORENCE EBERSOLE SMITH), BELIEVING SHE COULD BE OF MORE ASSISTANCE OUTSIDE THE PRISON CAMP, REFUSED TO DISCLOSE HER UNITED STATES CITIZENSHIP. SHE DISPLAYED OUTSTANDING COURAGE AND MARKED RESOURCEFULNESS IN PROVIDING VITALLY NEEDED FOOD, MEDICINE, AND SUPPLIES FOR AMERICAN PRISONERS OF WAR AND INTERNEES, AND IN SABOTAGING JAPANESE STOCKS OF CRITICAL ITEMS. TAKING A POSITION IN THE JAPANESE CONTROLLED

Philippine Liquid Fuel Distribution Union, she furnished vouchers, invoices, shipping tickets, and warehouse release orders covering quantities of gasoline, diesel fuel, oil, and alcohol, which were then used by loyal Filipinos. She constantly risked her life in secretly furnishing money and clothing to American Prisoners of War, and in carrying communications for them. In consequence, she was apprehended by the Japanese, tortured and imprisoned until rescued by American troops. Through her inspiring bravery, resourcefulness, and devotion to the cause of freedom, Mrs. Finch made a distinct contribution to the welfare and morale of American Prisoners of War on Luzon.

Presented on this SEVENTH day of NOVEMBER in the Year of Our Lord, One Thousand Nine Hundred and Forty Seven.

Although he couldn't be at the ceremony, Carl Engelhart had initiated the campaign for the medal to see that Florence was rewarded for her selfless sacrifice in not only saving his own life but indirectly hundreds of others at Cabanatuan and Santo Tomas, for which she had sought nothing in return after the war.

After their meeting in Washington, DC, in November 1945, he asked her for a detailed account of her underground activities and the people she had worked with in carrying them out. He also investigated the scope of the work she had done with Tony and Josefa Escoda and the Hunters' ROTC resistance organization.

As a result of Carl's inquiries, Florence learned that Josefa and Tony Escoda were executed by the Japanese and that she was probably the last person to see Tony alive in Bilibid prison before he was beheaded. She was deeply saddened to learn that Francisco Reyes was executed in a Kempeitai prison in December 1944. Ricardo de Castro had not been arrested, and survived the Battle of Manila.

After receiving the Medal of Freedom, life returned to its normal routine. In 1948, Bob received his chemistry degree from Long Island University and was immediately offered a job by his favorite professor to manage the laboratories in the chemistry department.

In 1949, Florence and Bob decided to have a family. Continuing to work until the final weeks of her pregnancy, Florence delivered their baby daughter, Elizabeth "Betty" Finch, on June 29, 1950.

In August 1950 she received a letter from Carl saying that he had retired from active army duty after a physical exam revealed that he could not stand for more than ten minutes without his knees buckling. Up to that point he had successfully hidden his weakness.

He was immediately hired by Marin County, California, to become their director of civil defense, and set to work developing a plan to cope with extreme emergencies resulting from fires, floods, storms, and earthquakes. A year later, he was appointed the field commander in the event of any type of natural disaster.

To contain their growing book collection, Bob purchased a set of floor-to-ceiling shelves from Montgomery Ward and their books soon filled one wall of the apartment, along with dozens of classical music albums.

Florence could not have been happier.

SEVENTY-TWO

1955
ITHACA, NEW YORK

In 1955, Charlie Clarke, one of Bob's army friends, contacted him to say that his brother Tom was looking for a chemist. Tom was an executive at the Grange League Federation (later to become the Agway corporation), an agricultural business based in New York that manufactured seeds and fertilizers.

At his job interview, Bob was told that the company was moving some of its operations to Ithaca, New York, and was asked if he would be willing to relocate. He agreed enthusiastically, and along with Florence and Betty made the journey upstate by train.

Aside from the dark and cold winters, Florence found Ithaca to be a wonderful place to live. It had the advantages of small-town life combined with the thriving creative and cultural community of a university town. She quickly made many new friends. Settling in for the long haul, she and Bob decided to try for a second child and in June 1955, she gave birth to their son Robert T. "Bobby" Finch Jr.

Using money carefully saved since the war, they bought their first home in 1956.

Seeking a new challenge, Bob applied for the master's program in chemistry at Cornell University and was accepted. His boss at GLF allowed him to adjust his working hours to do both. In December 1957, he braved a snowstorm to attend a class at the university only to find it had been cancelled. Feeling suddenly ill and disoriented, he asked the secretary to call an ambulance. At the hospital, doctors discovered he had suffered a severe heart attack and he remained there for six weeks.

Florence visited every day until his release at the end of January 1958, when he was sent home to further recuperate before returning to his job. On March 1, Bob sustained a second heart attack at home and returned to the hospital for another month.

Florence knew she needed to resume working. After applying for a position at Cornell, she was hired as an administrative assistant and secretary to Professor George Kahin, the director of Cornell's Southeast Asia Program. It was a perfect fit for her and led to a challenging portfolio of projects in the years ahead, including the creation of an English-Indonesian dictionary at the behest of the Ford Foundation.

In 1966, Bob accepted a position as a chemist in the Cornell Veterinary College, a job that he found less stressful and more rewarding. The reduced hours also gave him more time to spend with Betty, who was now in high school, and Bobby, who was ten years old.

To bond closer with his son, he began collecting tiny metal military figures. Together, he and Bobby painted on the soldiers' uniforms and insignias. With the two small armies, they spent many hours refighting famous battles on the living room floor.

Bob and Florence continued to savor the romantic side of their marriage and Bob celebrated every holiday and anniversary with beautifully written endearments to Florence in his carefully polished script. He never left the house without hugs and kisses for her and the children.

On Monday, August 12, 1968, as Betty was preparing to leave for her freshman year at the State University of New York at Potsdam, Bob awoke with severe chest pains. Florence called his heart doctor and asked him to come to the house. Instead, the doctor recommended that Bob take one of his nitroglycerin tablets and wait to see if he felt better.

When he slipped into unconsciousness, Florence called an ambulance and rode with him to the hospital. Bob died twenty minutes later in the intensive care unit. He was only fifty-three years old.

During the last ten years of their happy and fulfilling marriage, Florence had grown accustomed to the fact that Bob's connection to life was tenuous and each day together was to be cherished. After enduring many tragedies in her life, she now fully embraced a Christian faith that allowed her to take comfort in the belief that he was in heaven.

With Betty heading off to college and the house still mortgaged, Florence devoted herself to raising Bobby and freeing the family from debt. Finally learning to drive, she worked at Cornell until 1981, when she was required to retire at the age of sixty-five. Now able to pursue higher education for herself, she enrolled in college and began taking courses in environmental protection, English, and history.

Florence treasured her participation in church activities at First Presbyterian and the many friends she made there. Selected as a deacon by the pastor of the congregation, she assumed a similar mentoring role like the one she had enjoyed at Union Church Hall, counseling younger mestizas, only now she supported many of the young men and women in her new church family.

Through the years, Florence stayed closely in touch with Carl Engelhart and they traded letters every few weeks. Still active after his retirement from Marin County, he and his wife Margo moved to Seal Beach near Los Angeles. They loved to travel by car all over the country, visiting iconic national parks and wildlife preserves.

In early 1995, he passed away at his home at the age of ninety.

That same year, a letter arrived at Florence's home in Ithaca that transformed the relationship between her and her children. It was an announcement from the Commandant of the United States Coast Guard that they were planning to name their new Pacific headquarters building in Hawaii after Florence Ebersole Smith Finch.

Betty and Bobby had no idea why. Florence never told them what she had done during the war or that she had been the recipient of President Truman's Medal of Freedom in 1947. None of her friends or the people she worked with at Cornell knew either.

It was a revelation that led to many hours of conversation about her past life. Betty and Bobby didn't even know she had been married before. She told them about Bing and showed them his citation for the Distinguished Service Cross along with her own citation for the Medal of Freedom.

They could only look at their mother in awe, recalibrating everything they thought they knew about her with this other person she had been during the war, helping to save hundreds of lives.

The dedication ceremony at the Coast Guard headquarters took place in June, and Florence and Betty attended it in Honolulu. Returning to Ithaca, Florence felt uncomfortable after learning that the *Ithaca Journal* ran a feature story about her exploits in the war and the most recent honor bestowed on her by the Coast Guard. She didn't want people to look at her differently or to think she was seeking publicity. Her friends did subsequently look at her differently, and it was with unabashed admiration and a sense of pride in knowing her. When her bus arrived back at Ithaca, there was a cheering crowd waiting. Florence shyly waved before getting in Betty's car to go home.

SEVENTY-THREE

2001

ITHACA, NEW YORK

In the winter of 2001, eighty-five-year-old Florence felt the need to prepare for the possibility of her death. She felt fine but was determined not to be a burden to her children. She wrote her son Bobby in Colorado about the plans she had made.

Dear Bobby,

We are having another winter storm and a foot of new snow. My church meeting was cancelled Monday night and so I've used the last two days to catch up on high priority items.

Enclosed is a copy of the funeral arrangements I have just made. As I told you on the phone, I'm to be cremated instead of buried in a casket and all that. Cremation has lower costs and it's environmentally conscious. Now you and Betty will be spared the burden of determining the arrangements. I have a CD with the bank which is intended solely for burial expenses.

One more thing. The funeral parlor owner—Mr. Bangs—Betty went to school with his sister Patty—told me the box of my ashes could be put on top of your Dad's coffin. That would free up space for you and Betty. I hope this does not upset or depress you. These are necessary things to do so you won't be bothered with them. Lots of love and keep well. Mom

PS: I have enough mailing labels to last me all my days. Here are some you can use for future letters.

In March 2008, when Florence turned ninety-two, she was placed in hospice care at the urging of her doctor after a medical diagnosis determined that she was in the advanced stages of spinal paralysis and had perhaps a month or two to live.

She called Bobby at his home in Denver and told him that instead of waiting for death, she planned to stop eating and drinking. She said she was hoping to see him one last time before she began her fast. Bobby called Betty to say he was coming. She was just as horrified at the turn of events but both of them knew their mother's resolution after making a decision.

At the hospice facility, he found his mother lying in a comfortable room with a picture window looking out on a pond. She smiled broadly when he came in, and they kissed. He saw how weak she was, frail to the point of being feeble, even without having begun the fasting.

Florence begged him to support her decision.

"All right. You have my blessing," he said, finally. "But I want to spend the next three days here with you and I want to videotape your memories."

"Yes, all right," she agreed.

That same day he began filming her with his video camera.

"I'm not going to make this easy on you," he said. "I want you to say goodbye to me."

"Goodbye, Bobby," she said, her voice breaking. "I love you very much."

"Now the kids . . . Annie, Logan, say goodbye to them," he said through tears.

"Goodbye, Annie. Goodbye, Logan. I love you," she said to her grandchildren.

"All right," he said. "Let's start with your earliest memories."

She paused for a while, concentrating. "I remember my mother calling me Loring. I was in the woods and she was calling out to me. You know my real name is Loring, Loring May Ebersole."

Three days later, she was sitting up in a wheelchair, far more animated and alert than when Bob arrived. Now energized to give him additional recollections, she continued to eat and drink while he filmed her.

After reversing the decision to end her life, Florence found that the paralysis the doctors had said would only increase actually seemed to be abating. Her decision proved more prescient than she could have imagined when it turned out that the medical diagnosis had been wrong. A few weeks later, she was strong enough to leave the hospice facility.

Florence Finch cheated death once again.

The next nine years of her life were embraced as an almost miraculous gift, one that enabled Florence to witness the growth of her six grandchildren to adulthood, and for her to welcome a new generation of great-grandchildren into the world.

After she turned 101 on October 15, 2016, her strength and vitality finally began to ebb. Now a resident of a nursing home, her days of savoring hamburgers, pizza, Filipino dishes, and an occasional strawberry daiquiri were over. Only the daily visits by family kept her engaged in life.

Betty was tutoring schoolchildren on the afternoon of December 8, 2016, when she received a call from a nurse that Florence was significantly weaker. Her vital signs appeared to be fine but by the time Betty reached her, Florence said she felt very tired.

By 5 p.m. she began slurring her words and Betty called Bobby to express her fear that they might be close to the end. Bobby said he would fly back right away but Betty thought it would be too late.

At 7 p.m., her breathing became more labored and a nurse administered five milligrams of morphine to help calm her. Betty held her hand and began reciting the Lord's Prayer, Florence's favorite. When she finished the prayer and said "Amen," Florence stopped breathing.

It was the seventy-fifth anniversary to the day that Florence was awakened before dawn by the phone call from Commander Sam Cheek, informing her that the Japanese had attacked Pearl Harbor and the war had begun.

As with so many of the challenges she confronted in life, she was fully prepared for death. She organized the memorial service with her favorite bible passages and hymns. Concerned she might pass away during the harsh Ithaca winter when friends from far away would have to negotiate icy roads, she had left a final directive for Betty.

"Hold the service in the spring," she told her daughter.

It was Florence's favorite season, one of rebirth and renewal.

She was buried with full military honors on Saturday, April 29, 2017.

The United States Coast Guard summed up her deeds in a written statement: *Of the thousands of women who have served with honor in the Coast Guard, one stands out for her bravery and devotion to duty: Florence Ebersole Finch.*

Betty viewed it a bit differently. "Heroism had not defined her," she told the *New York Times*, "but it defined how she lived her life."

EPILOGUE

KIYOSHI OSAWA

Kiyoshi "Ken" Osawa survived the horrific accident in which his legs were crushed. After three weeks in a coma, he awoke to a different world. While unconscious, Japanese soldiers marauded through the hospital, randomly killing patients as well as civilians hiding there to escape the fighting. After many surgeries from American doctors, he eventually regained the ability to walk without crutches.

In August 1945, Osawa was thrilled to learn that Katsuko and his two children were spared from American firebombing. Repatriated to Japan in a prison ship, he struggled to start a new business and after several years found success selling chrome ore excavated in the Philippines to Japanese industrial companies.

In 1958, Osawa found himself yearning to return to the Philippines. Joining a Manila trading company, he once again became a respected member of the business community, living to see his grandchildren reach adulthood before passing away in January 2002.

NORMA EBERSOLE DELMAR

After the war, Norma, Jerry, and Bobby lived in Manila with Norma's mother, Maria Hermoso. As the city was slowly rebuilt from the sea of rubble, Norma found work in the sales department of the Philippine Refining Company, which made Lifebuoy soap. Maria Hermoso passed away in January 1954.

Norma moved to Los Angeles, California, in the 1970s and worked as a teacher's aide until her retirement. She and Florence visited each other many times over the years, and their children remain in close touch. Norma passed away in October 1999.

Norma's son Jerry volunteered for the US Navy in 1960 and served for twenty-one years, first as a submariner and later as a corpsman. After his retirement, he worked as a clinical laboratory technician. He now lives in San Diego with his wife, Flor. Bobby Delmar also came to the United States and worked at the VA Hospital in Long Beach, California, before moving back to the Philippines, where he now lives.

MABELLE EBERSOLE LEWIS

After the war, Florence's Aunt Mabelle continued working at the City Ice and Fuel Company and hosting family gatherings that often included Florence and her children, Betty and Bob. Mabelle passed away in 1977.

ACKNOWLEDGMENTS

I am indebted to Elizabeth Finch Murphy and Robert Finch Jr. for entrusting me with the opportunity to write the story of their mother's life. Without their support and full access to the "Florence archives," the task would have been impossible. I am grateful to them both. Their enthusiasm was a tonic, particularly through the long and productive research phase.

Although Florence didn't speak to her children about her wartime activities for almost fifty years after the Japanese surrendered in 1945, Betty and Bob made up for lost time in seeking to learn everything they could about her journey from young war widow to a member of the Philippine resistance movement.

Another significant debt is owed to the late Edward Carl Engelhart, who witnessed so much World War II history in the Philippines and recorded it in a memoir that deserves publication, along with those of so many other unsung heroes in that war. His sense of humility in these pages rivals that of Florence. It was serendipitous that Colonel Engelhart chose to give the original copy of his memoir, with photographs, to Florence, who passed it on to her son Bob.

In researching this book, I would like to also thank the many who helped fill in the holes that invariably emerge in trying to write a narrative of someone's life after all the principal figures have passed away. I'm deeply grateful for the contributions of Jerry Delmar, the son of Norma Ebersole Delmar, for his vivid recollections of his mother and grandmother, Maria Hermoso. I'm also grateful to Joan Yvette Ebersole Ronquillo, who is the granddaughter of Charles Ebersole Sr., and who lived for many years on the Ebersole plantation in Isabela Province.

I would also like to thank Maria Cecilia I. Ayson at the Filipinas Heritage Library in Manila; Philip Sanvictores at the Philippines-Japan Society, the

Philippines Veterans Affairs Office, the Philippines Veterans Memorial and Historical Division; Fred Roos, Kimberly Ann Hastings, Theresa Fitzgerald, and Cara Lebonick at the National Archives at St. Louis; Suzanne Christoff and Casey Madrick at the library of the US Military Academy at West Point; historian Robert K. Krick; Tami Biddle at the US Army War College in Carlisle, Pennsylvania; Marlea Leljedal at the US Army Heritage and Education Center in Carlisle; George Cabot, Dino Delmar, and Janice Young at the Genealogical Society of Linn County, Iowa; Theresa Kaminski, professor of history at the University of Wisconsin; Robert Gardner, the grandson of Marvin Gardner Sr.; Michael Musick, Chris Kolakowski, Director of the MacArthur memorial in Norfolk, Virginia; and Carlos Lugo, Barrett Tilman, Thomas C. Hurd, Heather Murphy, Christopher Rollins, Michael McGandy, Carolyn Mrazek, and Florencia Delmar.

I would also like to extend my appreciation to Mauro DiPreta, who believed strongly in this book and helped to guide it on its path to publication. This book has benefited enormously from the creative collaboration I have enjoyed with my editor at Hachette, Mollie Weisenfeld, a true line editor of the old school who made this book significantly stronger.

Lastly, I would like to express my appreciation to my incomparable literary agent, David Halpern at the Robbins Office, who has now shepherded me through ten books over the last twenty years. It's been a wonderful partnership.

BIBLIOGRAPHY

Of enormous benefit in researching and writing *The Indomitable Florence Finch* was an abundance of original source material that shed light on almost every facet of Florence Finch's extraordinary life.

Florence was a prodigious letter writer, and many of these notes were preserved by the recipients and returned to her. Her prolific correspondence with her Aunt Mabelle Ebersole Lewis began shortly after her father's death in 1928 and continued until December 1941, when the Philippines was cut off from the United States after the Japanese invasion. The scores of letters provided valuable insights into her maturation from a sheltered girl of thirteen at Union Church Hall to the independent young woman who met and fell in love with Charles "Bing" Smith.

Florence also saved her voluminous post–World War II correspondence with Colonel E. Carl Engelhart. Some of the early letters provided valuable information in the preparation of Engelhart's 1946 submission to the US Army's Decorations and Awards Branch, which led to Florence being awarded the Medal of Freedom. They corresponded faithfully up to 1994, the year before he passed away.

The life of Florence's father, Charles Ebersole Sr., was revealed from a number of original sources, including the personal diary he wrote in 1900 detailing his voyage as an eighteen-year-old across the world to Manila Bay and his subsequent service as a medic with the US Army. During the insurrection he began writing to his sister Mabelle Ebersole Lewis, and she saved the letters that continued up to his death in 1928. They were then given to Florence and eventually her children.

An original source that provided important insight into the disintegration of the Ebersole family was a trove of legal documents from Philippine court records dating back to 1930, which was when a legal battle began

315

between Florence's mother Maria and Maria's daughter Flaviana over who should inherit the bulk of Charles Ebersole's estate, including his substantial plantation and other properties. The legal battle went on for nearly half a century, and the court documents include sworn affidavits from Maria and other family members that revealed the convoluted marital relationships between Charles, Maria, and Flaviana.

Of critical importance in telling this story was the three-hundred-page personal reminiscence written by Colonel E. Carl Engelhart that focused on his experiences during the war, the original of which he gave to Florence. It recounts in depth his work as an intelligence officer before and during the war, his subsequent surrender at Corregidor, the harrowing three years he spent in Japanese captivity, and the assistance provided by Florence to him and the other prisoners, which saved their lives. The memoir culminates with his surviving the sinking of the Japanese "hell ships" that carried American prisoners to Japan and Korea.

This manuscript also benefited greatly from the writings of Kiyoshi Osawa, the managing director of the Philippine Liquid Fuel Distribution Union, who wrote four books about his life in the Philippines, all of them touching on his experiences in World War II. *A Japanese in the Philippines* and *A Japanese's Miraculous Life: 70 Years with the Filipinos* were particularly valuable in charting his transformation from a proud Japanese thrilled at the defeat of the American forces in the Philippines, to someone deeply mortified by his nation's conduct toward the Filipino people.

DIARIES/JOURNALS/PERSONAL LETTERS (UNPUBLISHED)

Charles G. Ebersole Sr. (1880–1928)
Collected writings including *The Journal of Charles G. Ebersole (August 1899–December 1900)* edited by Katrina Morse (April 2015).

Personal correspondence with Mabelle Ebersole Lewis (1922–1928) detailing his family life and business activities in the Philippines, interactions with family, friends, educators, and business associates, and the health conditions that led to his death.

Florence Ebersole Smith Finch (1915–2016)
Voluminous personal correspondence with her aunt Mabelle Ebersole Lewis (1928–1977), detailing many incidents in her life prior to the Second World War, her political views, her personal and working life, her meeting her first husband, their courtship, and their life together up to the attack on Pearl Harbor in December 1941.

Personal correspondence with E. Carl Engelhart (1945–1991), recounting friends they lost in the war, the diversion activities that Engelhart believed saved the lives of not only himself but many other prisoners of war, the results of his inquiries into the individuals who helped in her diversion efforts, including Ricardo de Castro, his interaction with the descendants of Charles E. Smith, and the details of their postwar lives and families.

A detailed written account of her arrest by the Kempeitai in October 1944, followed by her interrogations and torture at their hands at the Airport Studio, and her subsequent trial and imprisonment at Bilibid prison and the Women's Correctional Institution at Mandaluyong. (Written in May 1945.)

A forty-page reminiscence that begins with her years at Union Church Hall, her subsequent years working at the Army-Navy YMCA, meeting her husband Charles E. Smith, being hired by Carl Engelhart to work in the Office of Army Intelligence, her courtship and marriage to Smith, the opening weeks and months of the war, her notification of her husband's death by a Japanese officer, her diversion of fuel stocks with Ricardo de Castro at the Philippine Liquid Fuel Distribution Union, her personal and family life, her arrest and torture by the Kempeitai, her trial, imprisonment, and rescue in February 1945. (Written in 1995.)

A transcribed interview with daughter Elizabeth Finch Murphy detailing her life as a child in Manila after leaving her father's plantation, the academic courses she took, favorite friends and teachers, her business education, an account of her work at the Army-Navy YMCA, her subsequent relationship with E. Carl Engelhart, a lengthy remembrance of the morning she learned of the attack on Pearl Harbor, and the arrival of the Japanese army in Manila on January 2, 1942. (Written circa 1996.)

A reminiscence of her first meeting with Charles E. Smith before the war, her work for E. Carl Engelhart at the Office of Army Intelligence in Fort Santiago, her courtship by Smith and life as a new bride, the events surrounding the news of the Japanese attack on Pearl Harbor, and the events that occurred leading up to the death of her husband. (Written September 14, 1997.)

Numerous written recollections of her life in Manila after the death of her husband, the circumstances leading to her being hired by the Philippine Liquid Fuel Distribution Union, her interactions with its managing director Kiyoshi Osawa, her plans to begin diverting fuel to help the American prisoners at Cabanatuan and the internees at Santo Tomas prison, the successful fuel diversions carried out with Ricardo de Castro, how she balanced her personal life with her secret activities, and her move with her sister Norma and Norma's children to Tondo with the assistance of Francisco Reyes. (Written March 22, 1996.)

A transcribed account of her travelling alone from the Philippines culminating in her arrival in the United States and subsequent life for the next three months in Buffalo, New York. (Written June 12, 1997.)

Eighteen hours of videotaped memories of her years as a student at the Union Church Hall in Manila, her subsequent education, her daily life during the war, her secret diversion activities that led to her arrest, torture, and imprisonment, her rescue by soldiers of the 1st Infantry Division, and her postwar life with second husband Bob Finch, as well as her children and grandchildren. (Recorded in 2008.)

A reminiscence titled "WWII" in which she recounts the details of what happened in the hours after learning of the Japanese attack on Pearl Harbor, the subsequent weeks after her husband left for Corregidor, the witnessing of Japanese atrocities, the conditions at Santo Tomas prison where her friends were held, the circumstances leading to her being hired to work at the Philippine Liquid Fuel Distribution Union, her communications with Carl Engelhart and Ray Bibee through the underground courier service, her diversion activities in support of the American prisoners and the Philippine underground, her encounter with Tony Escoda in Bilibid prison, meeting fellow prisoner Dorothy Fuentes, the final battle for Manila, and her receiving the news from her Aunt Mabelle that led her to leave for America. (Written circa 2001.)

Colonel E. Carl Engelhart (1900–1995)

A 299-page personal reminiscence written after the war titled *Trapped on Corregidor*. It begins with Colonel Engelhart's life after his graduation from West Point and briefly dwells on the events that prepared him for the war, including a multiyear posting as a military attaché in Japan. The narrative primarily focuses on his work as a senior intelligence officer in the Philippines prior to the war, his intelligence-gathering activities that predicted the Japanese invasion, his confrontations with Colonel Charles Willoughby, his responsibilities as the controller of the minefields in Manila Bay during the siege of Corregidor, his final parting with Bing Smith, his interactions with the Japanese forces after the fall of Corregidor, his three years of captivity at Cabanatuan, and his survival of the "death ships" that carried him and his fellow POWs to Japan and Korea before his eventual release in September 1945.

Captain E. L. Sackett

The unpublished journal of the commanding officer of the USS *Canopus* at the time of the siege of Corregidor in 1942, describing all the events that occurred aboard the ship, including the construction of the two *Mickey Mouse Battleships*, and their actions supporting the American troops on Bataan, leading to the death of Charles E. Smith. (Written in May 1943 for the families of the men who served aboard the ship.)

OFFICIAL COURT DOCUMENTS

In the wake of the death of Charles Ebersole Sr. in 1928, a legal battle ensued between the two families that were potential heirs. The official court records date from the initial hearings in 1930 and later hearings in 1957 in the Court of First Instance Isabela, First Judicial District, Second Branch: **In the Matter of the Intestate Estate of Charles Ebersole, Sr.** The records include sworn testimony and sworn affidavits from a number of the principals, including Maria Hermoso, Charles Ebersole Jr., and Antonio Vasquez. Also included in the court documents is a 1950 inventory of the existing property still owned by the Ebersole estate.

MILITARY SOURCES

Complete Military Service Record of Charles E. Smith (1906–1942). National Archives and Records Administration, St. Louis, Missouri.

Military Service Record of Charles G. Ebersole (1898–1903).

Sworn statement by Florence E. Smith to the Judge Advocate General's Department–War Department detailing her experiences as an inmate at Bilibid prison, Philippines, between October 24, 1944, and December 18, 1944.

Posthumous Award of the Distinguished Service Cross with citation to Charles E. Smith, Chief Electrician's Mate, United States Navy. By direction of the President and by command of Lieutenant General Wainwright. April 9, 1942.

Official submission by Colonel E. Carl Engelhart to the US Army Adjutant General, Decorations and Awards Branch, Washington,

DC, in support of the award of the Medal of Freedom to Florence Ebersole Smith with supporting documentation detailing her wartime activities. August 12, 1946.

BOOKS

Armamento, Vidal Brigoli. *The Indomitable*. Quezon City: Hunters ROTC Association, Inc., 1972.

Baclagon, Uldarico S. *The Philippine Resistance Movement against Japan*. Manila: Munoz Press, 1966.

Batchelor, John F., and Shelly E. McAndless. *Cabanatuan: A Prisoner's Perspective*. Self-published, 2018.

Beck, John Jacob. *MacArthur and Wainwright: Sacrifice of the Philippines*. Albuquerque: University of New Mexico Press, 1974.

Borneman, Walter R. *MacArthur at War: World War II in the Pacific*. New York: Little, Brown and Company, 2016.

Brereton, Lewis H. *The Brereton Diaries: The War in the Air in the Pacific, Middle East, and Europe, 3 October 1941–8 May 1945*. New York: William Morrow, 1946.

Brines, Russell. *Until They Eat Stones*. Philadelphia: J. B. Lippincott Company, 1944.

Burton, John. *Fortnight of Infamy: The Collapse of Allied Airpower West of Pearl Harbor*. Annapolis, MD: Naval Institute Press, 2006.

Chun, Clayton K. S. *The Fall of the Philippines, 1941–42*. Long Island City, NY: Osprey, 2012.

Cogan, Francis B. *Captured: The Japanese Internment of American Civilians in the Philippines, 1941–1945*. Athens: University of Georgia Press, 2000.

De la Cruz, Jesselyn Garcia. *One Brief Shining Moment: An Eyewitness History*. Manila: James B. Reuter, S. J. Foundation, 1994.

Edmunds, Walter D. *They Fought With What They Had: The Story of the Army Air Forces in the Southwest Pacific 1941–1942*. Boston: Little, Brown and Company, 1951.

Frank, Richard B. *MacArthur*. New York: St. Martin's Griffin, 2007.

Hartendorp, A. V. H. *The Japanese Occupation of the Philippines*. Manila: Bookmark, 1967.

Hartendorp, A. V. H. *The Santo Tomas Story*. New York: McGraw-Hill, 1964.

Hernandez, Yolanda Canseco. *Josefa Llanes Escoda: Portrait of a Heroine*. Manila: Girl Scouts of the Philippines, 1998.

Ingles, Gustavo C. *Memoirs of Pain: Kempei-Tai Torture in the Airport Studio, Fort Santiago and the Old Bilibid Prison, to Redemption in Muntinlupa*. Manila: Mauban Heritage Foundation, 1992.

Jacinto, Pacita Pestano. *Living with the Enemy: A Diary of the Japanese Occupation*. Pasig City, Philippines: Anvil, 1999.

Kaminski, Theresa. *Angels of the Underground: The American Women who Resisted the Japanese in the Philippines in World War II*. New York: Oxford University Press, 2016.

Karig, Walter, and Welbourn Kelley. *Battle Report: Pearl Harbor to Coral Sea: Prepared from Official Sources*. New York: Farrar & Rinehart, 1944.

Labrador, Juan. *A Diary of the Japanese Occupation, December 7, 1941–May 7, 1945*. Manila: Santo Tomas University Press, 1989.

Larrabee, Eric. *Commander in Chief: Franklin Delano Roosevelt, His Lieutenants, and Their War*. New York: Simon & Schuster, 1988.

Legarda, Benito J. *Occupation 1942–1945*. Quezon City: Vibal Foundation, 2016.

Lichauco, Marcial Primitivo. *Dear Mother Putnam: Life and Death in Manila During the Japanese Occupation 1941–1945*. Hong Kong: Fung, Cornelia Beatrice Lichauco, 2005.

Manchester, William. *American Caesar: Douglas MacArthur, 1880–1964*. Boston: Little, Brown and Company, 1978.

Meixsel, Richard B. *Frustrated Ambition: General Vicente Lim and the Philippine Military Experience, 1910–1944*. Norman: University of Oklahoma Press, 2018.

Miller, Edward S. *War Plan Orange: The US Strategy to Defeat Japan, 1897–1945*. Annapolis, MD: Naval Institute Press, 1991.

Mojica, Procuol L. *Terry's Hunters: The True Story of the Hunters ROTC Guerrillas*. Manila: Benipayo Press, 1965.

Morton, Louis. *The Fall of the Philippines*. Washington: Department of the Army, 1953.

Osawa, Kiyoshi. *Dreams Are Endless: Living As I Wish, Entrusting Everything to Fate*. Manila: Bysch Corporation, 1994.

Osawa, Kiyoshi. *Go South, Japanese*. Manila: Joshu Bunko Library, 1994.

Osawa, Kiyoshi. *The Japanese Community in the Philippines Before, During, and After the War*. Manila: Joshu Bunko Library, 1994.

Osawa, Kiyoshi. *A Japanese in the Philippines*. Japan: Dai Nippon Printing, 1981.

Osawa, Kiyoshi. *A Japanese's Miraculous Life: 70 Years with the Filipinos*. Manila: Kalayaan Press, 1996.

Peralta, Laverne Y. *Who Is Who: Philippine Guerilla Movement 1942–1945*. Quezon City, 1972.

Petillo, Carol Morris. *Douglas MacArthur: The Philippine Years*. Bloomington: Indiana University Press, 1981.

Phillips, Claire, and Myron B. Goldsmith. *Manila Espionage*. Portland, OR: Binford's & Mort, 1947.

Salazar, Generoso P., Fernando R. Reyes, and Leonardo Q. Nuval. *World War II in the Philippines: Defense, Defeat and Defiance*. Manila: Veterans Federation of the Philippines, 1993.

Savary, Gladys. *Outside the Walls*. New York: Vantage Press, 1954.

Wainwright, Jonathan M. *General Wainwright's Story*. New York: Doubleday, 1946.

Walsh, John E. *The Philippine Insurrection, 1899–1902: America's Only Try for an Overseas Empire*. New York: Watts, 1973.

Weinstein, Alfred A. *Barbed Wire Surgeon*. Marietta, GA: Deeds Publishing, 1975.

NEWSPAPERS/PERIODICALS

Army-Navy YMCA 40th Anniversary Celebration Issue. 1938. Manila, Philippines.

"Astonishing Stories: Florence Ebersole Smith." *The Coast Guard Reservist*, January 2002.

"Buffalonian's Kin Rescued in Manila." UPI, February 11, 1945.

"Cedar Rapids Pays Tribute to War Dead." *Cedar Rapids Gazette*, May 30, 1942.

"Fall Causes Death of Local Lineman." *Cedar Rapids Gazette*, January 12, 1925.

"Florence Ebersole Finch, a Living Fil-Am World War II Hero." *Philippine Mahubay News*, March 12, 2011.

"Flying Squad Rescues 12 from Manila Asylum." UPI, February 10, 1945.

"Former Cedar Rapids Man Given Posthumous Award of Distinguished Cross." *Cedar Rapids Gazette*, May 19, 1942.

"Medal of Freedom for Heroic Underground Aid to U.S." *News and Views, Headquarters, First Army*, November 24, 1947.

"Only Spar to Wear Pacific Ribbon Tells About Japanese Cruelties." *Spar Magazine*, June 1945.

Scott, James M. "Battlefield as Crime Scene: The Japanese Massacre in Manila." *World War II Magazine*, December 2018.

"SPAR Florence Ebersole Smith, War Widow and Former Japanese Captive, Is Speaker." *The Record*, Washington, DC, September 13, 1945.

"Tortured, Sentenced to Prison by Japanese, Spar Now in Training." *U.S. Coast Guard Harpoon Magazine*, June 1945.

"Underground 'Vet' Becomes Recruit." *Buffalo Courier Express*, June 28, 1945.

"The Young Dead Soldiers Do Not Speak." *Cedar Rapids Gazette*, September 16, 1943.

TRANSCRIPTS (RADIO BROADCASTS)

Columbia Broadcasting System. "Report to the Nation." Sunday, August 5, 1945.

US Coast Guard Broadcasting Network (WWDC). "Spars on Parade." August 8, 1945.

WNEW Broadcasting System. "Meet the Coast Guard." Sunday, August 12, 1945.

INDEX